SHLOMO ALONI

JEZREEL VALLEY MYSTÈRES

The Mystere IVA in Israeli Air Force Service, Squadron 109, 1956-1968

Schiffer Publishing Ltd®
4880 Lower Valley Road • Atglen, PA 19310

Other Schiffer Books by the Author:
Ghosts of Atonement, ISBN: 9780764347566
Hammers, ISBN: 9780764336553
Vultures Over Israel, ISBN: 9780764339608

Other Schiffer Books on Related Subjects:
Debrief, ISBN: 9780764327858
The Israeli Air Force, 1947-1960, ISBN: 9780764303906
The Iran-Iraq War in the Air, 1980-1988, ISBN: 9780764316692

Library of Congress Control Number: 2015939361

Designed by Molly Shields
Type set in Akzidenz-Grotesk Condensed BQ/Georgia

ISBN: 978-0-7643-4825-9
Printed in China

Published by Schiffer Publishing, Ltd.
4880 Lower Valley Road
Atglen, PA 19310
Phone: (610) 593-1777; Fax: (610) 593-2002
E-mail: Info@schifferbooks.com

For our complete selection of fine books on this and related subjects, please visit our website at www.schifferbooks.com. You may also write for a free catalog.

This book may be purchased from the publisher. Please try your bookstore first.

We are always looking for people to write books on new and related subjects. If you have an idea for a book, please contact us at proposals@schifferbooks.com.

Schiffer Publishing's titles are available at special discounts for bulk purchases for sales promotions or premiums. Special editions, including personalized covers, corporate imprints, and excerpts can be created in large quantities for special needs. For more information, contact the publisher.

CONTENTS

ACKNOWLEDGMENTS

This presentation of events is a tribute to Squadron 109's Mystère era that spanned from 1956 until 1968; a time during which Squadron 109 Mystère was based at Ramat David, at the heart of the Jezreel Valley in northern Israel.

Special thanks to modeling maestro Asher Roth and to Ezra Aharon, Yossi Arazi, Zvi Avidror, Dror Avneri, Eli Bahat, Dan Barak, Michael Barzam, Isaac Barzilay, Asaf Ben-Nun, Shmulik Ben-Rom, Adi Benaya, Yehuda Borovik, Arie Dagan, Joel Dan, Uri Dekel, Gideon Dror, Samuel Dvir, Achikar Eyal, Eli Eyal, Arik Ezuz, Oded Flum, Jacob Gal, Avi Gilad, Shabtai Gilboa, Isaac Golan, Ran Goren, Albert Grandolini, Amnon Halivni, Reuben Harel, Rami Harpaz, Zvika Hess, Eelan Hight, ILDA, ILPO, David Ivry, Shlomo Kahana, Mati Kaspit, Abraham Kimchi, Ziv K, Uri Lis, Judah LevRan, Ruth Livneh, Gideon Magen, Judah Manor, Uri Margalit, Itamar Neuner, Isaac Nir, Haim Niv, Avi Oren, Guri Palter, Amos Peleg, Elisha Perry (Friedman), David Porat, Eliezer Prigat, Absalom Ran, Ilan Ron, Ran Ronen, Reuben Rosen, Meir Ruff, Ruth Shadmi, Noga Shadmi-Lavi, Yossi Sarig, Nathan Segall, Aviem Sella, Dan Sever, Jonathan Shahar, Amnon Shamir, Meir Sheffer, Samuel Sheffer, Pesach Shraga, Zeev Tavor, Raanan Weiss, Ran Yahalom, Iftach Zemmer, Ofer Zidon, and Levy Zur.

All photos originated from collections of the aforementioned; in many cases the same photo originated from the Personal Collection (PC) of several contributors.

To save space, as well as avoid confusion, the formal military style presentation of [rank] [name] was rejected in favor of the less formal [name] only presentation.

ILAF codes for radio call signs and operations were translated from Hebrew to English in order to ease reading.

ILAF names are presented in English with explanations in appendix A.

FOREWORD

by David Ivry

The Israeli Air Force took delivery of the Mystère IVA several months prior to Operation KADESH—or the Suez War—in October 1956. The Mystère was the most advanced aircraft Israel could get at the time, and the Israeli Air Foce (ILAF) procured the aircraft at the same time the French Air Force did; hence, experience operating the aircraft was nil.

At first, the ILAF was offered the Mystère II; however, following several test flights by ILAF pilots, it seemed the aircraft had many problems. The solution came with the ILAF procuring Dassault Ouragan aircraft, which would serve the ILAF until the Mystère IVA was mature. This was, in fact, the first French jet fighter. The first Ouragan aircraft landed at Hatzor in October 1955, and served as the backbone of operational training until the ILAF took delivery of the Skyhawk in 1956. The Ouragan launched the ILAF's French era and the ILAF adopted the French jargon. About six months later, the first Mystère IVA arrived and two squadrons were established very quickly: Squadron 101 at Hatzor and Squadron 109 at Ramat David. The establishment of two squadrons of first-line aircraft was a leap forward and the ILAF was intensively upgraded. At the end of 1955, many pilots were still piston-engine pilots, but by 1956, the ILAF was mostly jet. This meant intensive conversion courses for pilots. Some underwent conversion courses for three jet aircraft types in one year: conversion to the British Meteor and transfer to French aircraft via Ouragan to Mystère. The Meteor was a two-seater, and as such was very important to the process. The ILAF jet flight culture was provided by the Meteor, then developed by the Ouragan and Mystère

During Operation KADESH, two Mystère squadrons and one large Ouragan squadron were already operational. Some of the pilots had little experience with these aircraft during the war; however, their flight and operational experience covered for the lack of acquaintance with the aircraft.

The Mystère represented a new generation of aircraft, the generation of swept-back wings. This aerodynamic configuration gave the aircraft high speed in subsonic speed, since the speed of compression—the speed in which air reaches sonic speed on an aircraft's various surfaces—comes at a much higher speed. It should be noted that the Law of Areas, which enables the transfer of the speed of sound, was still under experiment and was in fact implemented in the Mirage aircraft.

Major David Ivry, Squadron 109 Commander, 1963-1964. (PC)

The speed of sound was a barrier in the past, hence named the "sound barrier." It was difficult to break the sound barrier, even when making a dive, with the energy produced by engines at the time. The compression speed in the Ouragan aircraft was 0.82 Mach in a clean aircraft. It could reach 0.94 Mach in the Mystère, naturally by making a sharp dive. Compression is characterized by strong trembling of the aircraft and stiff steering, and not always responding as expected.

We encountered the "pitch op" phenomenon for the first time in the Mystère, once again as a result of the swept-back wings, when during maneuvers the center of pressure moved back on the wings and the aircraft sharpened its nose movement faster than the aircraft had planned while losing energy and entering very

Major General David Ivry, ILAF Commander, 1977-1982. (PC)

high attack angles. This phenomenon was eventually overcome in the advanced aircraft by entering a computer system for handling. The self-sharpening was initially a disadvantage; however, we later learned to take advantage of it in air combat training.

The Mystère was designed at the time as a first line interception aircraft. As usual, we stuck to our doctrine regarding the multi-mission capabilities of a fighter aircraft. We procured the aircraft with payload capability for bombs and external fuel tanks. The aircraft was apparently not very appreciative of this configuration and would take-off in a heavy configuration at the end of the runway after a very long run, which was very risky during the hot summer. That was when temperature limits were entered for flights.

As for my own story with the Mystère, I only passed the conversion course in 1957. Return to Israel from a Pilot Attack Instructor course in the RAF—a course that was called a PAI course, but in fact was an air gunnery course—in September 1956 had made it impossible to have a conversion course on the Mystère before the October 1956 Suez War. For this reason I flew the Ouragan during Operation KADESH, an aircraft I had been flying before I left for England in March 1956. I passed the conversion course on the Mystère towards my transfer to Squadron 105, which took delivery of the first Super Mystère.

In 1963, after establishing the first Mirage III squadrons and being part of the delivery team of the Mirage III since 1961, I was assigned to command the Squadron 109 Mystère IVA—the famous "Emek" (Valley) squadron. I took over command from Amnon Halivni and passed it on to Ohad Shadmi in 1964. Shadmi led the squadron to impressive achievements during the June 1967 Six Day War while not losing a single air crew in the process.

An Air Force has one aircraft in each era that serves as the tip of the spear and that every pilot longs to fly. The ILAF Mystère era lasted from 1956 to 1958, until the arrival of the Super-Mystère. Nevertheless, being the leading aircraft during Operation KADESH, the Mystère was very well liked. The ILAF was relatively small in the 1950s, yet had two Mystère squadrons, which was exceptional at the time. Squadron 101 later transferred from Hatzor to Tel Nof and transformed into Squadron 116, so that by the June 1967 Six Day War, there were still two Mystère squadrons that constituted a natural transition to the more advanced aircraft: the Super-Mystère, the Vautour, and the Mirage. One cannot find an active fighter pilot at the time that did not fly the Mystère.

The ILAF owes a lot to the Mystère, an aircraft that helped stabilize a culture of jet flight. We all owe a lot to those we lost while flying the legendary aircraft.

Major General (retired) David Ivry
Squadron 109 Commander 1963-1964
Israel Air Force Commander 1977-1982

CHAPTER 1

FROM MOSQUITO TO MYSTÈRE

1951-1956

Squadron 109 was activated in 1951 as a Mosquito unit, subordinated to Wing 4 at Tel Nof air base at a time when the ILAF's 1 April 1951 ORBAT was as follows:

Base	Wing	Squadron	Type
Ramat David	1	101	P-51 Mustang
Ramat David	1	105	Spitfire
Tel Nof	4	69	B-17 Flying Fortress
Tel Nof	4	100	light transport
Tel Nof	4	103	medium transport

Wing 4 moved from Tel Nof to Hatzor in October 1951, and Hatzor was Squadron 109's home base until 1956. During this time the ILAF launched a few projects for acquisition of jet-powered combat aircraft. Implementation of these ILAF jet-powered combat aircraft purchase programs lasted longer than expected. Diplomatic difficulties and technological hurdles delayed deliveries, but eventually, it was this effort that enabled the transformation of Squadron 109 during 1956 from a piston-powered Mosquito unit at Hatzor to a jet-powered Mystère unit at Ramat David.

DAWN OF THE MIDDLE EAST JET AGE

Jet fighters entered the Middle East military balance from 1949. The UK Royal Air Force issued Vampires to the Suez Canal Zone based Middle East Air Force from October 1949 and Meteors followed from July 1950. Egypt took delivery of Meteors from October 1949 and Vampires followed from December 1950.

On 24 September 1950, ILAF Intelligence reported that Egypt already fielded 25 Meteors, 18 Vampires, and three Venoms; this report was probably exaggerated. Actually, deliveries to Egypt of 65 jet fighters—three Meteor T.7s, 24 Meteor F.8s, 22 Vampire FB.52s, and 16 Vampire NF.54s—were suspended in 1950 as a result of diplomatic friction between Egypt and the UK. Following in the footsteps of Egypt, more Middle East nations were expected to introduce jet fighters during the early 1950s. Obviously, Israel launched an effort to equip the ILAF with comparable first generation jet fighters.

Squadron 109's Mosquitoes flying over the Zebulun Valley—north of Haifa and west of the Jezreel Valley—in 1952; though Squadron 109 was activated in 1951, the unit only started flying the Mosquito in February 1952, after an initial cadre of crews graduated from a Mosquito Conversion Course in the UK. (PC).

Egypt was the first Middle Eastern nation to introduce jet fighters; EGAF's Number 1411 was a Meteor F.4. (PC)

Vampire EGAF Number 1529 as photographed during its delivery flight to Egypt. (PC)

THE FIRST JET FIGHTER SQUADRON

From 1950, Israel evaluated a few types of subsonic first generation jet fighters, but none of these were actually available to Israel. Diplomatic difficulties blocked the sale to Israel of the British Attacker, and development delays made the French Ouragan irrelevant to Israel at that time.

At some point, the ILAF considered skipping acquisition of the subsonic first generation jet fighters in favor of purchasing transonic second generation jet fighters—the F-86 was the ILAF's preferred type—but not a single type of transonic second generation jet fighter was available to Israel at that time.

Running out of options, Israel accepted a UK offer for Meteors and a contract was signed on 10 February 1953. Meteor deliveries to Israel started in June 1953; that same month, Squadron 117 was activated at Ramat David as the ILAF's first jet squadron.

Squadron 117's first pilots (left to right): Joe Alon, Daniel Shapira, Squadron 117 Commander Menahem Bar, Squadron 117 Deputy Commander Benjamin Peled, Aaron Yoeli, and Jacob Nevo. Previously serving as Squadron 105 Commander, Menahem Bar went on to serve as Squadron 109 Commander from 1956. (PC)

Squadron 109 deployed from Hatzor to Ramat David in October 1953 for the duration of ILAF MANEUVER 1953; this photo was taken from the Squadron 105 building as two Squadron 117 Meteors taxied past the deployed Squadron 109 Mosquitoes parked on the line that was normally occupied by Squadron 105 Spitfires. (PC)

TRANSONIC JET FIGHTER

From the second half of 1953, the ILAF's top priority operational requirement was swept wing, transonic second generation jet fighters. By then, Arab nations and Israel all operated subsonic first generation jet fighters, but the number of Arab jet fighters was significantly higher than the number of Israeli jet fighters; in other words, the ILAF faced numerical inferiority.

In order to balance this numerical inferiority, the ILAF aspired for technological superiority. If the ILAF would have introduced a transonic second generation jet fighter sooner than Egypt, then the resulting gap in technologies would have served the Israeli objective of technological superiority as a counterbalance to numerical inferiority.

The ILAF's preference was still the already combat proven F-86, but U.S. export policy of weapons to the Middle East ruled out the F-86 and the ILAF had to look for alternatives. The Swedish J29 and the French Mystère II were evaluated in early 1954: the J29 was an operational type that entered Swedish service in 1951, while the Mystère II was still under development and would eventually enter French service in July 1955.

In May 1954, AIR2 Chief Adam Shatkai suggested:

> In light of evaluation and comparison of aircraft, it has been concluded that it is advisable to acquire the F-86. If the F-86 will not be available for acquisition, it is recommended not to purchase the Mystère (especially due to lack of experience and metric system engineering) or the J29 (primarily because of supply concerns and metric system engineering), but to continue operating the

Meteor [as the ILAF's top fighter] until a more suitable type is available.

Meanwhile, the ILAF's 1 April 1954 ORBAT was as follows:

Base	Wing	Squadron	Type
Ramat David	1	101	Mustang
Ramat David	1	105	Spitfire
Ramat David	1	107	Spitfire
Ramat David	1	117	Meteor
Hatzor	4	69	B-17
Hatzor	4	109	Mosquito
Hatzor	4	110	Mosquito
Tel Nof	22	103	medium transport
Ramla	-	100	light transport

MYSTÈRE II ORDER

Also in May 1954, Air Department Chief Daniel Shimshoni issued the three-year ILAF ORBAT plan for April 1954 to March 1957. It was forecasted that Squadron 101 would convert to the Mystère during ILAF Year 1955, while Squadron 109 was not expected to change an aircraft type during the time frame of that plan.

Israel ordered the Mystère II. The 23 August 1954 contract covered the acquisition of six Mystères and an option, valid until December 1954, for nine more Mystères. The option was exercised in a 27 December 1954 contract. The delivery schedule was six aircraft during February to March 1955, six aircraft from August to September 1955, and the final three aircraft from February to March 1956.

GLOW IN TROUBLE

The ILAF code for the first phase of the Mystère II purchase program was Operation GLOW A. The planned follow-up purchase was coded GLOW B, and this was indeed inked on 18 August 1955 to cover the acquisition of fifteen additional Mystères.

Meanwhile, ILAF plans were slightly altered. On 16 November 1954, ILAF Commander Dan Tolkowsky reported that Squadron 113—a new unit to be activated at Hatzor—would operate the Mystère.

Mystère II deliveries to Israel did not start in February 1955. Mystère II development ran into troubles and deliveries to FRAF only started in July 1955. The delivery schedule to Israel was thus changed: six aircraft were planned for delivery in October 1955 and nine aircraft were planned for delivery in January 1956.

FROM II TO IV

Military tension between Egypt and Israel soared in September 1955. War seemed imminent, so both hawkish sides sought immediate induction of weapons: Israel turned to France, while Egypt turned to the USSR.

War between Egypt and Israel did not erupt at that time, but the high state of alert impacted both Squadron 109 and the Mystère II purchase project.

For the duration of the September 1955 readiness for war, Squadron 110 was amalgamated with Squadron 109. At the same time, Israel requested from France the immediate emergency delivery of jet fighters.

France offered immediate delivery of 24 used jet fighters—12 Ouragans and 12 Mystères from FRAF inventory—with 18 new Mystères—to complete the ILAF Mystère II contract for 30 aircraft—to follow at a later date.

Selected during the winter of 1954 to 1955 for conversion to the Mystère II in France and as the Squadron 113 setup team were (left to right and top to bottom): Daniel Shapira, Benjamin Peled, Dror Avneri, Dan Gonen, Ira Shmueli, and Jacob Nevo. Their departure to France was delayed due to GLOW difficulties, and it was then that Shmueli was killed in an accident on 15 May 1955. Jacob Morgan replaced Shmueli as a member of the team and the group travelled to France, where in August 1955 they attended a brief preparatory Ouragan conversion course prior to the start of Mystère II conversion course flights on 9 September 1955. (PC)

In light of this French offer, the evaporating risk of immediate war, the Mystère II's shortcomings, and the Mystère IV's progress, ILAF Commander Dan Tolkowsky recommended to accept the Ouragan offer but to replace the Mystère II with the Mystère IV.

SQUADRON 113 OURAGAN

Immediate acceptance of the Ouragan also impacted Squadron 109. The temporary amalgamation of Squadron 110 with Squadron 109 for the duration of the September 1955 crisis proved permanent, as Hatzor had to spare space for Squadron 113 Ouragan, which took over the facilities formerly serving Squadron 110.

Squadron 109 was also affected, even before the switch from the Mystère II to the Mystère IV had been finalized. As a result of the MiG-15's introduction in Egypt, the ILAF's past aspirations for acquisition of a small number of Mystères to create a technology gap was no longer relevant. The numerical issue had to be addressed as well and Israel was not only negotiating with France a switch from the Mystère II to the Mystère IV, but also aimed at more than double the number of acquired aircraft in order to equip two squadrons with Mystères, rather than one squadron as originally planned.

Accordingly, on 19 December 1955, ILAF Commander Dan Tolkowsky issued the "Half a Year Plan" to cover changes in ILAF ORBAT planning for December 1955 to April 1956.

MYSTÈRE FOR 109

In the 19 December 1955 "Half a Year Plan," ILAF Commander Dan Tolkowsky stated:

Due to delays in the ILAF's Mystère II purchase program, Israel was not the first Middle Eastern nation to induct transonic second generation jet fighters. In late September 1955, Egypt announced—perhaps in response to the "almost war" situation that erupted earlier that same month—the acquisition of Soviet weapons, including dozens of MiG-15s, with deliveries following almost immediately. This photo of an Egyptian MiG-15 was reportedly taken at Abu Sueir in late 1955. Egypt's MiG-15 introduction shattered the ILAF's plans to accomplish technological superiority and consolidated the EGAF's numerical superiority while also impacting Israeli acquisition of the Mystère. (PC)

Squadron 113 Ouragan was activated at Hatzor during October 1955 and took over the facilities of Squadron 110 Mosquito. This Ouragan was parked on the former Squadron 110 line from the direction of the former Squadron 110 six cells shed and looking north, towards the Squadron 109 Mosquito six cells sheds of similar construction; the Squadron 109 line was north of this shed. (PC)

The Squadron 109 Mosquito line at Hatzor, opposite the distinctive squadron shed; this is in the general direction of west to east—the squadron building was west of the line and shed. (PC)

> If enough Mystères to equip more than one squadron will be acquired, then Squadron 109 will reequip with Mystère and Squadron 110 will reopen as a Mosquito reserve unit.

Since Hatzor was able to accommodate two fighter squadrons, the ILAF's plan was to relocate Squadron 113 Ouragan from Hatzor to Ramat David, then reopen Squadron 101 at Hatzor as the first Mystère squadron and then convert Squadron 109 from Mosquito to Mystère, so that Hatzor would host two Mystère squadrons.

A major obstacle for this ILAF plan was the fact that the USA financed Mystère IV production for the FRAF; the contract covered 225 aircraft that were delivered from June 1954 until June 1956, though actual FRAF service introduction was from May 1955. This financing arrangement limited France's ability to commit for early delivery of a large number of aircraft to Israel. As a result, the first Israeli Mystère IVA contract, signed in late December 1955, covered only twelve Mystères, with Israel's request for 60 more Mystères set aside for subsequent negotiation.

THE END FOR SQUADRON 109 MOSQUITO

Uncertainty engulfed the ILAF ORBAT plan and adjustments had to be made. Squadron 101 was indeed activated as a Mystère unit; the first six Mystères for Squadron 101 landed at Hatzor on 11 April 1956, and the second sextet followed on 18 April 1956. AIR3 issued order Operation RAZIS on 5 April 1956 to cover these ferry flights from France to Israel; RAZIS was a combination of RAZ—Hebrew for Mystery in English and Mystère in French —and ISrael, so RAZIS was an abbreviation of the phrase Mystère for Israel.

Also during April 1956, a second Mystère IV contract was agreed to; this contract covered acquisition of a second batch of twelve aircraft. AIR3 issued the order for Operation SIZAR—backwards for RAZIS—on 1 May 1956 and the aircraft were flown from France to Israel on 27 May 1956 and on 15 June 1956.

By 8 May 1956, ILAF Commander Dan Tolkowsky assessed that the ILAF would acquire additional combat aircraft during the summer of 1956, but exact types and quantities were still unknown; the most likely acquisition plan at the time was 34 Vampires for Squadron 105 and 24 Ouragans or Mystères for Squadron 109. The projected ILAF ORBAT of jet combat aircraft squadrons for the fall of 1956 was as follows:

Base	Wing	Squadron	Type
Ramat David	1	105	Vampire
Ramat David	1	109	Ouragan or Mystère
Ramat David	1	117	Meteor
Ramat David	1	119	Meteor NF.13
Hatzor	4	101	Mystère
Hatzor	4	113	Ouragan

The December 1955 ILAF ORBAT had indeed been implemented, but with minor modifications that resulted from ongoing constraints: Squadron 109 Mosquito was closed—final

Israeli Prime Minister and Minister of Defense David Ben-Gurion (grey hair) greets a Squadron 101 pilot after completion of a ferry flight from France on 11 April 1956 at the Wing 4 Engineering Squadron complex. (PC)

flying day was 29 May 1956, and adjutancy assignments were cancelled on 1 June 1956—and its facilities were handed over to Squadron 101 Mystère; Squadron 110 Mosquito was activated as a reserve unit; Squadron 113 Ouragan did not move from Hatzor to Ramat David, but remained in the former Squadron 110 Mosquito facilities at Hatzor; and the reopening of Squadron 109 was on hold pending purchase developments.

HIGHTIDE MYSTÈRES

Suddenly, the ILAF's troubles turned around. From an inability to acquire enough combat aircraft to fulfill ILAF ORBAT requirements due to the reluctance of nations to export combat aircraft, to the inability of Israel to finance all combat aircraft on offer to Israel, offers now actually exceeded ILAF ORBAT requirements. Aerospace magazine *Flight International* reported on 18 May 1956:

> In order to redress the balance of air power in the Middle East—which has been in Egypt's favor since she obtained medium bombers built in Czechoslovakia—the Western powers have agreed to allow Israel to buy a limited number of modern fighters. It is believed that France will supply 12 Mystères (in addition to 12 delivered under an early agreement) and that 12 Sabres are to be provided by Canada.

Negotiation between France and Israel concerning a huge arms deal—Israeli code name HIGHTIDE—started on 22 June 1956; four days after deliveries to the FRAF of the USA-financed Mystères were completed on 18 June 1956, slightly ahead of schedule. Israel was interested in acquisition of 72 Mystères, but financial constraints restricted Israeli purchase to "only" 36 Mystères at a unit cost of 364,000 U.S. dollars.

MYSTÈRES TO RAMAT DAVID

At last, the ILAF was expected to have enough Mystères to reopen Squadron 109. HIGHTIDE Mystères departed France from 18 to 22 August 1956 and arrived at Hatzor from 18 to 23 August 1956. By then, the plan to relocate Squadron 113 Ouragan from Hatzor to Ramat David and to open Squadron 109 Mystère at Hatzor had been superseded by a new plan to open Squadron 109 Mystère at Ramat David. In line with this revised plan, Squadron 101 pilots, some of them flying three Mystère ferry flights in a single day, flew 24 Mystères from Hatzor to Ramat David on 23 August 1956; interestingly, the Mystères ferried from Hatzor to Ramat David were not all recently received aircraft, but a mix of RAZIS, SIZAR, and HIGHTIDE Mystères.

Previously, AIR1 issued an organization order that scheduled the reopening of Squadron 109 to September 1956, at Ramat David. Menahem Bar—his assignment as Squadron 117 Commander lapsed on 1 August 1956—was named for assignment as Squadron 109 Commander; Samuel Sheffer, Amnon Halivni, and Joel Dan were also selected for assignment to Squadron 109 Mystère.

AIR1 issued the Squadron 109 Mystère Standard A (Wartime) and Standard B (Peacetime) on 23 September 1956. The same

4xFQA	4525	4xFVW	4505
4xFQB	4526	4xFVX	4506
4xFQG	4531	4xFVY	4507
4xFQH	4532	4xFVZ	4508
4xFVD	5465	4xFWA	4509
4xFVE	4570	4xFWB	4510
4xFVF	4571	4xFWC	4511
4xFVG	4572	4xFWD	4512
4xFVH	4573	4xFWE	4513
4xFVJ	4575	4xFWF	4514
4xFVL	4581	4xFWG	4515
4xFVM	4582	4xFWH	4516

Mystères flown to Ramat David from 23 August 1956 included ILAF Numbers 4505 to 4516, 4525, 4526, 4531, 4532, 4565, 4570 to 4573, 4575, 4581, and 4582; these were issued civil style radio call signs in October 1956 as listed. (PC)

squadron structure applied to both standards: a commander, a deputy commander, Flight A, Flight B, headquarters section, flying section, and Technical Flight. Standard A (Wartime) specified 42 officers (one Major pilot, three Captain pilots, 32 1Lt pilots, one Captain TFC, one 1Lt adjutant, one 1LT signals officer, one 1LT ordnance officer, one 1LT intelligence officer, and one 1LT navigator) and 200 enlisted service people. Standard B (Peacetime) specified 17 officers (one Major pilot, four Captain pilots, ten 1Lt pilots, one 1Lt TFC, and one 1Lt adjutant) and 101 enlisted service people. The Standard B (Peacetime) was based on a monthly utilization of 300 flight hours, a figure that Squadron 109 would rarely accomplish during its Mystère era. The difference in officers and enlisted persons between Standard A (Wartime) and Standard B (Peacetime) resulted from report to squadron of enlisted people and reserves during an emergency situation, though there were a few unexplained discrepancies between the Standards A (Wartime) and B (Peacetime), such as four Captain pilots in Standard B (Peacetime) against only three Captain pilots in Standard A (Wartime), or the TFC, who was a 1LT in Standard B (Peacetime) and a Captain in Standard A (Wartime).

Then again, the reopening of Squadron 109 had to be delayed, this time not due to shortage in aircraft, as was the case prior to HIGHTIDE, but because, suddenly, the ILAF enjoyed an excess of new combat aircraft and had to reschedule, as it lacked the resources to activate so many new combat aircraft squadrons over such a short period of time.

CANADIAN SABRES

Having aspired for the F-86 purchase for so many years, the ILAF was determined to fully exploit the opportunity to acquire Sabres from Canada. Prime Minister and Minister of Defense David Ben-Gurion noted on 8 August 1956:

> An F-86 costs 320,000 U.S. dollars without spare parts. The cost for 24 aircraft with spares, including 12 engines, will be ten million U.S. dollars; type conversion flying training included but not operational training. Payments are 20% in advance with the balance over three years.

The ILAF ORBAT plan changed. The Ramat David based Squadron 117 Meteor was selected for conversion to the F-86, but the ILAF simply lacked human resources to activate four cutting edge units—Squadron 113 Ouragan, Squadron 101 Mystère, Squadron 117 F-86, and Squadron 109 Mystère—within only a year. The reopening of Squadron 109 Mystère was therefore rescheduled to December 1956, as priority shifted to F-86 acquisition. Also impacted was the planned location of Squadron 109; the original plan was to open Squadron 109 at Hatzor, but this changed to Ramat David; then, after the decision to prioritize Squadron 117 F-86, planning was updated so that Squadron 109 was to open at Ramat David prior to transfer to Hatzor. ILAF Commander Dan Tolkowsky explained the ILAF's intentions on 23 October 1956:

> Deficiencies in Mystère readiness and concentration of all efforts to support the current training of Squadron 101 preclude activation of Squadron 109 even at Hatzor, while it is planned to open the squadron at Ramat David during December 1956. Sabre introduction will compel, in due time, relocating Squadron 109 south and to concentrate the two Mystère squadrons at Hatzor, while the Sabre squadron will be based at Ramat David. However, for the time being, it is too risky to concentrate all Mystères in a single air base.

The Canadian government approved F-86 export to Israel on 12 July 1956, and an official Canadian statement concerning the contract with Israel was released on 21 September 1956. Canadair was quick to prepare for contract fulfillment and the first Sabre Mark 6 for Israel (6030) first flew on 5 September 1956; the depicted 6036 first flew on 15 October 1956. (PC)

Meanwhile, Wing 1 Engineering Squadron took care of the Mystères at Ramat David.

GEAR UP FOR WAR

The Squadron 109 Mystère set-up team was transformed into the Squadron 117 F-86 set-up team. F-86 purchase was such a high priority that even though military tensions in the Middle East were again soaring, three Squadron 117 F-86 set-up team pilots —Samuel Sheffer, Amnon Halivni, and Joel Dan—departed Israel on 4 October 1956 for a Sabre conversion course in Canada. As preparations for war accelerated, the three pilots were recalled from Canada and arrived in time to take part in Suez War operations as Squadron 113 Ouragan pilots. Samuel Sheffer recalled:

> We were planned to start Sabre flights on Monday [29 October 1956], but on Saturday [27 October 1956], when we were guests in the home of the Israeli Ambassador in Montreal, the Ambassador received a phone call from Israel, ordering us to return immediately, so we did not fly the Sabre. We arrived in Israel on the night of 29 to 30 October 1956 and were assigned to Squadron 113 Ouragan.

Previously selected for assignment as Squadron 109 Commander, and at the time named to command Squadron 117 F-86, Menahem Bar, who had not travelled to Canada, was posted to Squadron 101 Mystère during the Suez War.

On 25 October 1956, AIR3's issue of order Operation ABSALOM signaled the start of large scale ILAF preparations for war. Two days later, Squadron 117 Meteor deployed from Ramat David to Tel Nof and the Squadron 117 facilities at Ramat David—buildings and line—were reserved for a Mystère unit that was planned to operate from Ramat David during the impending war, though this was not to be Squadron 109, but a shadow unit that was named Squadron 199 and was actually a component of FRAF Fighter Wing 2, which deployed to Israel for the duration of the Suez War.

ILAF ORBAT on 29 OCTOBER 1956 was as follows:

Base	Wing	Squadron	Type
Ramat David	1	69	B-17
Ramat David	1	105	Mustang
Ramat David	1	110	Mosquito
Ramat David	1	119	Meteor NF.13
Ramat David	1	199	FRAF Mystère
Hatzor	4	101	Mystère
Hatzor	4	113	Ouragan
Hatzor	4	201	FRAF Mystère
Tel Nof	-	103	medium transport
Tel Nof	-	115	Mosquito PR.16
Tel Nof	-	116	Mustang
Tel Nof	-	117	Meteor
Lod	-	200	FRAF F-84F
Ramla	-	147	Stearman
Beer Sheba	-	100	Piper
Teman Field	-	140	Harvard

SQUADRON 199

The deployment to Israel of French combat aircraft was in line with the prewar agreement between the Suez War coalition members: France, UK, and Israel. AIR2 subsequently summed it thusly:

> French air forces in Israel composed of a Mystère squadron (Squadron 199) flying French aircraft, an F-84F squadron (Squadron 200), and a Mystère squadron (Squadron 201) flying Israeli aircraft. Squadron 199 deployed to Ramat David on 29 October 1956 and Squadron 201 deployed to Hatzor that same day. The F-84F squadron arrived on 30 October 1956 and was based at Lod.
>
> The intention was to utilize French aircraft solely for air defense in order to free our aircraft for offensive operations. Despite difficulties in command and control

Sinai stripes were painted on all military aircraft present in Israel during the Suez War. Painting of the first version of the stripes was ordered at 04:20 on 29 October 1956, and this version included a central yellow wider stripe with two narrower flanking black stripes. Painting of the second version was ordered at 06:45 on 1 November 1956—after Anglo-French forces joined the hostilities—and included the addition of two yellow stripes on either side of the first version; in this view of a FRAF Fighter Wing 2 Mystère, it looks like the outer yellow stripes were added in different shades than the central yellow stripe. (PC)

This FRAF Fighter Wing 2 Mystère had the number "201" painted on its rudder. (PC)

—a requirement for French speaking controllers and the different communication systems—the command and control system handled the situation in a way that enabled efficient control of French aircraft air traffic.

The Ramat David-based Squadron 199—a shadow squadron of Squadron 109, just as Squadron 201 was a shadow squadron of Squadron 101—settled down in the temporarily vacated Squadron 117 facilities. Initial operations indeed focused on air defense, but eventually, the French Mystères also flew offensive operations. The activity of all French Mystères in Israel during the Suez War engulfed 167 sorties, including 135 air defense sorties, 20 offensive operation sorties, and 12 training sorties (the ILAF Mystère unit, Squadron 101, flew 147 sorties during the Suez War).

CHANGE OF FORTUNES

Preparations for the Suez War delayed conversion of Squadron 117 from the Meteor to the F-86. The diplomatic and political repercussions of the Suez War finished off all prospects of the F-86 ever entering ILAF service. Previously, Flight International commented on 28 September 1956:

An FRAF Fighter Wing 2 Mystère taxis at Ramat David during the Suez War. (PC)

> On Friday last, September 21, the Canadian government announced that it had approved the sale to Israel of 24 F-86s. Mr. St. Laurent, the Prime Minister, said that after consultation with "certain friendly governments," the Canadian government had decided it would not be justified in refusing the request made some time ago by the Israeli government for the purchase of these aircraft.
>
> The Canadian government had been greatly influenced in its decision "by the fact that Israel's neighbor has recently received large numbers of jet fighters from the Soviet Union and, even more important, a considerable number of modern jet bombers, of which Israel possesses none. Assurances have been received from Israel that the intercepters in question will be used solely for defense against aggression."
>
> Mr. St. Laurent added that approval for the F-86s covers a period of six months, during which time the aircraft would normally be made available and shipped. If at any time during that period the political circumstances should change in such a way as to warrant cancellation or postponement of the outstanding part of the order, such action would be taken.

Obviously, from the Canadian point of view, "political circumstances" changed "to warrant cancellation or postponement of the outstanding part of the order," while from the Israeli perspective, the F-86 was no longer an attractive offering, as the ILAF had enough transonic second generation jet fighters and Israeli priority for the future re-equipment of the ILAF was to induct supersonic third generation jet fighters, rather than acquire more transonic second generation jet fighters.

Since the issue that disrupted original planning—Canadian Sabres—no longer existed, the ILAF's ORBAT plan had to be updated again: Squadron 117 would remain a Meteor unit, while Squadron 109 would reopen at Ramat David.

FROM 199 TO 109

Slight modifications had to be made in order to suit the then current situation. The prewar schedule for activation of Squadron 109 at Ramat David was not changed, remaining December 1956. However, adjustments to previous plans had to be made because tensions in the Middle East were still high and it took some time for the ILAF to return from wartime emergency deployment back to normal peacetime operations.

Squadron 117 returned from Tel Nof to Ramat David on 6 November 1956; not to its old squadron complex—at the time used by Squadron 199 and soon to be assigned to Squadron 109 —but to the former facilities of Squadron 105 Mustang.

The withdrawal of French forces was also not accomplished at a stroke, but was gradual; the last to remain in Israel was the French cadre of Squadron 199, flying the Squadron 109 Mystères from Squadron 117's facilities. On 15 November 1956, ILMD Director Simon Peres reported to Prime Minister and Minister of Defense David Ben-Gurion that France had agreed to continued deployment to Israel of 24 Mystère pilots and 40 Mystère maintainers. In an ILAF status report issued on 19 November 1956, ILAF Commander Dan Tolkowsky stated:

> The only French forces deployed to Israel during the Suez War to remain in Israel are:
>
> - 13 pilots and circa 40 support service persons at Wing 1 to enable the operation of Mystère aircraft assigned to [the ILAF's] second Mystère squadron (109).
> - Control officers posted to Central Control Unit 333, Signals Unit 501, and Signals Unit 503.
> - Liaison cell.

On 29 November 1956, Wing 1 Air Engineering Squadron Commander Israel Roth reported the 24 Mystères assigned to Squadron 109 were ILAF numbers 4505 to 4516, 4525, 4526, 4531, 4532, 4565, 4570 to 4573, 4575, and 4581 and 4582; these were all

Squadron 199 Mystères at Ramat David; the ILAF's 6600 range numbers were fictitious ferry numbers, while the true Mystère ILAF numbers were in the 4500 range. In order to confuse observers—concerning the number of Mystères that Israel acquired—the same fictitious ferry numbers were used during RAZIS, SIZAR, and HIGHTIDE. The trouble was that, for quite some time, false ferry numbers were not replaced with true ILAF numbers and this caused considerable confusion, especially among the technical ranks of the ILAF. (PC)

Squadron 199 Mystère 6645 in November 1956. Flown and maintained by FRAF Fighter Wing 2 service persons, the Squadron 199 Mystères were from the batch ferried from Hatzor to Ramat David on 23 August 1956 for assignment to Squadron 109, an assignment that had to be delayed for three months (September to December 1956) due to the Canadian Sabres affair and the Suez War. Four Mystères were ferried to Israel as "6645": one during RAZIS, one during SIZAR, and two during HIGHTIDE. (PC)

HIGHTIDE Mystères. Since the standard ILAF Mystère squadron was 24 aircraft, the ILAF ORBAT included a healthy reserve of twelve Mystères to cater to temporary grounding due to maintenance and to compensate for permanent loss due to attrition.

The pilots of Squadron 109's set up team reported to Squadron 199 and a nucleus of a Squadron 109 Technical Flight was assembled around an experienced skeleton of Ramat David service persons who had formerly served with Squadron 105 Mustang or Squadron 117 Meteor.

Initially, Squadron 109 pilots flew with French Squadron 199 pilots—Samuel Sheffer's first flight in a Squadron 199 aircraft was on 2 December 1956 in Mystère 32—and Squadron 109 support service persons maintained the Mystères alongside the French Squadron 199 maintainers. The handover process finished within ten days; the French were ready to depart and the time seemed right to transform Squadron 199 into Squadron 109.

CHAPTER 2

DEFENDERS OF THE NORTH

1957-1959

Squadron 199's farewell flyover was flown on 12 December 1956, and Squadron 109 Mystère's open flyover was flown on 13 December 1956. Squadron 109 opened with a full complement of twenty-four aircraft, but with only four pilots, so opening day was a symbolic milestone and a starting point towards accomplishment of the IOC and FOC.

ROADMAP TO IOC

The ILAF suffered from a shortage of jet pilots. This issue was discussed on 3 December 1956, in a meeting chaired by Air Department Chief Ezer Weizman and attended, among others, by Squadron 101 Commander Benjamin Peled and Squadron 109 Commander Menahem Bar. While ILAF ORBAT included five jet fighter squadrons and more than 100 jet-powered combat aircraft, the number of jet pilots was planned to reach fifty-seven by 1 April 1957; an average of only eleven jet pilots per jet squadron, or a ratio of only one jet pilot per two jet aircraft. The ILAF planned to increase the number of jet pilots to 102 by 1 April 1958, but also expected an ORBAT refreshment, so that 170 to 180 jet-powered combat aircraft would be in ILAF inventory during ILAF Year 1958; the ILAF graphs of jet pilots and jet aircraft were expected to cross in December 1958, when the number of jet pilots was planned to reach 170.

The Squadron 109 line a short while after opening on 12 December 1956; the Mystères are still painted with Sinai Stripes, but the Squadron 199 FRAF markings are gone: the tricolor rudder has been painted over and the FRAF badges are replaced with ILAF badges.

The Squadron 109 line a short while after opening on 12 December 1956; the Mystères are still painted with Sinai Stripes, but the Squadron 199 FRAF markings are gone: the tricolor rudder has been painted over and the FRAF badges are replaced with ILAF badges.

Squadron 109, as one of the two top frontline squadrons of the ILAF, was obviously prioritized in assignment of pilots, but it was impossible to completely drain pilots from other ILAF squadrons so that Squadron 109 would accomplish IOC and FOC as soon as possible. The set objective for IOC was twelve pilots by 1 April 1957.

FIRST MISSIONS

Long before accomplishment of IOC, Squadron 109 Mystère flew first missions. Its first thus far unearthed mission was flown on 24 December 1956, when Samuel Sheffer and Amnon Halivni flew MIOR Lamed108. That same day, AIR3 issued MIOR Lamed115, due to be flown on 25 December 1956. A Squadron 115 crew was tasked to fly a reconnaissance mission over Syria in a Squadron 117 Meteor; the objectives of the mission were to photograph Hamah and Mazzeh air bases from 30,000 feet (or lower in case of contrails, but not lower than 20,000 feet). A Squadron 109 pair was tasked to escort the Meteor and AIR3 MIOR Lamed115 stipulated:

> In case of contact with enemy aircraft the [retreat of the] reconnaissance aircraft should be covered and [the escort aircraft should then] disengage immediately.

Cooperation between Squadrons 109 and 117 was not limited to operations. Squadron 117 also suffered a severe shortage of pilots; by 28 December 1956, there were only five pilots assigned to the regular cadre of Squadron 117 that, besides being a frontline unit, also served as the Flying School Advance Training Squadron. Obviously, mutual assistance could benefit both parties, so Squadron 117 reported on 28 December 1956:

> The squadron was assisted by three instructors from Squadron 109 [Samuel Sheffer, Amnon Halivni, and Joel Dan] who are flying one instruction flight per day in Squadron 117 and one training flight per day in Squadron 109.
>
> The [Squadron 117 Meteor] instructors attended a six-sorty Ouragan conversion course from 24 to 28 December 1956 in preparation for a full [Squadron 109] Mystère training term from 1 January 1957, while continuing to serve as Squadron 117 instructors.

Cooperation was not limited to pilots, but also included maintainers:

> The squadron's ordnance and weapon specialists are currently undergoing a three-week Mystère conversion course at the Wing's ordnance flight; the course includes one week of theoretical studies and thereafter practical work at the squadron and at the wing's ordnance flight.

Mystères 81 and 25 depart Ramat David; both were at Ramat David from August 1956 and both are still flying with Sinai Stripes. (PC)

Mystères 90 and 92 depart Ramat David; both were not among the original batch transferred to Ramat David in August 1956, but were issued to Squadron 109 after the Suez War. (PC)

Overall, the Squadron 117 report highly praised cooperation with Squadron 109:

> Assistance of instructors from Squadron 109 enabled accomplishment of the Squadron 109 training program and the Squadron 117 instruction program; this scheme will run on a regular basis from 1 January 1957.

START OF FIRST TERM

ILAF Report October to December 1956 indicated the new Mystère squadron did not fly during October 1956, while accumulating ten flight hours in November 1956 and 208 flight hours in December 1956. Aircraft inventory by the end of December 1956 was twenty-nine—after 4530 (a Suez War Squadron 101 MiG killer), 4574, 4583, 4590, and 4592 were assigned to Squadron 109—and average serviceability over the three months was forty-one percent.

Squadron 109 Mystère's first full training term started on 1 January 1957, and was planned to run until the end of March. The number of Squadron 109 pilots more than doubled by 10 January 1957. First, three Squadron 117 instructors flew the Mystère on 3 January 1957—one of the three was Mati Kaspit, who soloed in Mystère 10. Then, two Squadron 101 pilots—Josef Zuk and Uri Dekel—reported to their new assignment as Squadron 109 pilots on 10 January 1957.

The three Squadron 117 instructors completed conversion on 10 January 1957 and started air combat training on 13 January 1957. Squadron 117 instructor Mati Kaspit accumulated 61:40 flight hours during forty-eight Meteor sorties and 19:35 flight hours during twenty-nine Mystère sorties in January 1957.

Small-scale operational activity continued, and on 9 January 1957, a Squadron 109 pair again escorted a Squadron 117 Meteor tasked to photograph Hamah and Mazzeh—in line with AIR3 MIOR Aleph37—in what was practically a repeat of MIOR Lamed 115, flown on 25 December 1956.

FUEL LEAKS

Though practically new aircraft, Mystère maintenance issues soon surfaced. On 11 January 1957, MAT2 authorized camouflaging of Mystères:

4582 was the first Squadron 109 Mystère to be treated against corrosion and then repainted in April 1957—this photo of Mystère 82 was possibly taken in December 1957—with Mystère 65 also treated against corrosion and then repainted in October 1957. (PC)

> Due to the fact that there are jet fuel leaks in most aircraft, and this problem will not be solved in the near future, a temporary authorization is granted to camouflage painting as follows:
>
> All upper surfaces are to be painted in camouflage [scheme].
>
> Leading edges of wings, tail and upper section of air inlet are to be painted.
>
> Lower surfaces of wings, fuselage and tail are not to be painted.

PUNCH PROPOSAL

Mystère entered ILAF service in April 1956, but before 1956 was over, Israel had already ordered SMB2. The days of the Mystère as an ILAF interceptor were numbered and, although not yet concerning Squadron 109, FRAF started to explore options to improve the punch of the Mystère as an attack aircraft to suit a future place one tier below SMB2. Air Attaché Josef Keidar reported from France on 14 January 1957:

> In the wake of recent testing of Mystère on fighter-bomber missions, the French decided that improvement is required. The French believe that the Mystère will serve for many more years as a fighter-bomber and therefore should be adapted to this mission. A study has been approved with an objective to increase range and ammunition. The current concept is to fit four external fuel tanks and increase ammunition from 150 to 250 RPG... The aircraft will then be able to attack targets 1,000 kilometers [621 miles] from base, with internal guns and belly rockets.

Two weeks later, on 28 January 1957, AIR2 Chief Nathan Eldar initiated a parallel ILAF study to better adapt the Mystère to the air-to-ground mission:

> Due to the fact that the French are currently studying suitability of the Mystère to attack missions ... Squadron 101 Commander is tasked to prepare a study concerning the subject under discussion ... The study should be handed to AIR2 Chief by 1 March 1957.

ILAF YEAR 1957 PLAN

Prime Minister David Ben-Gurion believed that war was highly unlikely during the years following the Suez War, so this time frame would be ideal for a defense budget cut. The planned budget cut surfaced a dispute between the ILDF Chief and ILAF Commander concerning Mystère flight hour allocation. The Prime Minister summed up on 7 January 1957:

> A Mystère flight hour costs 1,500 Israeli Pounds. [ILAF Commander] Dan [Tolkowsky] wants 7,000 Mystère flight hours plus, 12,000 flight hours in other jets. [ILDF Chief] Moshe [Dayan] proposes 4,000 Mystère flight hours, plus 10,000 flight hours in other jets.

In light of this dispute, the Prime Minister summoned the ILAF Commander for a meeting on 8 January 1957 and the following day, 9 January 1957, the ILAF Commander prepared for the Prime Minister—with a copy to the ILDF Chief—an ILAF position paper concerning Mystère flight hour allocation for ILAF Year 1957:

A view from a tanker along the arched line at Ramat David that was constructed in 1953 for Squadron 117 Meteor, which used the arched line until 1956, when Squadron 109 took over as the premiere Ramat David interception squadron. (PC)

Another view along the Squadron 109 arched line during refueling, with Mystère 32 first among at least fourteen aircraft. (PC)

Mystère 72 landing at Ramat David with Sinai Stripes visible on the right air brake. (PC)

> The ILDF Chief wants to allocate 4,000 Mystère flight hours for [ILAF] Year 1957, compared with my request for 7,000 and compared with 3,500 Mystère flight hours planned for [ILAF Year] 1956, with a considerably smaller number of pilots than planned for [ILAF Year] 1957. The implication is that a regular Mystère squadron pilot will fly 80 hours per year, or 100 hours at best. This solution, with all due respect, is not only dangerous, but also absurd. I understand that the intention is to save the cost of spare parts for 3,000 Mystère flight hours—that is, 2.1 million US dollars or 3.8 million Israeli Pounds. Such savings is an illusion. A decrease in Mystère pilot training will increase the chance of accidents. A pilot with 100 Mystère flight hours represents an investment (in spares only) of 210,000 Israeli Pounds since the start of his ILAF training. On top of this, the aircraft costs 325,000 US dollars or 590,000 Israeli Pounds. Therefore, a loss of aircraft and pilot is a loss of 800,000 Israeli Pounds. Obviously, the savings in flight hours can be quickly surpassed by the loss in accidents. To this should be added the severe morale blow to pilots, knowing that they were unable to maintain a proper standard of training, and this will erode ILAF readiness not only during [ILAF Year] 1957, but beyond.
>
> The decision we are facing is not about a budget for ILAF Year 1957, but whether to let or not let all that the ILAF has accomplished go down the drain, with full operational consequences and implications.

While the dispute was ongoing, the ILAF already planned ILAF Year 1957 as though the higher figure of Mystère flight hours had been approved. The 7 February 1957 iteration of the ILAF Plan For Year 1957 stated:

> Budget constraints forced preparation of a plan based on 120 flight hours per Mystère squadron regular pilot; a figure that is a third less than the required minimum. If a plan to train Mystère pilots in France will materialize, then it will be possible to increase the allocation of Mystère flight hours. The bottom line is that a slowdown in training of Mystère pilots results in a substantially smaller number of Meteor and Ouragan flight hours, thus resulting in substantial savings.

The French proposition to accept ILAF Mystère pilots for training in FRAF squadrons seemed a satisfactory solution for the ILAF's dilemma, but the problem was the ILAF did not have enough qualified Mystère pilots for training in France and maintaining a minimum readiness in Israel, as AIR2 summarized on 17 February 1957:

> France agreed in principle to induct 50 Israeli pilots for training in FRAF Mystère squadrons. Presuppositions:
>
> - At any given moment there will be eight regular pilots —one squadron commander, one flight commander, two pair leaders and four wingmen—assigned to each of the two Mystère squadrons.
> - France does not limit the size of the group; each group will be deployed to France for eight months.
> - The first group will depart to France in May 1957.
>
> The ILAF does not have fifty pilots who have finished Squadron 113 [Ouragan OTU] training and are ready for conversion to the Mystère.

AIR2's proposition was therefore to deploy to France three groups of pilots, one after another: twenty-six pilots in the first group, twelve pilots in the second group, and twelve pilots in the third group. Also, on 17 February 1957, AIR5 outlined a plan for the training of Mystère pilots during ILAF Year 1957.

AIR5's objective was a standard training syllabus for all Mystère pilots. For the first time in ILAF history, the ILAF Year was divided into three four-month terms. Every regular Mystère pilot serving with Squadrons 101 or 109 was planned to fly forty flight hours in fifty-six sorties during each term. The training syllabus for each term included eighteen sorties of basic air-to-air training; eight sorties of air-to-air gunnery; eight sorties of air-to-ground gunnery, rocketry, and bombing; and twenty-two sorties of tactical training, including air combat, air support, and SEAB. On top of training regular pilots, the squadrons were also to convert pilots to the Mystère and preserve the combat qualifications of EP pilots.

Planned pilot assignments to Squadron 109 were:

- Year 1957 Term 1: four regular pilots, seven trainee pilots undergoing conversion to the Mystère, and two EP pilots.
- Year 1957 Term 2: eleven regular pilots, twelve trainee pilots undergoing conversion to the Mystère, and two EP pilots.
- Year 1957 Term 3: eighteen regular pilots and seven EP pilots.

Ordnance allocated for training was:

- Year 1957 Term 1: 7,200 gun rounds, ninety-six T-10 rockets, 384 SNEB rockets, forty-eight 50-kilogram concrete bombs, and forty-eight napalm canisters.
- Year 1957 Term 2: 14,400 gun rounds, 192 T-10 rockets, 768 SNEB rockets, ninety-six 50-kilogram concrete bombs, and ninety-six napalm canisters.
- Year 1957 Term 3: 13,250 gun rounds, 172 T-10 rockets, 688 SNEB rockets, eighty-six 50-kilogram concrete bombs, and eighty-six napalm canisters.

The first change to the AIR5 plan surfaced on 22 February 1957, when MAN1 issued Squadron 113 Ouragan OTU graduate assignments: six (instead of seven) to Squadron 109, five (instead of six) to Squadron 101, and one to Squadron 103.

Gideon Magen first flew Mystère 4526 on 17 March 1957. (PC)

MYSTÈRE CONVERSION COURSE 1

Flying School Class 20 graduated in June 1956; all ten graduates were assigned to the Squadron 105 Mustang OTU course that ended in September 1956, with nine graduates who were all streamed to a Squadron 117 Meteor conversion course planned to run from September to November 1956. The Suez War broke out amidst this Meteor conversion course and the Class 20 graduates were "slipped back": seven to Squadron 105 Mustang and two to Squadron 140 Harvard. Once the Suez War ended, the combat-proven students completed the Meteor conversion course and were assigned to a Squadron 113 Ouragan conversion course from November 1956 to February 1957, at which point six were posted to Squadron 109 as Mystère Conversion Course 1 students: Asaf Ben-Nun, Arie Dagan, Gideon Magen, Yair Maor, Haim Niv and Levy Zur.

Squadron 109 Mystère Conversion Course 1's solo day was on 7 March 1957: Asaf Ben-Nun soloed in Mystère 16; Gideon Magen soloed in Mystère 26; and Levy Zur soloed in Mystère 14. Asaf Ben-Nun recalled:

> The Mystère was the first aircraft with a servo control system that we flew. Prior to the first flight, we were warned that the servo control system was sensitive and that pilots entered oscillations after take-off. It happened to a few pilots, but not to most pilots; the Mystère had a wonderful control system.
>
> There were no spare parts and there were only four batteries in the squadron, so when a four-ship formation flew, the next four-ship formation was ready with pilots in the cockpits until the first formation landed, then the four batteries were quickly transferred to the next formation.
>
> It was a very interesting era at Ramat David, an era when Menahem Bar invented the concept of turnaround—a small number of aircraft that generated many sorties.

ILAF REPORT JANUARY TO MARCH 1957

Squadron 109 reported 176 flight hours in January 1957, 115 flight hours in February 1957, and 197 flight hours in March 1957. All figures were well below the 300 flight hours per month that was used as baseline for compilation of the squadron's Standard B (Peacetime). Aircraft inventory by the end of March 1957 was still twenty-nine, and average serviceability from January to March 1957 was down to thirty-seven percent.

COMMAND HANDOVER BAR SHEFFER

Menahem Bar commanded Squadron 105 Spitfire from 1951 to 1953 and Squadron 117 Meteor from 1953 to 1956, prior to assignment as Squadron 109 Commander. Arie Dagan recalled:

> Menahem Bar often told us of the day when he graduated from a Palmach platoon commander course and his course commander told him "you will never be a commander"; an assessment that many ILAF service persons shared, but still Menahem earned high esteem in all of his command assignments. Menahem was a commander of an anti-commander cloth. His authority was based on personal example; his orders were accepted due to inherent rationale. His innovations—training terms, measurable accomplishments, fast turnaround, and combat day—were visionary.

Having overseen activation of Squadron 109 Mystère from December 1956 to March 1957, Menahem Bar handed over command to Samuel Sheffer, who graduated Flying School Class 5 in December 1951, attended a Squadron 105 Spitfire OTU from

A Squadron 109 Mystère over Acre, north Israel; Squadron 109 was viewed as "defenders of the north [Israel]," mostly facing Syria, while Squadron 101 was viewed as "defenders of the south," mostly facing Egypt. The principle reason for basing the two Mystère squadrons at separate air bases was due to defensive considerations, to enhance the chances of the ILAF's primary force surviving an enemy attack. (PC)

From the removal of Sinai Stripes until the painting of the squadron badge, Squadron 109 Mystères were devoid of distinctive markings, except for the last two digits of their ILAF number—75 in the case of 4575. (PC)

January to March 1952, served as a Flying School instructor from 1952 until 1955, attended a Squadron 117 Meteor conversion course from July to October 1955, converted to the Ouragan and Mystère during September 1956 in preparation for a F-86 conversion course in Canada, was attached to Squadron 113 Ouragan during the Suez War, and served as Squadron 109 Flight A Commander from December 1956 to March 1957. Samuel Sheffer recalled:

> The team assigned to the introduction of the Sabre was from Ramat David, so the three of us were reassigned to Squadron 109 Mystère. Menahem [Bar] joined us for a short while; officially he was squadron commander from December 1956 to March 1957. For a while the three of us flew with the French because our experience as Mystère pilots was limited to a short conversion we undertook prior to departure to Canada for Sabre conversion; we were Meteor pilots until then. The French handed all the equipment over to us as is, including all ground handling equipment and all the supplies they brought from France, including wine and various delicacies that we enjoyed for several months.
>
> I entered office as Squadron 109 Commander 20-22 March 1957. Squadron 109 was the flag bearer of ILAF doctrine in line with Menahem Bar's concept of how the ILAF should have operated, and he implemented his concept when he commanded Squadron 117 Meteor [from 1953 to 1956] and when he was Wing 1 Commander [from 1958 to 1963]. The concept was to accomplish air superiority through destruction of enemy air power by bombing runways and then destroying the enemy's aircraft on the ground. Obviously, Menahem Bar did not invent this concept, but he promoted this concept on two levels: the level of air crews and the level of ground crews.

Mystère 90 was initially assigned to Squadron 101, but transferred to Squadron 109 shortly after the Suez War; it was photographed before application of the yellow framing around the black numbers of the ILAF number's last two digits. (PC)

As for air crews, the main mission was attack of enemy air bases, but the enemy enjoyed numerical superiority, so [Menahem Bar's concept] was minimum time on the ground in order to fully exploit our force, generating a maximum number of sorties that resulted in a fast turnaround.

As for ground crews, the main mission was fast turnaround. At first, tractors towed bombs to aircraft along aircraft taxiways, so tractors and aircraft often created traffic jams. Fast turnaround required the delivery of many bombs to many aircraft over short time frames, so we created three levels of the ordnance supply system: a base level, an intermediate level, and in every HAS. Additionally, a separate system of roads was built in order to push bombs to aircraft without tractors having to use aircraft taxiways.

Menahem Bar introduced his concept when he was Squadron 117 Commander, but the Meteor was not well suited for implementation of this concept; at the time, the Meteor's only weapon was guns. The Mystère was armed with guns and bombs, thus enabling actual implementation of Menahem Bar's concept.

The emphasize was attacking enemy air bases, but other aspects of training were not ignored and we continued to train in air combat and air support, in line with a training plan along the guidelines that Menahem Bar introduced when he commanded Squadron 105 Spitfire [from 1950 to 1953].

At the end of every training term there was a combat day exercise; an exercise that emphasized fast turnaround. The aircraft were loaded with bombs, taxied to a line where the bombs were unloaded, and then the aircraft were taxied back as though returning from a combat mission. In order to hone the skills of ground crews, we organized fast turnaround competitions and pilots participated in these competitions, because it was an integrated system; it was impossible to implement this concept without ground crews.

There was "Air Force North" [at Ramat David] and "Air Force South" [at Hatzor]: while at Ramat David the emphasis was air superiority, and the emphasis at Hatzor was air combat; it was a matter of two different concepts.

ILAF ORBAT on 1 APRIL 1957 was as follows:

Base	Wing	Squadron	Type
Ramat David	1	109	Mystère
Ramat David	1	117	Meteor
Hatzor	4	101	Mystère
Hatzor	4	113	Ouragan
Tel Nof	-	103	transport
Tel Nof	-	115	Mosquito PR.16
Tel Nof	-	116	Mustang
Tel Nof	-	119	night fighter
Ramla	-	100	Piper

MIOR DALET14

AIR3 tasked a pair of Squadron 109 Mystères to escort a Squadron 115 crew in a Squadron 117 Meteor in line with MIOR Dalet14, issued on 3 April 1957. The Meteor's mission was to photograph five targets in Syria—including Mazzeh and Dumayr air bases—from an altitude of 30,000 feet, while escorting Mystères were to cruise at 32,000 feet. In case of contrails, the Meteor crew was briefed to descend, but not lower than 25,000 feet, while the Mystère pilots were also authorized to descend as long as eye contact with the Meteor could be maintained. The emphasized issue in briefing was air combat with enemy aircraft should be avoided.

STRIKE STUDY DISCUSSION

The Squadron 101 Mystère strike study evaluated endurance and ordnance options and was discussed during an AIR2 forum on 28 April 1957, in the presence of Squadron 101 Commander Benjamin Peled and Squadron 109 representative Samuel Sheffer.

The studied endurance options were a Mystère with four 625 liter (165 gallon) fuel tanks and a Mystère with two 825 liter (218 gallon) fuel tanks. Four 625 liter (165 gallon) tanks, 150 RPG, and fifty-five belly rockets enabled a radius of action ranging from 775 to 855 kilometers (482 to 531 miles), which covered all potential enemy air bases, except for Habaniya in Iraq. Two 825 liter (218 gallon) tanks with 150 RPG and fifty-five belly rockets, plus two 500 kilogram (1,110 lb) bombs, yielded a radius of action of 450 kilometers (280 miles).

Studied ordnance improvements suggested it would be possible to add twenty RPG without major modifications or 100 RPG with major modifications. The combination of guns and belly rockets was problematic, because links were ejected so that it was

Squadron 109 four-ship formation over an ILDF range; though at the time an ILAF interceptor, the Mystère was viewed as a versatile combat aircraft and was expected to shift to air-to-ground operations after the planned introduction of the SMB2 and Mirage. (PC)

Mystère 71 starred in an ordnance exhibition at Ramat David on 1 May 1957. The Mystère's external ordnance options—bombs, napalm canisters, and rocket pods—were displayed in front of the aircraft while T-10 rockets were attached to the outboard wing stations. (PC)

forbidden to fire the guns when belly rockets were deployed for fear that an ejected link would explode a rocket; thus, it was only possible to launch all the belly rockets and then fire guns or expend all guns ammunition and then launch the belly rockets; a proposed cure was to modify the Mystère to collect links, which would have limited the Mystère to 120 RPG. As for external ordnance, the options were bombs, napalm, or rockets:

Bombs could be loaded to all four external ordnance stations, with bomb release possible in a single salvo of four or in two salvoes of two; a peculiar release feature was that the inner left bomb and outer right bomb were dropped during the first salvo, with the outer left bomb and inner right bomb dropped in the second salvo.

Clearance for the carriage of four Napalm canisters was an ongoing program at the time, with Squadron 101's Mystère 29 used for tests.

Rockets—either 68 millimeter rockets in pods or T-10 rockets—could only be fitted to outer wing stations.

Samuel Sheffer flew Mystère 05 during the Israel Independence Day flyover on 6 May 1957; this photo was taken a short while later after introduction of the squadron badge. (PC)

The downside was that the radius of action without external fuel tanks or an inner belly tank was very short. With four 500 kilogram (1,100 lb) bombs and fifty-five belly rockets, the radius of action was a mere 120 kilometers (75 miles). With four 500 kilogram (1,100 lb) bombs and a 450 liter (119 gallon) inner belly tank instead of belly rockets, the radius of action was 170 kilometers (106 miles).

Based on the Squadron 101 Mystère strike study, the AIR2 forum decided to explore the feasibility of two 825 liter (218 gallon) tanks and four 625 liter (165 gallon) tanks, as well as the possibility of modifying the Mystère for the carriage of four rocket pods, 180 millimeter rockets, and for the collection of links rather than ejection.

OPERATION COMET

Israel Independence Day was exploited for a military show of force aimed at bolstering internal morale and to deter external enemies; it included a mass flyover. Since Israel's capital city of Jerusalem was divided and demilitarized, the Independence Day parade was rotated between major cities, and the 1957 event was set to take place at Tel Aviv on 6 May 1957.

On 4 March 1957, AIR3 ordered Squadrons 101, 109, 113, and 117 to prepare for a flyover of Tel Aviv with circa twenty Mystères, circa twenty-four Ouragans, and circa twelve Meteors, respectively. Specific details concerning Independence Day flyover timetables and the shapes of formations followed on 24 April 1957, when AIR3 distributed OPOR 17/57 COMET.

Squadron 109 managed to launch sixteen Mystères for the Independence Day flyover, including Samuel Sheffer in Mystère 05, Mati Kaspit in 65, Shabtai Gilboa in 74, Asaf Ben-Nun in 11, and Gideon Magen in 83.

MISSIONS OVER SYRIA

AIR3 issued MIOR He25 on 7 May 1957, tasking a Squadron 115 crew to photograph—in a Squadron 117 Meteor—the Lebanese and Syrian coastlines with a pair of Squadron 109 Mystères flying escort; the mission was scheduled to be flown on 9 May 1957 with TOT from 12:00.

A week later, on 16 May 1957, Squadrons 101 and 115 flew reconnaissance missions over Lebanon and Syria. Squadron 101 Mystère 76—flown by Dror Avneri, who would later fly as a Squadron 109 EP pilot—flew MIOR He37 to photograph four air bases in Lebanon and Syria, including Dumayr, Mazzeh, and Rayak, with an escorting Squadron 101 Mystère, while a Squadron 115 Mosquito flew MIOR He36 with a Squadron 109 escort—Samuel Sheffer in Mystère 72 and Asaf Ben-Nun in Mystère 70—in what was his first cross-border mission and his last flight from Ramat David prior to departure to France.

Seven Squadron 109 pilots—one regular and six trainees—departed for France in line with the aforementioned dispute concerning ILAF Year 1957 Mystère flight hours that was settled in favor of the ILDF Chief of Staff's view that suggested 4,000 flight hours and the French proposal to integrate ILAF Mystère pilots within FRAF Mystère squadrons. The departure of seven pilots to France at a time when the planned cadre of Squadron 109 Mystère pilots was four regulars, seven trainees, and two EPs left Squadron 109 with a skeleton staff of only three regulars and two EPs. It was then that Squadron 109 Mystères almost engaged Syrian MiGs twice.

The first close call was on 26 May 1957, when Amnon Halivni and Josef Zuk were scrambled to intercept Syrian aircraft that were flying close to the border but over Syrian territory, so at first, the Squadron 109 pair was not authorized to cross the border. Only when the Syrian MiGs turned tail—probably flying back to base—were the Squadron 109 pilots ordered to cross the border and chase, but by then the Syrian MiGs were too far away and the Mystères were unable to overtake the MiGs. Since the MiGs did not turn back, the Mystère pilots were recalled after a futile chase that lasted two or three minutes.

Level B maintenance of Squadron 109 Mystères at Ramat David Wing 1 Maintenance Squadron Mystère Workshop on 14 June 1957. (PC)

Joel Dan preparing for a flight in Mystère 30 on 14 June 1957; the kill marking dated back to Squadron 101 service during the Suez War and the yellow framing around the aircraft number had already been applied. (PC)

The second close call was on 27 May 1957, when Samuel Sheffer and Amnon Halivni in Mystère 14 flew MIOR He54 to escort a Squadron 115 Mosquito that was tasked to photograph Dumayr and Mazzeh. Syrian MiGs were scrambled to intercept the reconnaissance aircraft and closed to within visual range of the Mosquito, which by then was flying very close to the border and barely managed to escape as the MiGs turned back, perhaps to avoid crossing the border, or due to the presence of the Squadron 109 Mystères. Samuel Sheffer recalled:

> Radar coverage was very limited at the time. There were Mosquito reconnaissance flights photographing as deep as T-4; they penetrated [Syria] from Lebanon and returned over Syria [Golan Heights]. Our mission was to meet the Mosquito during egress and to escort the Mosquito so that Syrian MiGs would not harm it. Both ours and Syrian radar systems could detect aircraft, but without altitude data. The most interesting point was that there was a certain place and time for rendezvous, and although the Mosquito was on its way back when we took off from Ramat David, without proper ground control, we always rendezvoused as planned.

REVAMPED BADGE

The Squadron 109 Mosquito badge was a vulture grasping a bomb over a blue shield as the background; an appropriate badge for an attack unit. Since the Mystère was still viewed as an interceptor, the Squadron 109 Mosquito badge seemed inappropriate and was not painted on the Jezreel Valley Mystères.

Josef Zuk undertook to revamp the Squadron 109 Mosquito badge so it would suit Squadron 109 Mystère. The vulture was modernized, the grasped bomb was replaced with a grasped broken crescent, and the blue shield background was replaced by a blue circle. The revamped badge was introduced from 20 June 1957.

LONGER RUNWAYS

Mystère strike studies surfaced a potential safety hazard. Air Comptroller Branch Chief Judah Arbel stated on 27 June 1957:

> Reference to research concerning the Mystère's take-off run at a temperature of $42^{\circ}C$ ... Apparently, in order to safely take-off in a Mystère under such conditions, the runways must be lengthened or the temperature decreased, or the take-off weight limited. The only practical possibility for the time being, in order

Mystère 15—already adorned with the revamped Squadron 109 badge introduced from 20 June 1957—in an ordnance exhibition displaying (left to right) gun, fuel tank, new napalm, old napalm, 500 kilogram (1,100 lb) bomb, 250 kilogram (550 lb) bomb, rocket pod, and T-10 rockets. (PC)

to make a safe Mystère take-off, is to limit take-off weight at various temperatures.

ILAF REPORT APRIL TO JUNE 1957

Though from April 1957 the ILAF switched to three four-month long terms that overlapped the Israel Fiscal Year, the next ILAF report to the ILDF Chief of Staff was still in line with the old procedure of four tri-monthly reports overlapping the calendar year, so synchronization between the old three-month calendar year reporting system and the new four-month fiscal year system was yet to be accomplished.

By then, Squadron 109 no longer operated from the old Squadron 117 line, but from new HASs. Squadron 109 reported 117 flight hours in April 1957, 199 flight hours in May 1957, and 115 flight hours in June 1957. Aircraft inventory by the end of June was still twenty-nine, and average serviceability from April to June 1957 was up to 61.8%.

FLYING IN FRANCE

Squadron 109 pilots assigned to FRAF—Uri Dekel as team commander with Asaf Ben-Nun, Arie Dagan, Gideon Magen, Yair Maor, Haim Niv, and Levy Zur—last flew from Ramat David on 16 May 1957, but only started flying from Dijon—assigned to FRAF Fighter Wing 2 Squadron 1 (ESCADRON DE CHASSE 1/2 CIGOGNES)—on 3 July 1957.

The original objective of the deployment to France was to accumulate abroad as many flight hours as possible while enabling the ILAF to divide the allocated 4,000 Mystère flight hours amongst a smaller number of pilots, so that Mystère pilots would fly more than 120 flight hours during ILAF Year 1957. Surprisingly, FRAF flying was at an even slower tempo, so that by the end of July 1957, the seven Squadron 109 Mystère pilots deployed to Dijon flew only 5:35 to 9:05 flight hours, corresponding with 67 to 109 flight hours per year!

Flying in France exposed ILAF pilots to different operations and conduct culture, and to first-hand impressions of other combat aircraft, such as the Hunter and Sabre. Interestingly, ILAF Commander Dan Tolkowsky told Prime Minister David Ben-Gurion on 21 June 1957:

> The Mystère is better than the Russian MiG, better than the British Hunter, and better than the American Sabre.

But this was not the impression of the Squadron 109 pilots. Asaf Ben-Nun recalled:

> Flying in France was very interesting. First of all the language; prior to departure we learned French and we practiced flying using the French language.

ILAF service persons in France (left to right): Haim Niv, Gideon Magen, Arie Dagan, Isaiah Bareket, controller, Uri Dekel, Asaf Ben-Nun, and Levy Zur. (PC)

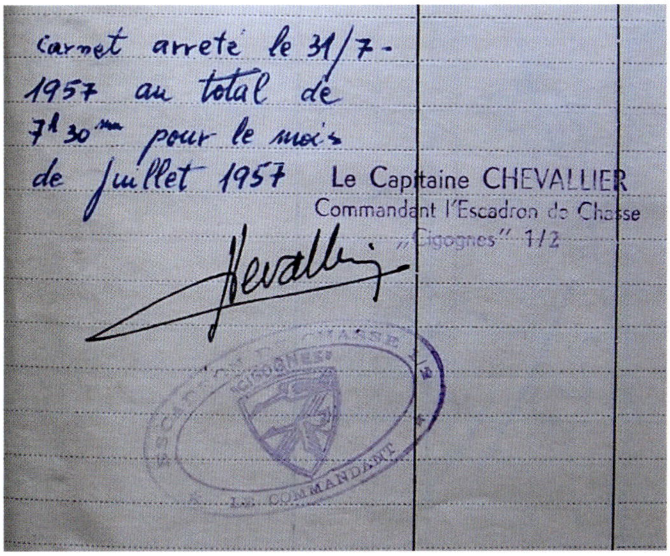

Carnet arrete le 31/7-1957 au total de 7h30mn pour le mois de Juillet 1957

Le Capitaine CHEVALLIER
Commandant l'Escadron de Chasse
„Cigognes" 1/2

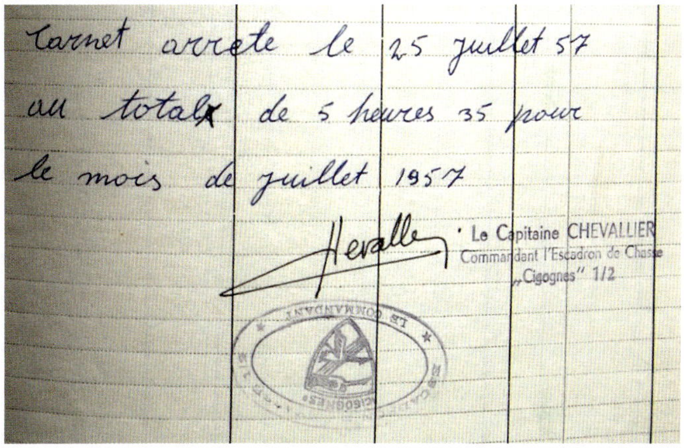

Carnet arrete le 25 juillet 57 au total de 5 heures 35 pour le mois de juillet 1957

Le Capitaine CHEVALLIER
Commandant l'Escadron de Chasse
„Cigognes" 1/2

Squadron 109 pilots flew less than ten flight hours each in France during July 1957—much less than the ILAF expected. (PC)

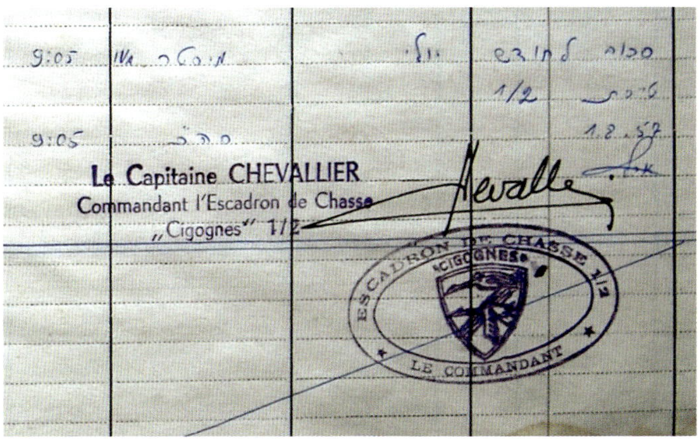

9:05

1/2

9:05

1.8.57

Le Capitaine CHEVALLIER
Commandant l'Escadron de Chasse
„Cigognes" 1/2

An interesting and important experience for Squadron 109 pilots deployed to Dijon was acquaintance with foreign procedures and aircraft, including the Canberra, F-86, and Hunter. (PC)

In France we flew in mixed formations; the French were very weak in air combat, but very strong in instrument flying, and we were exactly the opposite. We flew air combat training versus Sabres and they were superior; the Mystère's engine had a centrifugal compressor and the Sabre's engine had an axial compressor. The performance of the centrifugal compressor considerably decreased with altitude, while the axial compressor was much more efficient at high altitude.

CONVERSION COURSE 2

The ILAF planned to assign twelve pilots to Squadron 109 Mystère Conversion Course 2 during ILAF Year 1957 Term 2, but the actual intake was much smaller; Amnon Arad, Josef Henkin, Amihy Shmueli, and Jacob Yariv graduated Flying School Class 21 in December 1956, and attended a Squadron 117 Meteor conversion course and a Squadron 113 Ouragan OTU course prior to assignment to Squadron 109.

MYSTÈRE INTERCEPTION STUDY

Though SMB2 was already ordered and though the Mystère strike study was already discussed, on 25 August 1957 AIR2 ordered a Mystère interception study to be conducted by AIR3 staff officer Jacob Nevo, primarily because of second thoughts concerning SMB2 acquisition. A school of thought argued that in light of a tight budget and alleged marginal superiority of the SMB2 over the Mystère as an attack aircraft, it would be possible to skip the SMB2, so the Mystère would continue in service as an interceptor until the planned Mirage introduction from April 1961. The study objectives were to recommend:

- Improvements in air combat tactics and in interception procedures.
- Improvements through modifications to aircraft and systems.
- Improvements in aircraft performance.
- Improvements in services supporting combat and interception, such as control network and command system.

In response to the AIR2 requirement, on 5 September 1957 Jacob Nevo circulated a discussion paper asking for input concerning some suggestions:

- Changes to ILAF air combat training and tactics.
- Changes to aircraft systems: how to improve serviceability of the radar range finder, whether to replace the sight, how to enable gunnery and rocketry, how to add ammunition, whether to fit three mirrors, and whether to replace the pilot helmet.
- Changes to aircraft: RATO and repainting.
- Changes to support elements: telebriefing, expanded radar coverage, QRA complexes at the start of runways, and IFF introduction.

The date and pilots involved in this taxi accident between Squadron 109 Mystère 31 and Squadron 117 Meteor 03 are not yet known. (PC)

VAUTOUR CONNECTION

The presence of ILAF pilots at the FRAF base in Dijon prompted an interesting report dated 13 September 1957 from the British Embassy, Paris, France:

> In his letter ... of 11 July the Ambassador referred to a report that nine Israeli pilots had arrived at the FRAF base at Dijon. You may like to know that, on 16 August, the nine pilots were still at Dijon. They were all officers, the most senior being a Captain; they were using false names and had been issued with new identity cards by the Israeli Air Attaché in Paris. Although they had been flying Mystère 4As, they had not been doing anything worthwhile with them or learning very much. The source was convinced that they were not at Dijon for this purpose. A possible explanation of the presence of these officers in France has occurred to the Air Attaché. He thinks they may have come here to ferry back to Israel the ground attack version of the Vautour. About 15 of these have recently been built at St Nazaire, but it seems that the FRAF already has no use for them. They might, however, be extremely useful to the Israelis, for instance, in taking action against the forts guarding the Straits of Aqaba. A piece of supporting evidence is that one of the officers (a Lieutenant of German extraction) left for Tours, where the Vautour had started to arrive from the St Nazaire factory about the middle of August. This is of course only a theory, but it seems sufficiently plausible and interesting to bring to your notice.

The British were correct that the ILAF pilots were present at Dijon, but they were the seven Squadron 109 Mystère pilots, and they had nothing to do with the Vautour; the most interesting piece in this report was probably the sentence:

> Although they had been flying Mystère 4As, they had not been doing anything worthwhile with them or learning very much.

On top of that, Israel did acquire the Vautour and Squadron 109 did have a connection with the Vautour. Squadron 110 was opened at Ramat David to operate the Vautour, and Vautour deliveries to Israel started in August 1957—obviously, at the time this fact was not known to the British—but Vautour flights in Israel only started in April 1958. In the meantime, Squadron 110 Vautour setup team pilots flew Squadron 117 Meteors and Squadron 109 Mystères; Squadron 110 Vautour set up team pilot Zeev Tavor soloed in Mystère 73 on 22 September 1957.

Squadron 109 pilot Haim Niv beside an FRAF Fighter Wing 2 Mystère during Dijon deployment days, circa September 1957. (PC)

ILAF REPORT JULY TO SEPTEMBER 1957

Disharmony between ILAF reporting and ILDF and ILAF training terms continued when the ILAF tri-monthly report was issued on 28 October 1957, amidst ILAF Year 1957 Term 2.

Squadron 109 reported 241 flight hours in July 1957, 201 flight hours in August 1957, and ninety-five flight hours in September 1957. Three pilots graduated the Squadron 109 Mystère conversion course in September 1957, and upon graduation they were assigned to QFI Course 30 and subsequent service as Flying School instructors and Squadron 109 EPs, so that Squadron 109 staff was down to three senior pilots and was planned to remain at this low level until the return of pilots from France. Aircraft inventory at the end of September 1957 increased to thirty aircraft and average serviceability from July to September 1957 was up to 73%.

MYSTÈRE VERSUS SUPER MYSTÈRE

Apparently Israel had to decide whether to go ahead with SMB2 acquisition or not by 15 December 1957, so on 22 November 1957 AIR2 Chief Nathan Eldar started an accelerated staff study to compare the performance of the Mystère and SMB2 in typical ILAF interception profiles and attack missions. The rationale was that if the Mirage would be available from 1961, then the SMB2 would serve as a stopgap interceptor until the Mirage's introduction and as an attack aircraft afterward. The question the ILAF faced was whether to invest more than 17 million US dollars for the acquisition of twenty-four SMB2s that would only serve as interceptors from 1959 until 1961.

In addition to a theoretical comparison, AIR2 also recommended conducting five comparative test flights of the Mystère and SMB2 in order to yield actual data.

Squadron 109 was assigned with thirty Mystères by the end of September 1957, including 4514 and 4525. (PC)

Squadron 117 Meteor instructor Yossi Sarig performed his Mystère solo flight in 4592 on 11 December 1957. Mystère 92 was photographed the following day during Squadron 109 Day. (PC)

TRAINING TERM PLAN

The ILAF Year 1957 budget forced a scale down of training term flight hours from an ideal sixty per regular squadron pilot to a tolerable forty. In anticipation of a better financial reality, on 23 November 1957, AIR5 issued an ideal plan for a Mystère conversion course and a Mystère training term.

The Mystère conversion course was planned to cover eleven flight hours in sixteen sorties.

The Mystère training term was planned to cover sixty flight hours in ninety-three sorties: 14:40 flight hours in twenty-two sorties for basic air-to-air training; 6:00 flight hours in eleven sorties for air-to-air gunnery; 9:30 flight hours in nineteen sorties for air-to-ground gunnery, rocketry and bombing; 25:30 flight hours in thirty-eight sorties for tactical training; and 4:30 flight hours in three sorties for end of term combat day exercise.

ANNIVERSARY 1

By the end of ILAF Year 1957 Term 2, a group of five Flying School Class 22 and Squadron 113 OTU Course 4 graduates was assigned to Squadron 109: Rami Eyali, Baruch Haviv, David Hochman, Aaron Markman, and Jacob Terner; a sixth Class 22 graduate named Ezra Dotan was also planned for assignment to Squadron 109, but was reassigned from Squadron 113 OTU Course 4 to Squadron 113 OTU Course 5 and, as a result, his assignment to Squadron 109 was delayed.

At the start of ILAF Year 1957 Term 3, the seven Squadron 109 pilots assigned to FRAF since May 1957 returned to Israel. From July to November 1957 they flew a little—only 42:15 to 48:00 flight hours—but learned a lot while training in different weather, flying over unfamiliar terrain, and practicing against the F-84, F-86, F-100, T-33, Canberra, and Valiant.

Squadron 109 Mystère Anniversary 1 was marked on 12 December 1957 and included two major events: a turnaround competition and a mass flyover. Among the Mystères participating in the turnaround competition were 4575 and 4583. Gideon Magen flew the flyover in 4583. (PC)

Squadron 109 Mystère's Anniversary 1 flyover included twenty-four aircraft—thus signaling accomplishment of the FOR—as well as a low pass over Ramat David in four-ship formations. (PC)

With the completion of Squadron 109 Mystère Conversion Course 3, with the return from France of the seven pilots deployed to Dijon, and within one year of activation, Squadron 109 Mystère accomplished FOC with a cadre of assigned pilots larger than twenty-four.

Squadron 109 Mystère's first anniversary was celebrated on 12 December with a turnaround competition that the visiting team from Squadron 101 won, with a twenty-four aircraft flyover at ILAF air bases, and with an evening ball.

The regular cadre of pilots was then diluted when the seven "French" pilots were assigned to Flying School for the QFI course and subsequent service as flying school instructors in parallel with service as Squadron 109 EPs.

THUMBS UP FOR SUPER MYSTÈRE

An evaluation in flight of the SMB2 for comparison with the Mystère was approved. Jacob Nevo flew the SMB2 evaluation in France and filed his report on 17 December 1957, at which point he was already Acting Squadron 101 Commander:

> The SMB2 is superior to the Mystère at all points and in all aspects: a double rate of climb in all combinations of fuel and temperatures; level speed the same as the Mystère and top speed in a dive; longer range; and modern weapons (missiles) ...

The conclusive recommendation was to purchase the SMB2, but SMB2 acquisition was not yet included in ILAF Year 1958 Plan Draft 2, issued on 22 December 1959 and anticipating 5,900 Mystère flight hours during ILAF Year 1958; obviously, a decision to introduce the SMB2 would have implications on Mystère flight hours, as pilots would be assigned from the Mystère to the SMB2.

The SMB2 purchase recommendation also made a Mystère strike study relevant and on 29 December 1959, AIR2 circulated an invitation to discuss proposed Mystère modifications: a BDA camera, the collection of gun links, a sight modification to enable bombing or replacement with a sight with a bombing mode, and RATO in order to cut short the take-off run at high weights and temperatures.

The ILAF's ambivalent acquisition of the SMB2 resulted in an initial plan to introduce only twelve aircraft from May 1958, with a follow up purchase of twelve additional aircraft. The introduction of only twelve SMB2s at a time when the ILAF standard for a combat aircraft squadron was twenty-four aircraft resulted in a debate concerning optimal exploitation. Three options surfaced:

- Activation of a new SMB2 squadron that would operate twelve aircraft.
- Activation of a Squadron 101 SMB2 flight with twelve SMB2s.
- Activation of a Squadron 101 SMB2 flight and a Squadron 109 SMB2 flight with six aircraft each.

Mystère 07 landing at the end of Squadron 109 Mystère's Anniversary 1 flyover on 12 December 1957. (PC)

An AIR2 forum discussed these options—as well as other SMB2 introduction issues—on 6 January 1958, and AIR2's recommendation was to activate a separate SMB2 squadron; thus ended the first proposition for Squadron 109 to operate the SMB2, but a second proposition would surface in due time.

MUSTANG 13

The training term syllabus was divided into five chapters: basic air-to-air training; air-to-air gunnery; air-to-ground attack; tactical training; and end of term combat day exercise. Air-to-air gunnery required a target tug aircraft, so squadrons used to borrow Mustangs from Squadron 116 with senior pilots—practically all Flying School graduates including up to Class 20 were qualified Mustang pilots—flying the demanding target tug mission.

The ILAF Year 1957 Term 3 air-to-air gunnery training chapter ran from 29 December 1957 until 15 January 1958. Tasked to fly a target tug mission on 14 January 1958 in Mustang 13, Amnon Halivni reported:

> I performed a short take-off with a towing target on runway 09 at Ramat David. At 400 feet [altitude], I reduced power to 46" 2,100 RPM. At 900 feet [altitude], I started to turn left; airspeed was 160 [mph], coolant [temperature was] 110 [degrees], and engine indicators were OK. At 1,000 feet, after completion of 40 degrees of the turn, I lifted flaps and as a result the aircraft sunk some 30 feet; I was flying over Nahalal [village] when the engine stopped. I immediately transmitted "Damn! Engine cut; emergency landing; I will release the target nearby Nahalal and I hope to reach [runway] 15."
>
> The engine cut was sudden, but immediately afterwards it started to cough, as though only some of the cylinders still functioned. A little bit of white smoke emanated from the right side of the engine. I felt the engine was not delivering power except during the coughs. The [engine] coughs were at first frequent and then slowly subsided until [the engine] almost completely stopped coughing.
>
> I was over Nahalal and I decided to release the [towed] target, but I was unable to do so because I was over a village. I flew west beyond the perimeter of the village, even though this kept me away from the circuit of the runways [at Ramat David], and as I overflew beyond the buildings I released the target and turned left to an emergency landing. I had two options: land straight ahead in a field or to turn left 110 degrees to land on runway 15. I was doubtful if I would make it to the runway, especially as there was a deep ditch in front of it. My situation was 600 feet altitude at 130 MPH. I was afraid to land straight ahead because of the mud, so I continued turning towards runway 15.
>
> The control tower suggested I should detract the undercarriage, but I replied "I will not detract because my speed is slow and I may not make it." I flew very low over the ditch at 125 MPH and I managed to see the runway, so I was trying to pull the aircraft in order to align it along the axis of the runway. I was unable to complete the turn and I had to level the wings. I tried to land gently, placed my left hand on the sight, and touched down on the runway right at the start of the runway at roughly 100 MPH. The impact was weak, and only after the aircraft veered off the runway did I start to sense significant slowdown. I faced no problem keeping my head away from the sight and the aircraft stopped its run with a 90 degree swerve to the right.

Mustang 13 was not a total loss, but the Israeli Mustang force was approaching the end of its ILAF career, so there was no need to repair 2313.

Squadron 109's average air-to-air gunnery score was 10.9%; the parallel Squadron 101 air-to-air gunnery training chapter lasted from 26 December 1957 until 16 January 1958 and yielded an average score of 14.9%.

RAMI EYALI

On 28 February 1958, during the tactical training phase of ILAF Year 1957 Term 3, Mystères 08 and 15 collided during interdiction

Squadron 116 Mustang 13—on loan to Squadron 109 for target towing during air-to-air gunnery training—was written off in an accident on 14 January 1958. (PC)

practice over the Negev Desert. Josef Zuk, in Mystère 15, landed at Hatzor; Mystère 15 suffered severe damage in the empennage and was grounded for repairs for a prolonged period; the thus far unearthed first flight of Mystère 15 after repair is dated March 1959. Mystère 08 crashed and pilot Rami Eyali was killed.

EXERCISE MAN

ILAF Year 1957 Term 3's concluding maneuver was Exercise MAN. AIR Department Chief Ezer Weizman outlined its objectives:

> To test the ILAF's ability in operation of force at maximum tempo, [to test the ILAF's] emergency deployment, and [to test the ILAF's] command and control system.

The exercise involved all ILAF units—reserves were mobilized for the duration of the exercise and training was suspended for duration, with EPs reporting to squadrons—but did not include enemy simulation, apart from "red" radar tracks to train the command and control system. Emphasized issues were:

- Maximum number of sorties
- SEAB and air support
- Deployment of units
- Functionality of the ILAF command post
- Command and control system's ability to operate in an environment of increased traffic
- Air mobility
- Passive defense (camouflage and deception)
- AAA battalions
- Intelligence reports
- Battle damage repair

In order to maximize its realism, AIR3 was planned to distribute MIORs to squadrons; distributed MIORs specified which missions would be flown with ordnance and which missions would be flown without ordnance. Missions flown without ordnance were mostly tasked to fly SEAB against ILAF air bases and BDA was based on the output of gunnery cameras. Missions flown with ordnance were tasked to attack targets on ILAF ranges, with range teams monitoring each attack and evaluating results.

Exercise MAN started the morning of 12 March 1958 with Operation REACTION, a SEAB offensive against an imaginative enemy air force with ILAF bases and ranges as targets; formations attacking ranges simulating air bases actually attacked with bombs, napalm, rockets, and guns, while formations attacking bases did not utilize ordnance. Squadron 109 was tasked within the frame of Operation REACTION to launch two SEAB packages:

- an eight-ship formation tasked to raid Teman Field with gunnery cameras from H+5 until H+25.
- an eight-ship formation tasked to raid Tel Nof with gunnery cameras from H+25 until H+45.

On 12 March 1958, EP pilot Gideon Magen flew the Operation REACTION mission against Teman Field in Mystère 10 and subsequently flew three more Exercise MAN missions (rocketry and gunnery in Mystère 82, napalm in 70, and bombing and gunnery in 10) for a total of four sorties (3:30 flight hours).

EP pilot Asaf Ben-Nun also flew four sorties on 12 March 1958: MAN MIOR 301 (bombing and strafing in Mystère 31), MAN MIOR 304 (bombing and strafing in 65), MAN MIOR 307 (SEAB in 74), and a scramble to intercept Meteors in Mystère 72; his total time was 3:35 flight hours.

Exercise MAN's main objective was to generate as many sorties as possible; in order to cope with the considerably higher number of flights, reserves bolstered the ranks of regular maintainers. (PC)

At the time of Exercise MAN, the number of Mystères assigned to Squadron 109 exceeded the ILAF's standard of twenty-four aircraft per fighter squadron—the balance between standard and inventory compensated for aircraft grounded during maintenance; Mystère 05 was undergoing Level B maintenance at the Ramat David Wing 1 Maintenance Squadron Mystère Workshop. (PC)

EP pilot Ohad Shadmi flew five sorties on 12 March 1958: SEAB Teman Field in an eight-ship formation in Mystère 13, the rocketry range at Halutza in Mystère 25, bombing and strafing Halutza range in Mystère 74, a simulated attack against AAA emplacements defending Tel Nof in Mystère 25, and SEAB Teman Field in an eight-ship formation in Mystère 10; his total time was 4:15 flight hours.

Mystère 07 landing at Ramat David. By March 1958, the ILAF was preparing for the conduct of large scale daytime operations, but also started to explore options for enhanced effectiveness during nighttime warfare. (PC)

NOCTURNAL WARFARE

Exercise MAN's primary objective was to generate a high tempo of sorties, but all of its sorties were flown during daytime. The ILAF's inability to operate efficiently during nighttime was viewed as a major deficiency in light of ILDF doctrine. AIR2 Chief Nathan Eldar elaborated on 28 March 1958:

> Due to ILDF emphasis concerning nocturnal warfare and the attributes of a short war that compel maximum effort, it is important to secure an option for our aircraft to fight at night.

Illumination of a target was vital to enable aircraft to fight at night, not only for attacks, but also for positive identification prior to attack. The ILAF explored illumination from the ground and the air.

Artillery and searchlights were suggested for marking targets, with artillery marking already tested and searchlight marking—with two searchlights crossed over the target—proposed for testing. Both options were relevant for marking with aircraft and then dropping flares in order to attack.

Flares were only available for piston-powered combat aircraft—the Harvard and Mustang—and one MI-2 flare illuminated an area one to three kilometers (one half to two miles) in diameter for three minutes. A flare for jet-powered combat aircraft was in development; the original schedule anticipated introduction from April 1958, but by March 1958, it was clear that the schedule had slipped and service introduction of the MI-3 flare was not expected before April 1959. AIR2 Chief Nathan Eldar summarized:

> The ILAF invested in development of a means to enable operations at night. Among other things, the ILAF solved issues concerning phases of a mission at night [other than attack], such as take-off, flying, homing, and landing.
>
> Development of illumination systems has not been prioritized ... MI-2 flare development has lagged and [the ILAF] order has not been fulfilled yet; development of MI-3 flares is facing a schedule slip of more than a year.
>
> Delayed delivery of this basic means forces the ILAF to avoid tests and training concerning aircraft operations at night; it must be said that a maximum number of tests has been conducted in line with the means supplied to the ILAF.

AIR2 thus recommended accelerating development and production of MI-3 flares to test combined operations at night with ILDF marking and ILAF illumination. The acquisition of the Decca navigation system was also suggested to enable target attacks deeper within enemy territory.

ILAF YEAR 1958 TERM 1 PLAN

Four Flying School Class 23 graduates—Eli Bahat, Oded Einav, Kochav Hess, and Simi Saar—reported to Squadron 109, along with Class 22 graduate Ezra Dotan, at the end of the Squadron 113 Ouragan OTU Course 5 that ran during ILAF Year 1957 Term 3. Three Class 23 graduates—Bahat, Einav, and Saar—were actually planned to convert to the Mystère and fly one term with Squadron 109 as a stepping stone prior to assignment to Squadron 110 Vautour at the start of ILAF Year 1958 Term 2; Simi Saar's first Squadron 109 Mystère flight was in 4513 on 27 March 1958.

Additionally, at the start of ILAF Year 1958 Term 1, Squadron 110 Vautour's team pilots were still flying Squadron 109 Mystères pending authorization to start Vautour flights in Israel. Therefore, Squadron 109's plan for ILAF Year 1958 Term 1 was as follows:

Simi Saar's Mystere first flight was flown in Mystere 13—which was photographed in June 1957—on 27 March 1958. (PC)

This included two peaks in aircraft availability, as twenty-four aircraft were required for the Israel Independence Day flyover on 23 April 1958 and for the end of term combat day exercise on 9 July 1958.

Interestingly, the Squadron 109 plan for ILAF Year 1958 Term 1 covered 1,360 flight hours or, excluding flight hours planned for Squadron 110's setup team, 705 flight hours. Simple extrapolation would have yielded 2,115 flight hours for Squadron 109 during ILAF Year 1958 or 4,230 flight hours for Squadrons 101 and 109 during ILAF Year 1958, while actual Mystère utilization during ILAF Year 1957 was 4,879 flight hours and the proposed Mystère utilization for ILAF Year 1958 was 5,900 flight hours.

As always, planning was sensitive to changes; Vautour flights in Israel started earlier than planned and Squadron 109's flight hour allocation for Squadron 110's setup team pilots during ILAF Year 1958 Term 1 was no longer relevant.

Month	Aircraft	Regulars	EPs	Squadron 110	Total
April	16	150 flight hours	25 flight hours	70 flight hours	245 flight hours
May	18	215 flight hours	60 flight hours	150 flight hours	425 flight hours
June	18	215 flight hours	60 flight hours	150 flight hours	425 flight hours
July	18	75 flight hours	150 flight hours	40 flight hours	265 flight hours

SUPER MYSTÈRE ACQUISITION RECOMMENDATION

The ILAF's hesitancy concerning the SMB2's purchase finally evaporated on 14 April 1958, when AIR Department Chief Ezer Weizman issued a position paper in favor of acquiring not twelve or twenty-four SMB2s, as previously discussed, but thirty.

Arguments supporting SMB2 acquisition were the Mystère's absolute inferiority versus the MiG-17, the total superiority of the SMB2 over the Mystère, and delayed development of the Mirage.

SQUADRON 101'S TENTH ANNIVERSARY

Squadron 109 escorted a Squadron 115 Mosquito reconnaissance mission over Jordan on 23 April 1958; EP pilot Ohad Shadmi flew the hour and thirty minute mission in Mystère 90. The following day, Israel celebrated its tenth Independence Day and the ILAF staged a massive flyover; Squadron 109 EP pilots Asaf Ben-Nun

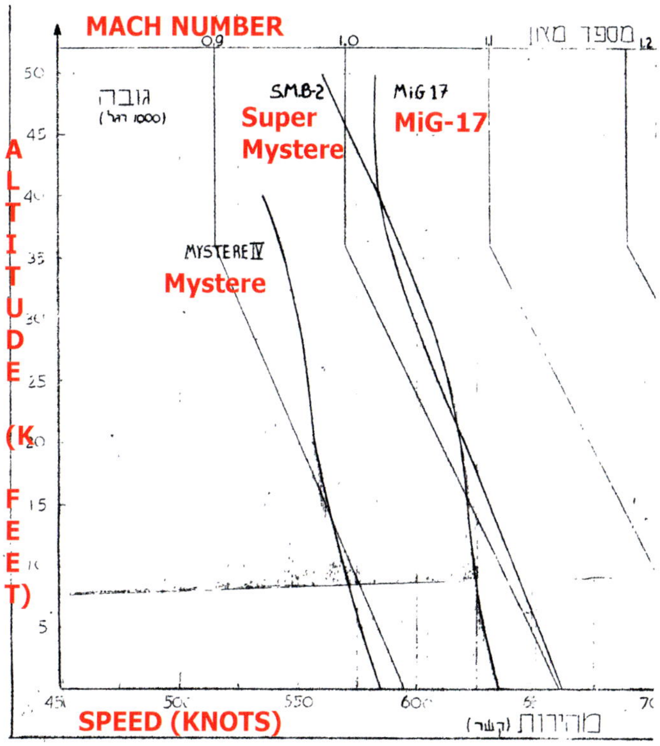

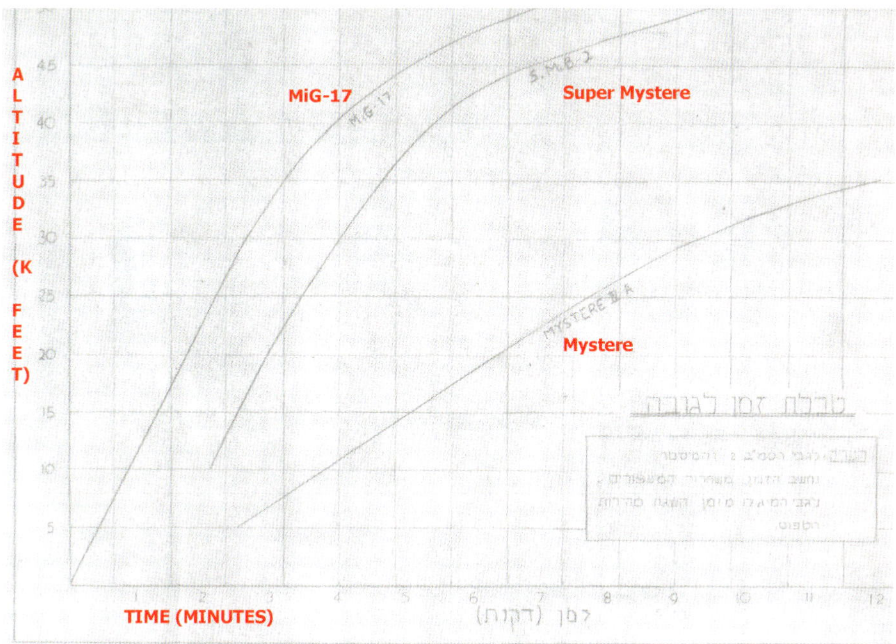

On 14 and 17 April 1958, the ILAF circulated graphs that emphasized the MiG-17's superiority over the Mystére in climb and speed to support SMB2 acquisition. (PC)

34
71
72

07

Squadron 109's sister Squadron 101 celebrated its tenth anniversary on 29 May 1958, and Squadron 109 was invited to participate in the turnaround competition; it is possible this visit to Hatzor prompted Squadron 109 to introduce a red flash along the fuselages of its Mystéres, as influenced by Squadron 101's red fuselage flash. (PC)

and Ohad Shadmi participated in the flyover in Mystères 71 and 72, respectively.

Also celebrating its tenth anniversary was the ILAF's First Fighter Squadron, so Squadron 109 deployed four Mystères to Hatzor—including 07, 71, and 72—for the turnaround competition during Squadron 101's tenth anniversary celebration on 29 May 1958.

DAVID HOCHMAN

ILAF Year 1958 term 1's tactical training phase included support of ILNF: Yossi Sarig flew an ILNF support practice on 4 June 1958 in Mystère 25, and Asaf Ben-Nun and Yossi Sarig practiced ILNF support on 6 June 1958 in Mystères 90 and 07, respectively. On 5 June 1958, Mystère 74 was lost during ILNF support training and pilot David Hochman was killed.

Mystère 74 was lost in a fatal accident during training with the ILNF on 5 June 1958 and pilot David Hochman was killed. (PC)

EXERCISE RAID

The scale and size of end of term combat day exercises was continuously expanded; Wing 1's ILAF Year 1958 Term 1 concluding combat day maneuver was Exercise RAID, which ran from 8 to 10 July 1958. Exercise RAID's objectives were to test:

- Wing 1 transition to C level readiness and emergency deployment
- Mobilization of reserves
- Activation of a dummy squadron
- Maximum tempo flying day, including training missions with live ordnance
- Level B maintenance during dispersion of aircraft
- Supply of services, fuel, and ordnance to HAS
- Damage control
- Activation of the wing command post
- Activation of the ILAF command post
- Practice with intelligence communication channels

So flying and fast turnaround—emphasized the most at squadron level—were only at the heart of the combat day concept, which also exercised many more related issues that actually enabled squadrons to implement fast turnaround and to accomplish a maximum number of sorties per day. RAID was divided into three phases:

- Phase A on 8 July 1958: mobilization of reserves; dispersal of aircraft; and transition to Readiness State C.
- Phase B on 9 July 1958: practice missions from dawn to dusk.
- Phase C on 10 July 1958: return to routine.

The targets were three ranges for practice missions with live ordnance and five airfields—Betzet, Megiddo, Plugot, St Jean, and Teman Field—for dummy attacks.

EP pilot Ovadia Nachman flew four RAID missions: MIOR Gimel 3 with napalm in Mystère 05, plus a dummy strike against Teman Field; MIOR Gimel 10 with rocket pods in Mystère 75, plus a dummy attack against Plugot; MIOR Gimel 17 with napalm in Mystère 25, plus a dummy attack against Teman Field; and MIOR Gimel 24 with T-10 rockets in Mystère 75, plus a dummy attack against Betzet, for a total time of 4:45 flight hours.

EP pilot Yossi Sarig flew four RAID sorties: MIOR Gimel 4 with two 250 kilogram (550 lb) bombs in Mystère 25; MIOR Gimel 13 with two napalm canisters in Mystère 70; MIOR Gimel 20 with rocket pods in Mystère 70; and MIOR Gimel 27 with T-10 rockets in Mystère 26, for a total time of 4:20 flight hours.

EP pilot Asaf Ben-Nun flew four RAID sorties: MIOR Gimel 9 with rocket pods in Mystère 32; MIOR Gimel 11 with napalm in Mystère 14; MIOR Gimel 24 with T-10 rockets in Mystère 07; and MIOR Gimel 32 with napalm in Mystère 65, for a total time of 4:25 flight hours.

EP pilot Ohad Shadmi flew five RAID sorties, all as leader of a four-ship formation: MIOR Gimel 3 with napalm in Mystère 75; MIOR Gimel 11 with rocket pods in Mystère 32; MIOR Gimel 17 with T-10 rockets in Mystère 06; MIOR Gimel 21 with napalm in Mystère 26; and MIOR Gimel 32 with napalm in Mystère 14, for a total time of 6:00 flight hours.

PRESIDENTIAL FLYOVER

Israeli President Isaac Ben-Zvi departed for a visit to the Netherlands, Belgium, and Switzerland on 14 July 1958. In line with MIOR Ayin 47, Squadron 109 was tasked to fly over Lod International Airport in a four-ship formation and then escort the El Al Britannia airliner; Yossi Sarig flew MIOR Ayin 47 in Mystère 10.

Squadron 109 EP pilots Ohad Shadmi and Asaf Ben-Nun flew Mystére 14 on 9 July 1958 during Exercise RAID MIOR Gimel 32 and Gimel 11, respectively. (PC)

ILAF DAY 10 (OR 11)

ILAF Day 2 was celebrated on 27 October 1949, and the tradition of commemorating ILAF Day during autumn continued until 1953; but from 1954, ILAF Day was celebrated during the summer and ILAF Day 10 was set to be marked on 10 August 1958. At the heart of the celebration was a flyover and firepower demonstration at a special set near Beer Sheba, in the Negev Desert, that was open to the public. Squadron 109's contribution included an "11" formation, though it is not clear if this formation included eleven aircraft or was shaped to represent the number "11," perhaps for ILAF Day 11; among the pilots participating in the flyover were Yossi Sarig in Mystère 81, Jonathan Shahar in Mystère 65, and Eli Bahat in 73.

POWER FOR THE MYSTÈRE

The Mystère lacked power, and this deficiency placed the Mystère in a precarious position compared to the MiG-17, the Mystère's main air-to-air competition for rule of Middle Eastern skies at the time. The issue of being underpowered was exacerbated when the Mystère strike study surfaced. While for air-to-air missions weight was minimized, during air-to-ground operations maximum weight was emphasized to accomplish better endurance and/or a heavier punch. Assaf Ben-Nun recalled:

> The Mystère's major weakness was that it was underpowered; it was aerodynamically smooth but it lacked power. The joke was that with two external fuel

The Verdon's lack of power was viewed as a major Mystère handicap and was addressed in September and October 1958, when a proposal to replace the Verdon 350 with the Atar 8 was discussed and rejected. This photo of a Mystère Verdon engine was taken at Ramat David in June 1957. (PC)

tanks and two 250 kilograms [550 lb] bombs, the Mystère was barely able to climb the taxiway up from the HAS; on heavy-weight take-off during hot days, the Mystère generated a cloud of dust at the end of the runway as the aircraft lifted off over the end of the runway.

A radical proposal to add power to the Mystère suggested replacing the Verdon 350 engine with the Atar 8, so that thrust would be increased from 3.5 tons to 4.4 tons. The Atar 8 proposition was explored, but on 7 September 1958 AIR2 concluded that replacement of the Verdon 350 with the Atar 8 was not worthwhile.

An AIR2 forum discussion on 8 October 1958 endorsed the AIR2 conclusion from 7 September 1958 and decided against replacement of the Mystère's Verdon 350 engine with the Atar 8.

EXERCISE FOCUS

ILAF Year 1958 Term 2 actually ran from 15 August 1958 until 12 November 1958, when the end of term combat day Exercise FOCUS took place. As usual, FOCUS concentrated on fast turnaround and a high tempo for flights.

FOCUS was planned to take place from 11 to 13 November 1958; in addition to typical combat day objectives, the main emphasis during FOCUS was BDA, especially in debrief reports compiled after flights. All FOCUS flights were to be with ordnance for real attacks against dummy targets at three ranges, while on the way back from the range to Ramat David, FOCUS formations were to fly dummy attacks against Megiddo, Plogut, and St Jean airfields.

Safety limitations emphasized minimum altitudes—3,500 feet above ground level in bombing, 150 feet in strafing, and 450 feet in rocketry—and weather limitations: no bombing at more than 5/8 clouds below 8,000 feet and no flying at more than 5/8 clouds below 3,000 feet. The number of strafing passes was restricted to two per aircraft per sortie. Remaining external ordnance not used over the ranges was to be jettisoned over the Mediterranean Sea.

The exercise was not two-sided, but Squadron 101 was tasked to maintain Mystères on readiness to practice the interception of Wing 1 aircraft flying Exercise FOCUS missions. However, only interception was to be practiced and two-sided mock air combat was strictly forbidden, primarily because the Wing 1 aircraft were armed with cocked guns.

FOCUS allocations to Squadron 109 included 360 reserve days to enable mobilization of 120 reservists, 3,120 gun rounds, 104 250-kilogram (550 lb) explosive bombs, fifty-two 250-kilogram (550 lb) sand bombs, and 104 sixty-eight millimeter rockets.

EP pilot Haim Niv flew four FOCUS sorties on 12 November 1958: bombing and strafing in Mystère 32; pod rocketry and strafing in Mystère 14; napalm attack and strafing in Mystère 82; and pod rocketry and strafing in Mystère 06.

EP pilot Asaf Ben-Nun flew five FOCUS sorties on 12 November 1958: dive bombing and strafing in Mystère 65; dive bombing and strafing in Mystère 70; pod rocketry and strafing in Mystère 75; low altitude bombing and strafing in Mystère 65; and napalm attack and strafing in Mystère 25.

OPERATION RUTH

The Cold War and Eastern and Western issues impacted Middle Eastern nations from May 1958, with a civil war in Lebanon followed by a regime change in Iraq during July 1958. United States and British intervention in Lebanon and Jordan, respectively, seemingly stabilized the situation, but the withdrawal of US and British forces from Lebanon and Jordan during October and November 1958 may have encouraged Middle Eastern nations to test the tolerance of local forces and global players.

Six Flying School Class 25 graduates were posted to Squadron 109 at the end of ILAF Year 1958 Term 2 Squadron 113 Ouragan OTU Course 7: Yair Ben-Sheffer, Judah Cohen, Uri Even-Nir, Rami Harpaz, Abraham Kimchi, and Haggai Koren. Their Mystère solo day was on 20 November 1958, and Kimchi soloed in 4515, here flying inverted over Ramat David. (PC)

Israel and Syria exchanged fire on 6 November 1958 and again on 3 December 1958. In preparation for potential deterioration, AIR3 issued OPOR RUTH to cover an air superiority offensive against Egypt and Syria since, at the time, the two nations were confederated as the United Arab Republic. Operation RUTH tasked Squadron 109 to assign sixteen aircraft to two SEAB missions, with one eight-ship formation tasked to attack an Egyptian air base and one eight-ship formation tasked to raid Mazzeh air base near Damascus.

United Arab Republic aircraft—Egyptian and Syrian—intensified activity, possibly to monitor ILDF intentions or to deter Israel from launching a reprisal attack against Syria in the wake of the skirmish on 3 December 1958, to the point that Egyptian MiG-17s and Squadron 101 Mystères clashed on 20 December 1958. Squadron 109 was not involved in the 20 December 1958 air combats, but due to soaring tensions all EPs reported to squadrons and readiness was stepped up, including patrols; on 21 December 1958, EP pilot Asaf Ben-Nun flew a dawn patrol over the border of Israel and Syria in Mystère 07.

As often happens, the December 1958 round of escalating tensions did not escalate to war and OPOR RUTH was not activated.

DANNY KAYE VISITS THE VALLEY

Tensions between Israel and the United Arab Republic did not escalate and Operation RUTH was not activated, but clashes continued. On 8 January 1959, Squadron 101 was involved in yet another air combat versus Egyptian MiGs. This time the engagement was inconclusive and all involved MiGs and Mystères returned safely to their bases, even though an Egyptian official statement claimed two Israeli aircraft were shot down—a statement that was evidently false, as all Squadron 101 Mystères involved in air combat versus Egyptian MiGs that day returned to Hatzor.

Squadron 109 was not involved in air combat versus Egyptian MiGs and did not take part in any action against Syria, but benefitted from the situation on 11 January 1959, when American actor Danny Kaye "dropped by" to visit Ramat David—accompanied by ILAF AIR Department Chief Ezer Weizman—on his way north to cheer up children in villages that suffered Syrian bombardment during the 3 December 1958 clash between Israel and Syria.

Squadron 109 junior pilots during the winter of 1958 to 1959 (standing left to right): Koren, Haviv, Harpaz, and Even-Nir; and crouching (left to right): Kimchi and Ben-Sheffer. (PC)

Asaf Ben-Nun flew Mystère 07 during a dawn patrol over the Israeli Syrian border on 21 December 1958. (PC)

American actor Danny Kaye visiting Squadron 109 on 11 January 1959 (left to right): Kimchi, Koren, Yariv, Cohen, Weizman, Kaye, Zuk, Harpaz, and Haviv. (PC)

Mystère 25 was damaged in an accident, possibly on 18 January 1959. The thus far unearthed last pre-accident flight is dated 12 November 1958 and thus far unearthed first post-accident flight is dated 23 November 1959. (PC)

Mystère 25 was damaged in an accident, possibly on 18 January 1959. The thus far unearthed last pre-accident flight is dated 12 November 1958 and thus far unearthed first post-accident flight is dated 23 November 1959. (PC)

MYSTÈRES 25 AND 12

Mystère 25 was damaged in a landing accident, possibly on 18 January 1959. Abraham Kimchi recalled:

> It was during one of my first flights in the Mystère; the nose wheel fell away right after take-off. I orbited to expend fuel while all the wise guys convened in the control tower and decided I should land "as is," and so I did. The nose gear collapsed shortly after touchdown and I used the brakes in an attempt to steer the aircraft on the runway, but then the main landing gear collapsed and the aircraft continued to run until it stopped beside the end of the runway in a huge cloud of dust. I collected my personal gear and walked to the squadron.

Mystère 12 was lost in an accident on 22 January 1959. Two pairs practiced two-on-two air combat over the Mediterranean Sea west of Nahariya; Amnon Halivni and Uri Even-Nir engaged Josef Zuk and Judah Cohen when Mystère 12 entered a spin and pilot Judah Cohen was forced to eject. The aircraft crashed into the sea but the injured pilot landed ashore.

AIR COMBAT LESSONS

AMV2 claims that Egyptian MiG-17 pilot Omar Farouk Abdel Salam engaged Israeli Mystères in February 1959 and was credited with a confirmed kill. This narrative should be dismissed, because ILAF Mystères are not known to have engaged enemy MiGs—Egyptian or Syrian —during February 1959.

AIR3's Jacob Morgan analyzed potential lessons from the 20 December 1958 and 8 January 1959 air combats and circulated five issues for discussion on 8 February 1959: formations; tactics; rear hemisphere warning in the MiG-17; performance comparison between the MiG-17 and Mystère; and a summary:

> Formations: From all engagements thus far, and from other sources, we learn that the United Arab Republic air force does not operate MiG-17 aircraft for operational missions in formations smaller than a four-ship; until not long ago, the Egyptians used to conduct interceptions in pairs, but now they conduct interceptions in four-ship formations at least, and sometimes in two separate four-ship formations.
>
> Most engagements versus MiGs (including during the Suez War) were against four-ship formations or large formations. In most cases, the second pair "disappeared" at the start of combat that was subsequently fought in numerical balance. On the other hand, it would be wrong to assume that this situation will last; therefore, there is room to consider the worthiness of operating our aircraft in four-ship formations. Information at hand indicates the MiGs are flying at a vertical separation of 3,000 feet between pairs, so it is possible an attack against one pair will be launched in ignorance of the second pair and without the "disappearance" of the second pair as they used to do in the past.
>
> However, operating our aircraft in four-ship formations will impair squadron training. Therefore, it is proposed to continue QRA in pairs for the time being, but to launch four-ship formations for other types of missions, such as escort, patrol, and reconnaissance. In light of this proposition, there is room to decide whether to dispatch four-ship formations—instead of a pair—to escort a reconnaissance mission, or that the photographing aircraft will be one of the four-ship formation aircraft in order to secure more maneuverability for the formation in case of engagement.
>
> Tactics: A pair of aircraft in combat can operate using one of three options:
>
> - Close formation, with the wingman always within fifty to 200 meters (160-650 ft.) from the leader.
>
> - Open formation, in which the wingman demonstrates more initiative, can distance from the leader up to two kilometers (one and a quarter miles), and can take the lead if they are in a better position to attack. The shape of the formation changes during the engagement for as long as at least one of the aircraft is in visual contact with the other aircraft.
>
> - Break of formation, with each aircraft selecting a target and attacking that target even if visual contact between the pair is lost.
>
> As already indicated, in all engagements thus far, one pair of MiGs remained to fight and one pair of MiGs disengaged at the start of combat. On occasion, the MiGs break in opposite directions, with one pair breaking right and one pair breaking left. Such a situation tempts us to break formation so that each one of our aircraft can follow one pair. This action would be right for a four-ship formation, which would split into two pairs, with each pair engaging an enemy pair, but is potentially dangerous in case of a pair. The advantage is more maneuverability for each aircraft, since they are no longer dependent on their mate, which restricts movement; but there is considerable danger of an attack against one of our aircraft by more MiGs that were not seen by our aircraft and managed to get right behind the tail of one of our aircraft. Overall, this

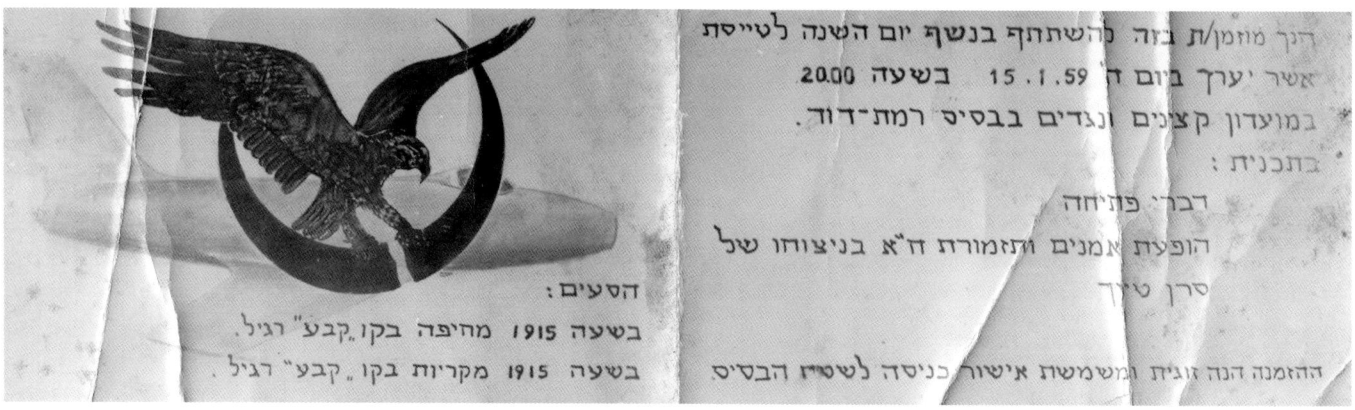
הנך מוזמן/ת בזה להשתתף בנשף יום השנה לטייסת
אשר יערך ביום ה' 15.1.59 בשעה 20.00
במועדון קצינים ונגדים בבסיס רמת-דוד.
בתכנית:
דברי פתיחה
הופעת אמנים ותזמורת ח"א בניצוחו של
סרן טייך
ההזמנה הנה זוגית ומשמשת אישור כניסה לשטח הבסיס.

הסעים:
בשעה 1915 מחיפה בקו "קבע" רגיל.
בשעה 1915 מקריות בקו "קבע" רגיל.

An invitation to Squadron 109 Day—actually an evening event starting at 20:00 on 15 January 1959. (PC)

Standing on a balcony (left to right): Ben-Nun and Dagan. Standing (left to right): Halivni, Dotan, Sheffer, Zuk, Yariv, and Shmueli. And crouching (left to right): Harpaz, Kimchi, Haviv, Ben-Sheffer, Even-Nir, and Koren. (PC)

Squadron 109 reserve maintainers push Mystère 75 in a HAS taxiway; the Ramat David Wing 1 Maintenance Squadron hangars are visible at the top right corner and the control tower is visible at the top left corner. (PC)

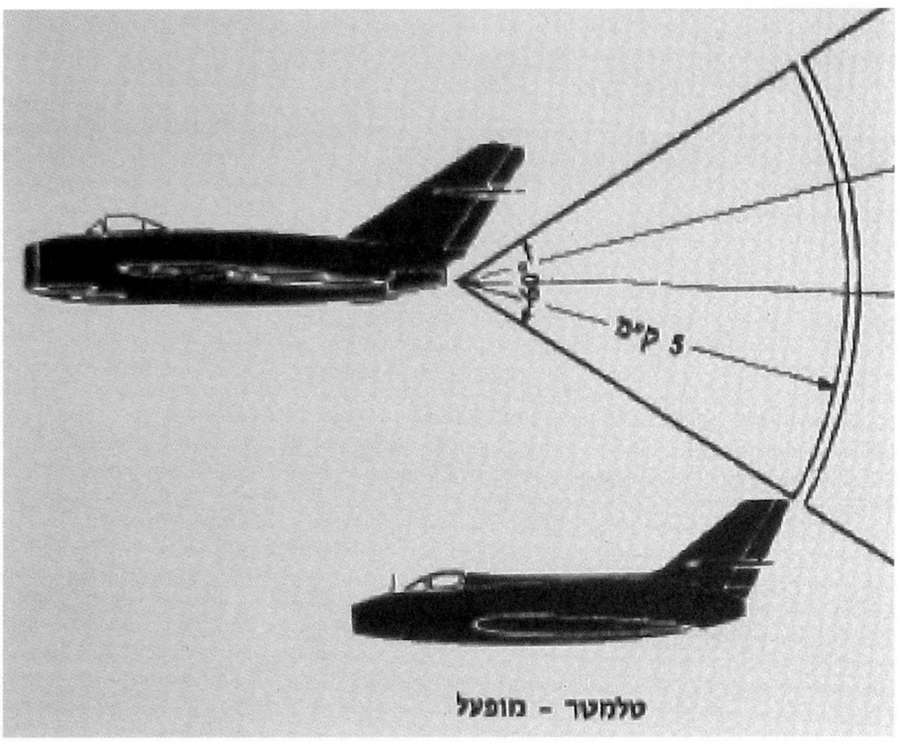

The ILAF's evaluation of the MiG-17's rear hemisphere warning system was a Mystère range radar detection range of five kilometers (three mile) in a sixty degree cone. (PC)

tactic may increase the number of kills, but may also result in the shooting down of our aircraft, and for this reason alone it should be rejected except in special circumstances.

Only the leader can decide on a course of action based on evaluation of a number of parameters at the start of engagement: the number of enemy aircraft; the relative tactical situation; the behavior of enemy aircraft; the weather; and the competence level of their wingman.

Therefore, it is recommended that a break of a pair will only be ordered under the following special circumstances:

- The leader is convinced that there are no more MiGs.
- The tactical situation is fit for a break in formation.
- The engagement is over our territory or near our territory.
- The leader believes the wingman can be trusted to get along alone.

Under other circumstances, the formation should not be broken and combat will be fought in close or open formation. The selection of the formation type are under authority of the leader in line with combat developments and especially based on the competence level of the wingman. In any case, the basic formation will be a close formation until the leader decides otherwise.

Rear hemisphere warning in the MiG-17: There are clear indications that the MiG-17 is equipped with a passive rear hemisphere warning system that reacts to radar beams, including range radar. This system is definitely installed in United Arab Republic aircraft, but there is no information whether it is active and what its attributes are. Professional evaluation suggests that such a system has a range of several kilometers [miles] and wide angle coverage that may reach 180 degrees with the ability to detect any radar. The only engagement during which it was possible to evaluate if such a system was active was during the final combat on 20 December 1958, but our indications are that the Egyptian pilots were not warned that our aircraft were approaching. From this, we cannot conclude that the system is not active because it is possible that:

- The aircraft in question had an unserviceable system.
- The system functioned, but the pilot did not pay attention, as he was busy with the GCI of our other aircraft.
- It is possible that the coverage angle is not wide but narrow—up to forty to sixty degrees—in which case there would have been no warning, as the attack was initiated at a high angle.

In light of the aforementioned discussions, there are two potential courses of action:

- To switch off range radar whenever we approach enemy aircraft from behind in a situation that we may be unnoticed.
- To wait for another engagement or more intelligence information that will convince us the system is active.

In case it is decided to switch off range radar, then a modification will be required to stop the transmission of a beam while maintaining range radar hot so that it will be possible to switch it on again.

Performance comparison between the MiG-17 and Mystère:

- The MiG-17's net weight is 5.7 tons with a thrust of 2.7 to 3.3 tons with afterburner, so that T/W at low altitude is 0.47 without afterburner and 0.58 with afterburner.
- The Mystère's net weight is 8.3 tons with a thrust of 3.5 tons, so T/W at low altitude is 0.42.

At 40,000 feet, the Mystère's thrust decreases to 0.9 tons. It is reasonable to assume there is a similar decrease in the MiG-17 (the two engines are very similar), which yields a dry thrust of 0.7 tons, but afterburner thrust does not decrease with altitude, and may even increase a little. As a result, the MiG-17's total thrust at 40,000 feet is 1.3 tons ... Therefore, T/W at 40,000 feet is 0.11 for the Mystère and 0.12 for the MiG-17 without afterburner and 0.23 with afterburner.

Thus, at all altitudes the MiG-17 has a minor advantage over the Mystère in dry T/W; an advantage that is increased with afterburner, especially at high altitude, because dry thrust decreases considerably with altitude, while afterburner thrust remains constant.

There are reports that the MiG-17's top speed at sea level is 630 knots. It is unclear if this speed is practical (other reports indicate 590 knots) or if it is a record number. In the Mystère, it is possible to accomplish 640 knots, but safety considerations limit speed to 585 knots, and it is possible the same applies to the MiG-17.

Maximum speed at high altitude is reported as Mach 1.2, but it is known that in normal flight the MiG-17 is limited to Mach 0.98, and it is certainly known that at high speeds it is possible to lose control; there is an arrangement for the automatic deployment of air brakes at Mach 0.98 that can be switched off in the cockpit.

The MiG-17's elevator servo system—unlike in the Mystère—is a system of hydraulic boosters, and this is probably the main reason for the restriction of maximum speed and the phenomenon of "stiff controls" to the point of loss of control as reported by several sources. There are reports of instability at high speeds that result in gunnery difficulties.

The MiG-17's internal fuel capacity is 1,400 liter [370 gallons] plus 800 liters [210 gallons] in two external tanks. Fuel consumption at 35,000 feet is 20 liters [6 gallons] per minute without afterburner and 80 liters [21 gallons] per minute with afterburner. At low altitude, the respective figures are 60-70 and 150. Thus, a MiG-17 that takes off from an air base near the Suez Canal will consume all the fuel in its external tanks by the time it reaches the Egyptian/Israeli border; if it patrols over the border for ten to fifteen minutes at 20,000 feet, then in case of engagement, it will not be able to fight with afterburner for more than three to four minutes, especially at low altitude, and then it will have to disengage with at least 600 to 700 liters [158 to 185 gallons] in order to return to base, or with 300 to 400 liters [eighty to 106 gallons] in order to land at El Arish. Thus, in case of return to base, it will be able to fight for two to three minutes, and in the case of landing at El Arish, it will be able to fight for four minutes. If we can catch it with less than 1,000 liters [264 gallons], it is realistic to assume it will not be able to use afterburner at low altitude, except for a disengagement attempt.

Turning at 30,000 feet at Mach 0.8, the MiG-17 can tolerate more than 2.5 G, compared with 1.8 G in the Mystère. We have no data concerning turning at low altitude, but it is obvious that the gap is lower due to a smaller disparity between engine thrusts at low altitude.

One of the MiG-17's most important positive points is its high rate of climb: 12,000 feet per minute without afterburner and 24,000 feet per minute with afterburner at low altitude. Time from brakes off to 40,000 feet is six minutes without afterburner and four minutes with afterburner. In pull up from low speed the Mystère cannot follow the MiG-17, but at speeds higher than 450 knots, the Mystère can follow the MiG-17 and even hit it during the start of its climb.

Summary of the comparison between the MiG-17 and Mystère: In an engagement versus the MiG-17—with pilot quality ignored and based only on aircraft performance—it is recommended to avoid slow speeds because of the MiG-17's lower wing load (the stall speed of a clean aircraft is 115 knots and the stall speed of a clean aircraft with minimum fuel is only 105 knots) and due to higher T/W that results in superior climb performance. Therefore, in slow speed maneuverability such as scissors, the MiG-17 is better than the Mystère. At high speed the Mystère has an edge because of the MiG-17's "stiff controls."

The MiG-17's edge in turn rate improves with altitude due to thrust; the minimal difference is at low altitude.

Fuel capacity is a major limitation in the MiG-17, and this limitation gets worse at low altitude.

Control stiffness is also more noticeable at low altitude and high indicated speeds, since at high altitude this phenomenon depends on a high Mach number.

At high speed, the MiG-17 is not stable and this impacts gunnery.

To this comparison we should add two factors: the average level of ILAF pilots is higher than the level of

Squadron 105 SMB2 flights from Hatzor started on 11 February 1959, when the first four Squadron 105 SMB2 pilots flew from Hatzor; among them was Ohad Shadmi in SMB2 04. (PC)

> Egyptian pilots; the Egyptians do not properly practice air combat.
>
> It seems that with an aggressive manner and proper pilots, a Mystère can attack and shoot down a MiG-17 at any altitude and speed, but if hitting a MiG-17 at the start of combat is not accomplished then it is recommended to engage the MiG-17 at low altitude and high speed through a high speed spiral dive, during which the MiG-17 will not be able to overtake the Mystère due to the Mystère's aerodynamic smoothness and will not be able to hit the Mystère because of the MiG's high speed control difficulties. During the dive, the Mystère should try to shake the MiG-17 with high G, as the Mystère enjoys better control at high speed. If the Mystère fails to shake off the MiG-17 during the dive, then at low altitude and high speed the performances of the two aircraft types are roughly equal, while the MiG-17 is limited in use of its afterburner due to the afterburner's high fuel consumption and the MiG-17's low fuel capacity.

On 12 February 1959, AIR3 Chief Moshe Peled chaired a forum that discussed the implications of the MiG-17 versus Mystère comparison; among the six staff officers and five squadron commanders in attendance was Squadron 109 Commander Samuel Sheffer. The forum discussed formations, tactics, and the comparison of the MiG-17 and Mystère.

Formation size for QRA was to remain a pair, but it was recommended to scramble a pair after each pair at a short time interval when the prospects of engagement were high; the formation size for escorting reconnaissance missions was also to remain a pair, except for mission profiles that would require more escort aircraft, but the proposition to integrate a reconnaissance aircraft with the escort formation was rejected.

Tactical decisions concerning combat were left to the leader's real time consideration, though it was recommended to try and preserve the elementary pair formation in combat. Breaking of the pair was the only discussed subject that resulted in two opinions. One opinion agreed to breaking the pair in certain circumstances: when the only way to accomplish the mission is to break a pair; when breaking the pair is beneficial in light of the tactical situation; when the combat is over friendly territory; and when there is absolute certainty that there are no more enemy aircraft. Another opinion was that the pair must be preserved and not broken under any circumstances.

The MiG-17 versus Mystère comparison pointed out a high speed low altitude advantage, but this advantage was based on still-unsubstantiated reports that the MiG-17 suffered serious control issues at high speed. The forum suggested it would not be wise to rely on such unsubstantiated reports and recommended to confirm or rule out the alleged MiG-17 issues at high speed while meanwhile engaging the MiG-17 in a way that would highlight the supposed superiority of ILAF pilots over United Arab Republic pilots.

OPERATION SERGEANT YORK

Air-to-air gunnery was practiced every term. The Mustang, then the Meteor, and then the Ouragan were all used as target tugs. Pilots took turns, and each participating Mystère had its rounds painted a different color so, at the end of practice, the number of colored holes in the drogue were counted and attributed to individual pilots. The number of hits was compared to the number of expended rounds and yielded a hit percentage; an average result was 10%. Known results for Squadron 109 pilots at the end of the training term that lasted from 15 August to 12 November 1958 are 3.3% and 3.4%—well below average.

Mystère squadron commanders complained the Mystère weapons system was inefficient in air-to-air gunnery and that there was a small number of "good" hitting aircraft and a large number of "bad" hitting aircraft, so:

- Senior pilots usually scored higher results than junior pilots, but when a senior pilot flew a "bad" hitting aircraft the score was not good.

Mystère 75 participated in Operation SERGEANT YORK as a "bad" hitting aircraft, flew five sorties, and accomplished 6.5%—sixth among the seven Squadron 109 Mystères that took part in SERGEANT YORK. (PC)

Mystère 16 participated in Operation SERGEANT YORK as a "good" hitting aircraft, flew five sorties, and accomplished 21%—first among the seven Squadron 109 Mystères that took part in SERGEANT YORK. (PC)

- Harmonization of weapons systems was not standard, but specific, so a "good" hitting aircraft may be harmonized not in line with standard procedures, while an aircraft harmonized in line with standard procedures may be a "bad" hitting aircraft.
- The replacement of weapons system components would not transform a "bad" hitting aircraft into a "good" hitting aircraft.

MAT2 was therefore tasked to:

- Define the components of the Mystère weapons system
- Improve Mystère weapons system efficiency in air-to-air gunnery
- Issue guidelines for Mystère weapons system maintenance.

Operation SERGEANT YORK was planned to test Mystère air-to-air gunnery as follows:

- Each Mystère squadron commander would select three "good" hitting aircraft and three "bad" hitting aircraft, and each aircraft would fly six sorties.
- Six senior pilots per squadron would participate, but in a mix of four local pilots and two visiting pilots.
- Each pilot would fly six sorties with 25 RPG, firing from 350 to 400 meters (1,140 to 1,312 ft) at a target towed by a Meteor flying at 160 knots at 20,000 feet.

Preparations for Operation SERGEANT YORK were to include: zeroing of the range radar for an accuracy of ±5 meters (16 ft) at 450 meters (1,476 ft), versus squadrons' practice of zeroing for ±50 (164 ft) meters at 450 meters (1,476 ft); harmonizing of the weapons system in range radar mode, versus squadrons' practice of harmonizing the weapons system in manual mode; utilization of accurate test equipment; and the zeroing of all guns in participating aircraft to within a standard tolerance of ±5.

MAT2 reported Operation SERGEANT YORK results on 9 March 1959. The report contained implicit criticism concerning the commitment of squadrons to test. Both squadrons included junior pilots on their teams. Squadron 101 prepared six aircraft in line with MAT2 guidelines and completed all flights in good weather within three days, but Squadron 109 included seven pilots and seven aircraft, some of which were not prepared for the test in line with MAT2's guidelines, and completed sorties within seven days in weather conditions that ranged from fair to bad.

Squadron 109's participating pilots were Ramat David Wing Commander Menahem Bar, Squadron 109 Commander Samuel Sheffer, Amnon Halivni, Josef Zuk, and Amihy Shmueli, while Squadron 109 pilots Jacob Yariv and Ezra Dotan flew Squadron 101 Mystères during Operation SERGEANT YORK. The top scoring Squadron 109 pilot was Menahem Bar with 22.8%; the Squadron

109 scores ranged from 7.5% to 22.8%, while the Squadron 101 scores ranged from 14.3% to 32.6%.

Squadron 109's participating Mystères were 14, 26, and 75 as "bad" hitting aircraft and 16, 31, 73, and 83 as "good" hitting aircraft; the scores of the "bad" hitting aircraft ranged from 6% to 16.9%, while the scores of the "good" hitting aircraft ranged from 12.9% to 21%.

The results concerning Squadron 101's aircraft were conclusive: All aircraft are "good," and only the human factor impacted results.

The results concerning Squadron 109's aircraft were inconclusive due to the deviation from test prerequisites in selection of aircraft, preparation of aircraft, continuity, weather, and the number of sorties per pilot.

MAT2 therefore rejected the myth of "bad" and "good" hitting Mystères, recommended weapons system maintenance procedures as applied during preparations for Operation SERGEANT YORK, and suggested reevaluating practice during training pilots in air-to-air gunnery.

MYSTÈRES 65 AND 73

On 11 March 1959, two versus two air combat training resulted in the loss of Mystères 65 and 73. Shy Egozi and Aaron Markman engaged Amnon Arad and Eliezer Prigat when Egozi (Mystère 73) and Prigat (Mystère 65) collided over the Mediterranean Sea, west of Nahariya. Both pilots ejected and were brought ashore onboard a fishing boat and an ILNF torpedo boat; Mystère 65 crashed into the sea and Mystère 73 crash-landed near Maalot Tarshiha in the Galilee, some twenty kilometers (twelve miles) inland east of the Mediterranean Sea coastline. Eliezer Prigat recalled:

> Egozi was a senior pilot in the squadron and I was a junior pilot. We started scissors and slowed down to the slowest possible speed, and our aircraft descended due to low speed. In scissors, one follows the other and the winner is the first to follow the other while at the same time sight aiming and opening fire. At a certain phase when the aircraft was barely controllable, flying at very slow speed, I noticed that he was about to hit my empennage. I tried to turn away, but he hit me in the tail and my aircraft started to spin down to the sea. I tried to recover from the spin, but this proved impossible and I was forced to eject at a relatively low altitude. Everything functioned, including the Mae West and dinghy, and while I was in the water I saw his parachute, because he ejected at a higher altitude and I ejected later, at lower altitude.
>
> A fisherman from Acre fished me out of the water and I took charge of his boat until an ILNF torpedo boat arrived. I transferred to the torpedo boat which then picked up Egozi and then a rescue helicopter arrived. We passed a medical examination in a hospital at Haifa and the helicopter flew us to the squadron at Ramat David, where Squadron [109] Commander Samuel Sheffer debriefed us.

OPERATION SUMMER

The combat day exercise that concluded ILAF Year 1958 Term 3 was Operation SUMMER, from 16 to 18 March 1959; this time there were two flying days and EP pilot Asaf Ben-Nun flew three sorties—low altitude bombing and strafing in Mystère 82; low altitude bombing and strafing in Mystère 72; and dive bombing and strafing in Mystère 26—on 17 March 1959 and two sorties on 18 March 1959—napalm attack and strafing in Mystère 90 and napalm attack and strafing in Mystère 06—for a total of 2:45 flight hours.

The importance the ILDF attached to the ILAF combat day concept was emphasized during a visit by Prime Minister and Minister of Defense David Ben-Gurion to Squadron 109 on 17 March 1959. Arie Dagan recalled:

> Combat Day practiced the complete system: air crews and ground crews, as well as command and control. There were many sorties tasked to attack ground targets with internal and external ordnance: general purpose bombs, napalm, heavy rockets, belly rockets, and guns. The [combat day] MIOR profile simulated an operational mission, with many characteristics of real combat: radio silence; low altitude flying; offensive and defensive combat formations at high altitude; and unexpected events on the way to the target and on the way back. We flew air support and air combats and patrols, but the main mission was SEAB: dummy attacks against real air bases and live ordnance attacks against dummy air bases at the ranges.
>
> SEAB focused our attention and was constantly improved and updated. It included large formations—eight-ship formations and split formations that raided the same target in perfect coordination. Also attacks from a single direction along a runway axis and attacks from different directions perpendicular to a runway. Turn back, turn inside, pull up and turn back in different directions and in line astern. Days and hours were spent in the squadron's veranda and in the briefing room, discussing SEAB theory and practice [in order to accomplish] more complication, more complexity, and more surprise: engaging the maximum number of targets simultaneously, spreading the risk of AAA fire, strafing immediately after the release of bombs, attacking aircraft with rockets, and dropping napalm on heavy engineering equipment. Imagination was not limited and every proposition was evaluated and tested.
>
> Ground crews set new records on every combat day. Turnaround time frame—refuel, rearm, repair of malfunctions, and preflight inspections—was cut shorter and shorter. Competition between teams and between squadrons fueled motivation. The number of sorties rose higher and higher. Dummy sorties—taxiing armed aircraft to a preset spot [where the aircraft was disarmed and defueled] before returning to the squadron after an approximate time of a sortie had elapsed—were introduced to challenge efficiency and productivity preparing aircraft for missions.

Combat day exercises such as the March 1959 Operation SUMMER were exploited to generate a general group photo (left to right, top to bottom): Avneri, Dagan, Eyal, Henkin, Even-Nir, Ben-Nun, Terner, Lidor, Arad, Sheffer, Ben-Sheffer, Harpaz, Hess, Niv, Dotan, Markman, Technical Flight Commander Josef Kvodi, Halivni, Zuk, Shmueli, Egozi, Yariv, Prigat, Kimchi, Haviv, and Koren. (PC)

Our aircraft were concentrated at a few air bases, so HASs were constructed to enable continued operations of our aircraft even under enemy attack. Our intention was to strike first and destroy the enemy's air power on the ground, but it was impossible to overlook a scenario of a surprise enemy attack against our air bases. A huge amount of money was invested in construction of HASs, since every single aircraft was invaluable. In the glory days of turnaround, the output of every single aircraft reached up to seven sorties per day. The potential was immense, as a small number of aircraft generating so many sorties could counterbalance the numerical superiority of the enemy.

Combat days attracted many visitors; everyone wanted to have a look at the perfectly functioning ILAF machine. Among the visitors was Prime Minister and Minister of Defense David Ben-Gurion. His love of the ILDF and his pride in the ILDF's soldiers shined. Behind the mat concrete walls and shining metal aircraft, he looked for people, and he was genuinely interested in our backgrounds and in our Zionist roots. When [Squadron 109 Commander] Samuel Sheffer—himself from moshav Beer Tuvya—introduced pilots to Ben-Gurion, he only mentioned the residence of those who grew up in moshav [an Israeli village type at the time mostly associated with Ben-Gurion's political party MAPAI, an acronym for the Hebrew of Workers' Party of the Land of Israel] —Kfar Yehushua, En Vered, Bet Shaarim, etc.—thus creating an impression that all of the squadron pilots were moshav natives. When I arrived at the HAS to prepare for flight, Ben-Gurion was already there and the meeting between the two of us was inevitable. I was excited to shake his

Mystère 25 sometime after application of the fuselage flash in 1959 and before the installation of the parachute pack in 1961. (PC)

hand and introduce myself as a native of [a kibbutz, an Israeli village type at the time mostly associated with Ben-Gurion's rival political party MAPAM, an acronym in Hebrew for the United Workers Party] Merhavya. Ben-Gurion turned sharply towards Sheffer with a big question mark on his face, but Sheffer did not lose his temper; he remained calm and retorted "yes, Merhavya, from moshav Merhavya" [thanks to the fact there was kibbutz Merhavya and moshav Merhavya, and ignoring the fact that Dagan was actually from the kibbutz] and the awkward moment evaporated into sweeping laughter.

Every combat day ended in a solemn evening feast that gathered together all the pilots from all squadrons. Competition between squadrons continued during the solemn evening feast. Pilots from different squadrons sat at separate tables, and despite the best efforts of [Wing 1 Commander] Menahem Bar, every evening feast ended in a battle between squadrons; the weapons were bread crumbs, seasonal fruits, cakes, leftovers, and even dishes thrown and tossed from one table to another. Only the shouts of the wing commander ended the ceremonial battle, but did not end the war, as another such battle was to be fought at the end of the following term.

END OF ILAF YEAR 1958

The ILAF's annual ORBAT report listed fifty-one Mystères in inventory on 1 April 1959. The Mystère fleet accumulated 6,237 flight hours during ILAF Year 1958, an all-time record for the ILAF. This peak coincided with the introduction of a new top interceptor, the SMB2. Since the ILAF viewed the SMB2 as a stopgap interceptor to bridge between the Mystère and Mirage, only a single squadron of SMB2s was acquired; it was opened at Hatzor during ILAF Year 1958 Term 3 and would accomplish IOC during ILAF Year 1959. As a result, Squadron 101 Mystères and Squadron 109 Mystères continued to back up Squadron 105 SMB2 QRA, with Squadron 109 usually first to scramble against air space violations over north Israel. However, in planned patrols, such as for the protection of reconnaissance missions over enemy territory, the SMB2 mostly superseded the Mystère. ILAF ORBAT on 1 April 1959 was therefore as follows:

Base	Wing	Squadron	Type
Ramat David	1	109	Mystère
Ramat David	1	110	Vautour
Ramat David	1	117	Meteor
Hatzor	4	101	Mystère
Hatzor	4	105	SMB2
Hatzor	4	113	Ouragan
Tel Nof	-	103	transport
Tel Nof	-	116	Mustang
Tel Nof	-	119	night fighter
Tel Nof	-	124	helicopters
Dov Field	-	100	Piper

CHAPTER 3

FROM AIR-TO-AIR TO AIR-TO-GROUND

1959-1962

Squadron 109's transition from air-to-air to air-to-ground started in 1959, when the ILAF introduced the SMB2, and concluded in 1962, when the ILAF introduced the Shahak. The SMB2 was only viewed as a stopgap interceptor pending the introduction of the Shahak and, for this reason, Israel, the ILDF, and the ILAF at first evaluated skipping the SMB2 acquisition, since the Mirage's availability was nearly secured from 1956 and the Shahak's introduction was at first planned for 1961. Thus, a single SMB2 squadron (Squadron 105) was operated from Hatzor, with a profound impact on Hatzor-based Squadron 101 Mystère, but with less impact on Ramat David-based Squadron 109, which continued to serve as the ILAF's "Air Force North" top interception unit in northern Israel.

This situation changed dramatically in 1962 when the ILAF introduced the Shahak, at first activating two squadrons—one at Hatzor and one at Ramat David—and eventually operating three Shahak squadrons that rendered the Mystère obsolete for the air-to-air mission and forcing Squadron 109 to seek reinvention to the air-to-ground mission.

SYRIA SKIRMISH APRIL 1959

Class 26 graduates Ephraim Ashkenazi, Uzi Hochman, Judah Lev-Ran, and Moti Yeshurun were assigned to Squadron 109 at the end of Squadron 113's ILAF Year 1958 Term 3 OTU Course 8. While flying a Mystère conversion course practice flight on 5 April 1959, Judah Lev-Ran was involved in an incident over the Syrian border, as AIR3 Chief Moshe Peled reported on 8 April 1959:

> At noon on 5 April [1959], 2LT Liberman flew a routine training flight in a Mystère over the Bet Netufa Valley. 2LT Liberman noticed an aircraft with two engines flying east and reported to ground control. Ground control ordered to identify the aircraft and to leave it alone if it was a UN aircraft, as well as [reminding the pilot] not to cross the border.
>
> 2Lt Liberman lost contact with the aircraft, but then saw it landing at Mahanaim. While circling over Mahanaim, the Mystère probably got close to the border and Syrians opened fire; the aircraft was not hit and the pilot did not notice [that Syrians opened fire aimed at his aircraft]. This was reported by [ILDF] Command North.
>
> It should be noted that on 2 April [1959] the ILAF issued an order banning ILAF aircraft flying training flights from getting closer than five kilometers [three miles] to the borders, as well as banning flights over the Galilee Panhandle.

The ILAF's cutting edge combat aircraft force from February 1959 to April 1962 was composed of the Meteor, Ouragan, Mystère, SMB2, and Vautour. (PC)

In this case, the pilot acted in line with ground control's order to identify an aircraft and without doubt, the pilot did not get close to the border for the purpose of crossing it.

The ILAF's order not to fly close to the borders was aimed at easing tensions, but occasional clashes continued and Squadron 101 Mystères again engaged Egyptian MiG-17s in an inconclusive combat on 28 April 1959.

FORMER FRENCH PRIME MINISTER VISIT

Guy Mollet was France's Prime Minister from February 1956 until June 1957, and it was during his term in office that diplomatic and military relations between France and Israel tightened. No longer Prime Minister but still a respected socialist leader, Mollet visited Israel from 11 May 1959. An expression of Israeli gratitude was a welcome party at Lod International Airport that included, among many others, Prime Minister and Minister of Defense David Ben-Gurion, ILDF Chief of Staff Haim Laskov, and ILAF Commander Ezer Weizman.

On 18 May 1959 Mollet toured northern Israel, and it was possibly then that the former French Prime Minister visited Ramat David in general and Squadron 109 in particular.

ILAF Commander Ezer Weizman presenting Mystère 09 to former French Prime Minister Guy Mollet in a Squadron 109 HAS at Ramat David, May 1959. (PC)

INTERCEPTIONS OF LEBANESE AIRCRAFT

Squadron 101's slice of air-to-air activity was larger than Squadron 109's, primarily because most of the encounters between Mystères and United Arab Republic MiGs were over the Egyptian-Israeli border. While the Hatzor-based Mystères engaged Egyptian MiGs, the Ramat David-based Mystères' moment of glory—at the time—involved interception of Lebanese piston-powered aircraft that allegedly violated Israeli air space not once, but twice within less than ten days in May 1959; perhaps pure coincidence, but more probably two related incidents with a seemingly innocent cover story.

The first incident happened on 18 May 1959, when a Lebanese Middle East Airlines DC-3 departed El Arish, Egypt, at 12:30, to transport UN service persons stationed in Sinai to vacation in Beirut, Lebanon. Onboard the DC-3 was a crew of three—two Lebanese pilots and one Lebanese stewardess—plus twenty-seven UN service persons: fifteen from India and twelve from Yugoslavia.

About an hour after departure from El Arish while cruising over Mediterranean Sea opposite Haifa, a pair of Squadron 109 Mystères intercepted the DC-3 and the Lebanese crew was ordered to divert to and land at Lod International Airport. The DC-3 flight from

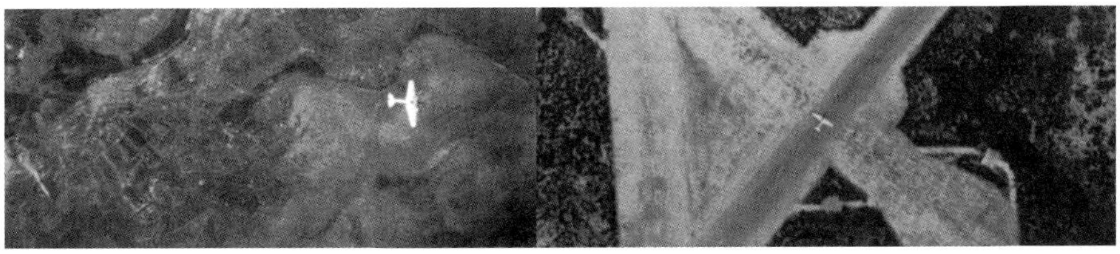

Squadron 101 Commander Aaron Yoeli photographed the LBAF's SM79 as it was flying over Galilee (left) and landing at Haifa (right). (PC)

LBAF SM79 was at Haifa from 27 May until 9 June 1959; the interception of two Lebanese aircraft within less than ten days was probably not a coincidence. (PC)

Squadron 109 pilots Josef Zuk (taller) and Jacob Yariv (without moustache) visited Haifa to inspect their catch. (PC)

the interception point to Lod took some time, so the first pair of Mystères—Amihy Shmueli and Ephraim Ashkenazi—was relieved by a second pair—Jacob Yariv and Moti Yeshurun—that oversaw the landing of the DC-3 at Lod and then returned to Ramat David.

Down at Lod, the Lebanese captain, Adel Salim Qawass, rejected the possibility that he deviated from his planned route during what was the second of three round trips between Beirut and El Arish planned for that day. The Israeli official statement actually avoided reference to any air space violation:

> A Lebanese Middle East Airlines aircraft that flew over [the Mediterranean] Sea within the control space of Lod Airport was intercepted at 13:30 by ILAF aircraft and forced to land at Lod Airport. The investigation concluded that the aircraft transported UNEF troops to Beirut.

While the unpleasantness was sorted out, the crew and passengers were served lunch and then the Israeli media interviewed the Lebanese captain and stewardess and a UNEF officer from Yugoslavia before the incident concluded at 16:55, when the DC-3 departed Lod on its way to Beirut.

The second incident took place on 27 May 1959, and again involved Squadron 109's interception of a Lebanese aircraft, this time military. The Squadron 109 log referred briefly to this incident as follows:

> A Savoia Marchetti [SM79]—a Lebanese aircraft with three [piston] engines—entered the northern Israel "by mistake" armed with cameras. Josef [Zuk] and Jacob [Yariv] were in the air, caught the catch, and dragged it to Haifa.

While the incident actually also involved Squadron 101 Mystères, the Squadron 101 log offered a more detailed and humoristic account of the incident:

> Squadron 109 pilots always complain that they do not have opportunities for engagements with enemy aircraft as does Squadron 101. Well today, the LBAF decided to "do something" to fix the situation and dispatched a grandpa Savoia Marchetti to boost the morale of Squadron 109.
>
> This morning, at 09:30, a [Squadron 101] four-ship formation—radio call sign PANTHER—took off to practice two versus two air combat. Prior to the start of practice, ground control ordered PANTHER leader to [abort training and to] fly north in the direction of Ramat David. Flying at 28,000 feet, PANTHER was ordered to patrol [over Ramat David], and it was then that PANTHER heard a Squadron 109 pair flying at 9,000 feet reporting a bogey over Ayelet HaShahar... [Ground control ordered to force the aircraft to land at Haifa] ... The bogey—identified as a Lebanese Savoia Marchetti—received the usual signals of interception—gear down and a few warning shots—and responded with gear down.
>
> Meanwhile, PANTHER 2 reported a fuel transfer malfunction, aborted the mission, and returned to base [Hatzor]. The Squadron 109 wingman also suffered malfunction and could not retract his landing gear, so he too aborted the mission and returned to base [Ramat David]. At this point [Squadron 101 Commander Aaron] Yoeli, who was flying [a test MIOR] reconnaissance, joined in, took photos of the Savoia Marchetti, and contacted the Lebanese pilot over the radio, explaining that it was being shepherded to land at Haifa ... in a conversation that was conducted in perfect English. Yoeli ... reported [to the Lebanese pilot] the direction of the runway [at Haifa], the length of the runway, and the direction of wind while all this time two Mystères were escorting the Savoia Marchetti, which made a perfect landing at Haifa.

The LBAF Savoia Marchetti pilot was actually not Lebanese, but an Italian named Gabriel Rivalta. Also onboard the Savoia Marchetti were a Lebanese copilot named Josef Saada and three crew members, including a photographer. The Savoia Marchetti departed Rayak air base in Lebanon on a reconnaissance mission, with Israel claiming the LBAF aircraft violated Israeli air space and Lebanon rejecting the Israeli claim, stating that the aircraft was flying over Lebanese territory at the time of the interception. ILDF statements seem to support the Lebanese view; the first ILDF statement was released at 11:10 and reported:

> A Lebanese military aircraft that flew this morning over Israeli territory was intercepted over kibbutz Ayelet HaShahar. After refusing to obey the orders of our pilots, several warning shots were fired and then the aircraft turned in direction of Haifa and landed there at 10:05. Onboard the aircraft was a crew of five and equipment for aerial photography. The aircraft type was a SM79; it is a light bomber with three engines. The aircraft and crew are in custody.

Subsequent ILDF statements were:

> A Savoia Marchetti aircraft—a Lebanese light bomber—was intercepted at 09:37 while flying over [Galilee] Panhandle (Metula and surrounding area) for photographic reconnaissance of our territory. At first, the aircraft did not obey the orders of our aircraft and they opened fire in its direction. As a result, the aircraft changed heading and flew to Haifa. It landed at Haifa airfield at 10:25.

And:

> The Lebanese aircraft that penetrated [Israeli air space] circa 09:35 penetrated four or five times into our territory over the Galilee Panhandle. The Lebanese

Squadron 109 Technical Flight service persons in the summer of 1959—Squadron 109 Commander Samuel Sheffer and Squadron 109 Technical Flight Commander Josef Kvodi (center)—in front of the QRA aircraft—4506 on the right and most likely 4575 on the left—that were parked on the line beside the squadron building and had their cockpits shielded from the sun during summer to cut reaction times shorter. (PC)

Aircraft number and unit badge were covered when ILAF aircraft were placed on public display; the Squadron 109 Mystère in this ILAF Day display is probably 4511. (PC)

notified via cease-fire committee that their aircraft was photographing the Malkiya area...

While at 15:00 it was added that:

A flight plan map was found in the aircraft with a flight line along the border inside Lebanon.

One way or another, the crew returned to Lebanon while the Savoia Marchetti remained in Israel until 9 June 1959, when Rivalta, aged 56, and Saada arrived from Lebanon, departed Haifa at 12:35, and flew to Lebanon with a Squadron 109 pair—Amihy Shmueli and Uri Even-Nir—escorting the Savoia Marchetti until it exited Israeli air space.

QRA ODDITY

The SMB2's introduction minimized the Mystère pilots' prospects to engage enemy aircraft. Squadron 105 SMB2 took over protection of ILAF special missions—mostly reconnaissance over enemy territory—and progressively took over the first tier of Hatzor QRA, with Squadron 101 shifting to a backup position. Up north, Squadron 109 remained the ILAF's premiere interception unit and the first line QRA at Ramat David. However, at the time, encounters with enemy aircraft were rare and the few engagements that took place involved

Squadron 101 Mystères or Squadron 105 SMB2s versus Egyptian MiGs over the Egyptian-Israeli border to the south. Squadron 109 Mystères were indeed scrambled from time to time, but most scrambles did not result in engagements. Arie Dagan recalled:

> The QRA aircraft were parked beside the squadron building, ready to scramble and track and foil any attempt to penetrate Israel's air space. Dozens—and maybe hundreds of times—at the sound of the siren, the QRA duty pilots jumped from the squadron's veranda, ran across the lawn [that surrounded the squadron's building] and hopped over the fence [that surrounded the lawn], rushing to the ladders that were attached to the QRA aircraft. A contest and a test of quickness, readiness, and ambition to have a chance at a real interception against an unidentified target. We dreamt during the night about real engagements and shooting down enemy aircraft.
>
> One autumn Saturday, I was assigned as QRA wingman with big Shumi [Amihy Shmueli] as leader. It was a cold cloudy morning and I was in my room, still in bed, reading newspapers, when the siren's scream kicked me out of bed "as is"—short pants and a T-shirt—dash in the direction of the "crash tender."
>
> Shumi arrived first at the dressing room and while he was wearing the G suit, I put on flying boots. The noise of a generator starting the engines of the QRA aircraft cut short our preparations. We grabbed our helmets and ran to the aircraft: Shumi in his G suit but barefoot, and I with my boots, but with short pants and a T-shirt. Within seven minutes of the siren's start we were in our cockpits; our ejection seat belt was not tightened yet, as we planned to tighten the belts immediately after take-off, all while asking permission from the control tower to line up on the runway and take-off.
>
> We took off, climbed with maximum engine power, and followed ground control orders: "heading to target 050, north of Sea of Galilee, altitude 25,000 feet."
>
> Shumi ordered to close formation as we entered clouds at 9,000 feet, heading 050 and climbing, and then "gunnery switches on, make sure that guns fuse in" while ground control asked for our position and altitude: "crossing 15,000 feet in clouds"; "change heading to 060."
>
> I opened formation as we broke out of the clouds at 18,000 feet. Shumi reported our altitude and heading, but ground control was silent until, after what seemed like eternity, ground control said "lost contact with target." I dropped a wing and had a look at the ground below, and an unfamiliar terrain was visible between shreds of clouds: to our left was Mount Hermon; Mazzeh air base was visible at our 11 o'clock; and Damascus spread [right in front of us] as a big green spot surrounded by [yellow] desert [terrain].
>
> We turned left and back to return to base. Shumi reported our position, asked for a vector to descend, and said that his legs were frozen, that he could not move his toes; this was the downside of our hasty scramble. We circled for a while below the cloud base to defrost and then we landed.
>
> Most scrambles were indeed futile; [the exception was when] Josef Zuk and Jacob Yariv intercepted a Lebanese Savoia Marchetti. A related special story were the pointless pursuits after American U-2 spy planes—we [ILAF] called them JULES VERNE—that photographed the Middle East while cruising at 70,000 feet, mocking our service ceiling of only 50,000 feet.

Actually, at the time, the exact identity of JULES VERNE was unknown to the ILAF; the first visual view of a JULES VERNE was accomplished during a Squadron 105 SMB2 scramble on 11 March 1959 that AIR Department Chief Gideon Elrom reported on 20 April 1959:

> Interception of JULES VERNE accomplished; for the first time a visual view. The aircraft was identified, with reservation, as a Valiant.

EXERCISE LANCE

ILAF training terms ended in combat days that exercised one base or one wing at a time. From time to time, the ILAF also exercised full scale operations. Exercise LANCE was a full scale ILAF maneuver that ILDF General Staff Branch Chief Isaac Rabin described to newspaper editors in a background brief on 7 August 1959:

> Training: There were several major exercises lately. The ILAF conducted a large scale exercise; as a matter of fact, this was the largest scale exercise since the Suez War. The objective was, unlike during the Suez War, that the ILAF would operate in full force without mobilization of reserves. The scenario was a surprise—the State of Israel was surprised [by an enemy attack] and the ILAF was ordered to immediately operate in full force while at the same time mobilizing its reserves to enable continuous operations over a longer time frame.
>
> This exercise proved that our air space is very small, even for the number of aircraft in ILAF service. The duration of the exercise was similar to the Suez War, but the number of sorties was higher. There were positive aspects as well as mishaps; we learn from every exercise in order to improve our standards for the next exercise.

The mishaps mentioned were not elaborated on, but referred to a collision in the air between two Vautours, a collision on the ground between two Mustangs, and to a Squadron 109 Mystère that caught fire in flight but landed safely.

Exercise LANCE emphasized the ILDF's doctrine of a separate ILAF air superiority campaign at the start of war. Squadron 109 EP pilot Asaf Ben-Nun flew four LANCE sorties on 21 July 1959—MIOR Lamed4, MIOR Lamed13, MIOR Lamed23, and Lamed33—

Reservists loading a Mystère—possibly 4516—with a bomb during a combat day exercise. The ILAF's switch from line to HAS improved maintainers' environment, shielding them from sun in summer and rain in winter. (PC)

Squadron 109 pilots during Exercise LANCE in July 1959 (standing left to right): Zur, Dagan, Markman, Dotan, Henkin, Ben-Nun, Arad, Eyal, Zuk, Egozi, Halivni, Sheffer, Shmueli, and Avneri. Crouching (left to right): Even-Nir and Niv. Sitting (left to right): Terner, Ashkenazi, Yeshurun, and Yariv. And sprawled: Prigat. Tents were erected during combat days to accommodate EPs and reserves. (PC)

Israel emphasized diplomatic relations with African states from the late 1950s. One aspect of these special relations was ILAF support to African states that included hosting visits, as illustrated, with ILAF Commander Ezer Weizman as chief host. This visit was at Ramat David with a Squadron 109 Mystère in an ordnance exhibition. (PC)

and one LANCE sortie (Lamed39) on 22 July 1959 for a total flying time of 4:30 flight hours, or an average of 0:54 flight hours per sortie. Squadron 109 EP pilot Levy Zur flew nine LANCE missions with a total flying time of 7:45 flight hours, or an average of three sorties per day and 0:52 flight hours per sortie.

Overall, Squadron 109 generated 198 sorties that summed up to 165:45 flight hours—an average of 0:50 flight hours per sortie—while respective ILAF figures for Exercise LANCE were 1,246 sorties, 1,153:52 flight hours, and an average of 0:56 flight hours per sortie.

SHEFFER DEPARTURE TO AFRICA

Squadron 109 Commander Samuel Sheffer flew the final Exercise LANCE sortie in Mystère 26 on 23 July 1957; this was his last flight in a Squadron 109 Mystère during the five following months. Samuel Sheffer recalled:

> I was a bit of an adventurer at the time, so I asked ILAF Commander Ezer [Weizman] for three months leave to tour Africa. I bought a Jeep, shipped it from Eilat to Ethiopia and, together with another pilot [Zeev Sharon from Squadron 110 Vautour], we covered 35,000 kilometers [21,748 miles] in five months, I knew that three months would not suffice, but [I did not dare ask for more] and I planned to blame technical troubles for the delay.

PESSIMISTIC FORECAST

On 1 April 1959, ILAF ORBAT included fifty-one Mystères, and this number did not change by 30 July 1959, when ILAF Commander Ezer Weizman issued a gloomy forecast that anticipated a decline in ILAF ORBAT from 150 combat aircraft in April 1960—including forty-eight Mystères—to only 103 combat aircraft by April 1962, including only forty Mystères. Intermediate forecasted Mystère inventory was forty-four in April 1961, so this forecast expected an average attrition of four Mystères per one ILAF Year.

Since Shahak was planned for ILAF introduction from 1962, ILAF Commander Ezer Weizman argued—in light of forecasted attrition—that a stopgap acquisition of twenty-four SMB2s was essential, so that the number of combat aircraft in ILAF ORBAT would not drop below 125 until the introduction of the Shahak.

Purchase of at least twenty-four SMB2s would have probably resulted in the conversion of Squadron 109 from the Mystère to the SMB2, but a large scale stopgap acquisition of SMB2s was not approved. The ILAF's attrition forecast proved pessimistic, as the actual number of ILAF ORBAT Mystères was forty-nine in April 1960, forty-seven in April 1961, and forty-three in April 1962.

SENIOR LEADERS COURSE 1

Squadron 101 ran Senior Leaders Course 1 from 16 August until 20 November 1959; among the six students—two from Squadron 105 SMB2, two from Squadron 110 Vautour, and one each from Squadrons 101 and 109—was Josef Zuk of Squadron 109.

As a result of Squadron 101's commitment to Senior Leaders Course 1, the Hatzor-based Mystère squadron did not run a Mystère conversion course during ILAF Year 1959 Term 2, so graduates of ILAF Year 1959 Term 1 Squadron 113 Ouragan OTU Course 9 were streamed to a Squadron 109 Mystère conversion course.

ILAF REPORT APRIL TO JULY 1959

ILAF Commander Ezer Weizman reported ILAF Year 1959 Term 1 on 15 September 1959. Squadron 109 accumulated 944 flight hours during this time frame, including 166 in April, 245 in May, 213 in June, and 320 in July, of which more than half (165:45

Squadron 101 Senior Leaders Course 1, August 1959 (back row left to right): Zorik Lev, Squadron 101 Deputy Commander Ran Ronen, Squadron 101 Commander Joe Alon, and Dror Avneri; and front row (left to right): Yossi Sarig, Josef Zuk, Shlomo Bet-On, and Reuben Harel. (PC)

ILDF Chief of Staff Haim Laskov visited Hatzor in November 1959, where he was photographed with ILAF senior commanders and Squadron 101 Senior Leaders Course 1 (standing, left to right): Personnel Department Chief Gideon Shochat, Material Department Chief Judah Rabin, Hatzor Wing Commander Moshe Peled, ILAF Commander Ezer Weizman, ILDF Chief Haim Laskov, Squadron 101 Commander Joe Alon, Air Department Chief Gideon Elrom, Zorik Lev, and Shlomo Bet-On. Crouching (left to right): Josef Zuk, Reuben Harel, Dror Avneri, Squadron 101 Deputy Ran Ronen, and Yossi Sarig. (PC)

flight hours) were accumulated during ILAF maneuver Exercise LANCE. Thus, July 1959 was the first month—in line with thus far unearthed data—during which Squadron 109 surpassed the 300 flight hours per month mark planned in the Squadron 109 Standard B (Peacetime) issued in September 1956. The overall impression of Squadron 109's accomplishments during ILAF Year 1959 Term 1 was:

> There is progress in air-to-air and air-to-ground operations of [Squadron 109] regular pilots; [Squadron 109] gunnery standard, except for air-to-air, has improved; and an investment in additional flight hours is required in order to improve the standard of [Squadron 109] air-to-air gunnery.

PRESIDENTIAL ESCORT

On 18 October 1959, Israeli President Isaac Ben-Zvi departed Lod International Airport in an El Al Britannia on the way to visit Burma. On 15 October 1959, AIR3 Achikar Eyal issued MIOR Kaph17, which tasked four Squadron 109 Mystères to escort the president's Britannia. The specified configuration was full internal ammunition and two external fuel tanks. The four-ship formation was to be ready from 07:15 on 18 October 1959:

> Central Control Unit 333 will be in touch with Lod control tower and will scramble the aircraft ten minutes prior to Britannia take-off.
>
> The aircraft will escort the airliner up to a distance of 50 nautical miles from the coastline. If the cloud base is lower than 2,000 feet and if cloud cover will be more than 4/8, then the aircraft will only rendezvous above the clouds.
>
> The estimated departure time of El Al airliners is 07:45. If the aircraft will arrive over Lod prior to take-off, then they will fly over the airfield at an altitude not lower than 100 feet.

IFF

The importance of electronics was growing to the point that the ILAF requested to equip aircraft with an IFF system as outlined in a detailed memo that ILAF Commander Ezer Weizman forwarded to ILDF Chief of Staff Haim Laskov prior to their monthly meeting on 19 October 1959:

> Identification has always been a prerequisite for efficient operations in the defense of Israeli air space and for safe control of our aircraft during offensive operations. The problem of identification is exacerbated through the introduction in theatre of fast jet aircraft armed with missiles.
>
> The objective is to outline a purchase plan of an IFF system for the ILDF.
>
> The operational requirement:
>
> - Warning time is reduced as aircraft speed is increased, so the identification time frame should be minimized in order to maximize interception time.
> - Range of air-to-air missiles is up to five to eight kilometers [three to five miles], so a pilot cannot visually identify a target; identification should be accomplished on the ground and reported to the pilot.
> - If the interceptor and target are close, it is impossible to identify any of them with separate [radar] tracks; therefore, identification should be permanently attached to the echo on the radar screen.
> - The same applies to the identification of ships by aircraft and vice versa.
>
> Thus far, we were unable to acquire IFF, but recently Britain authorized Marconi to offer us a modern system —the Mark 10—that is in NATO use. This system fits French aircraft that are in ILAF service. This system is compatible with ILAF radars. The IFF Mark 10 can be operated with or without code and Britain authorized the sale of the system without code, which is an essential element, as it secures identification.
>
> There is reasonable probability that the code can be developed locally, but it is suggested to make an effort to secure authorization for the purchase of the original code.
>
> The acquisition of IFF Mark 10 will cost approximately 1.4 million US dollars and 700,000 Israeli Pounds. IFF system efficiency and safety can only be guaranteed in fullness—IFF in every aircraft and in all radars—so if the IFF acquisition is approved, it will be necessary to implement the full plan.

The ILAF planned to accomplish IFF FOC by 1961 and the Mystère's allocation was to be forty IFF sets, each valued at 2,000 US dollars.

LEBANESE RAPIDE

Ramat David was referred to as "Air Force North," in charge of operations over northern Israel, while Hatzor was treated as "Air Force South," with responsibility for operations over southern Israel. This distinction was not sharp, because the Hatzor-based Squadron 105 SMB2s were tasked to fly pre-planned missions over northern Israel that involved a requirement for escort or patrol. However, in operations that were not pre-planned—mostly QRA scrambles—the distinction of territorial responsibility between Ramat David Air Force North and Hatzor Air Force South was mostly adhered to.

An exception occurred on 19 November 1959, when a target was tracked west of Haifa in what was traditionally Ramat David Air Force North territory. Instead of scrambling the Squadron 109 QRA from Ramat David, Central Control Unit 333 retasked Squadron 101 Mystères and Squadron 113 Ouragans engaged in air combat training to intercept the tracked target: a Lebanese Rapide on a commercial flight from Port Said to Beirut that was forced to land at Haifa, where the British pilot stated that interception took place thirty nautical miles west of Haifa, while the ILDF stated the intercepted Rapide was flying ten miles west of the coastline to the south of Haifa and the Squadron 101 pilots reported that interception took place west of Nahariya.

Rubbing salt into Squadron 109's wounds, the Squadron 101 Mystères and Squadron 113 Ouragans had to land at Ramat David for fuel prior to their flight back south to Hatzor.

EXERCISE SHOULDER

Wing 1 ILAF Year Term 2's combat day was Exercise SHOULDER, from 25 to 26 November 1959. Squadron 109 was planned to fly 100 sorties during Exercise SHOULDER, but actually flew 118 sorties and up to 99:10 flight hours, or an average of 0:50 flight hours per sortie. EP pilot Asaf Ben-Nun flew three sorties on 25 November 1959 and two sorties on 26 November 1959 for a total time of 4:55 flight hours. Ordnance consumption was 2,375 rounds, ninety-four 250 kilogram (550 lb) bombs and ninety-two 250 kilogram (550 lb) napalm canisters.

SQUADRON 109 SHAHAK?

The ILDF did not fully approve the ILAF's request for acquisition of twenty-four SMB2s to bridge the ORBAT ebb until the introduction of the Shahak. The acquisition of six SMB2s during ILAF Year 1959 was indeed approved, while the acquisition of twelve SMB2s during ILAF Year 1960 was still on the table. In case a total of eighteen SMB2s were acquired during ILAF Years 1959 and 1960, and taking into account attrition, the forecast was thirty-six SMB2s in service by ILAF Year 1961—substantially more than the ILAF's standard twenty-four airframes per combat aircraft squadron, but not enough to equip two full standard squadrons.

In an ILDF meeting on 6 November 1959, ILAF Commander Ezer Weizman was evidently pro one "big" SMB2 squadron, while in an ILMD discussion on 12 November 1959, ILDF Chief Haim Laskov advocated two "small" SMB2 squadrons.

On 18 November 1959, this issue was seemingly settled, for the time being, when the ILDF Chief ordered the ILAF Commander to prepare a staff study concerning the Shahak's introduction that included a presupposition of two "small" SMB2 squadrons by ILAF Year 1962.

Squadron 109 EP pilot Asaf Ben-Nun flew enemy simulation sortie Exercise DOME in Mystère 09 on 2 December 1959. (PC)

The requested ILAF staff study was promptly issued on 30 November 1959, but actually offered two options: two paths for ORBAT changes, with both paths planned to impact Squadron 109.

Option A expected the acquisition of six and twelve SMB2s during ILAF Years 1959 and 1960, respectively, so that by ILAF Year 1961, Squadron 105 would be one "big" SMB2 squadron, Squadron 109 would transfer Mystères to Squadron 101, and would then convert to the Shahak, while the ILDF Chief's objective of two "small" SMB2 squadrons would be accomplished during ILAF Year 1962, when Squadron 117 would convert from the Meteor to the SMB2.

Option B anticipated the purchase of six and fourteen SMB2s during ILAF Years 1959 and 1960, respectively, so that by ILAF Year 1960, Squadron 109 would transfer Mystères to Squadron 101 and would convert to the SMB2 as a second "small" squadron.

The ILAF Commander's recommended path was Option A.

REPORT ILAF YEAR 1959 TERM 2

A summary of ILAF Year 1959 Term 2 was issued on 27 December 1959. Squadron 109 accumulated 897 flight hours, including twenty-seven flight hours during August 1959, 326 flight hours during September 1959, 200 flight hours during October 1959, and 326 flight hours during November 1959. There were fifty MIOR sorties, including forty-three training, three tests, and five operations. The overall impression of Squadron 109 during ILAF Year 1959 term 2 was: "The standard of regular and EP pilots is improving; gunnery standards have improved."

NIGHTTIME FIGHTING PROGRESS

ILAF Commander Ezer Weizman reported progress in night fighting qualifications—air-to-air, air-to-ground, and reconnaissance —on 30 December 1959. The only qualification relevant to Squadron 109 Mystère was air-to-ground with MI-2 flares—already approved for use—and the more powerful MI-3 flares still under development.

Progress was slow, since only senior pilots were authorized to train in nighttime air-to-ground attack; the number of senior pilots—pilots who had completed three training terms—was small and the number of allocated flight hours was inadequate.

YEAR 1959 ACCIDENTS

The ILAF's Comptroller Branch summarized the accidents during 1959, and Squadron 109 experienced fourteen accidents in all categories, including three total loss accidents in which all three pilots ejected, or one accident per 178.6 flight hours. Comparative data for Squadron 101 was forty-five accidents (including one total loss accident in which the pilot was killed), or one accident per 61.8 flight hours.

AARON MARKMAN

Josef Zuk, Aaron Markman, and Jacob Terner practiced air-to-air on 1 January 1960, when Mystère 13 dived and crashed and pilot Aaron Markman was killed. The ILAF Flight Safety Branch notedd:

> Three Mystères took off to practice air-to-air photography at an altitude of 28,000 feet. The pilot was Number 2 in the formation. After take-off, the pilot experienced troubles with undercarriage retraction. Leader ordered [the formation] to activate cockpit pressurization and the three ship formation continued to climb to exercise at a specified altitude. In this practice, Number 1 was the target that Numbers 2 and 3 attacked.
>
> While flying the third pass, Number 3 noticed that Number 2 dived vertically towards the ground. Number 3 immediately called Number 2 and reported his situation but received no reply. Number 1 then intervened and the two pilots ordered Number 2 to pull up. There was no answer; the aircraft continued diving, hit the surface, and the pilot was killed.

The second major accident for Squadron 109 was on 15 January 1960. Mystère 83 suffered CAT3 damage when an engine turbine broke in flight. Subsequent vibrations were so severe that the engine had to be completely shut down, but the aircraft landed safely and was flying again by March 1960.

SHEFFER RETURNS FROM AFRICA

On 24 December 1959, an Israeli newspaper reported on the completion of Squadron 109 Commander's adventure in Africa, though the occupation of the adventurer was not revealed:

> The two Israeli youngsters who had covered 24,000 kilometers [14,912 miles] while touring Africa are [Samuel] Sheffer and [Zeev] Schwartz [Sharon]. Sheffer, aged 28, is a bachelor born in [moshav] Beer Tuvya; he and his friend Schwartz meticulously planned the voyage [that was accomplished] during a vacation from their work. They bought a jeep, shipped it from Eilat to Masawa, and then toured Ethiopia, Kenya, Uganda, Tanganyika, Rhodesia, and South Africa, and from there travelled to west Africa. Their success in realizing their dream evoked joy at Beer Tuvya. Sheffer and Schwartz will return to Israel within several weeks. They are currently at Ghana, waiting for the sailing to Israel of a Black Star merchant ship.

Squadron 109 Commander Samuel Sheffer returned to Israel almost a month later and resumed Squadron 109 Mystère flights on 24 January 1960 in Mystère 72.

OPERATION GRASSHOPPER

The escalation in clashes along the border between Israel and Syria resulted in the issue of an order at 12:00 on 30 January 1960 to prepare aircraft for attack missions against Syria, while EPs were ordered to report to their squadrons. Readiness State C—one level below war—was in force from 15:30 on 31 January 1960 until 3 February 1960. This time frame covered ILDF Operation GRASSHOPPER during the night of 31 January to 1 February 1960, which was an Israeli reprisal action against Syrian fortifications at Taufik, southeast of the Sea of Galilee. ILAF activity was restricted to reconnaissance and patrols; Squadron 109's share in this operational activity was a few QRA scrambles, and EP pilot Asaf Ben-Nun was scrambled in Mystère 70 on 2 February 1960. These scrambles did not result in engagements with Syrian aircraft.

OPERATION RETAMA

Tension between Israel and Syria actually built up towards United Arab Republic Day on 22 February 1960. The Israeli Prime Minister and Minister of Defense stated on 21 February 1960:

> We assume that [Egypt President Gamal Abdel] Nasser and Arab League threats to use force in order to prevent Israel from exploiting River Jordan water to irrigate the Negev Desert are empty threats, but if they are indeed intending to attack us then let them try.

Unknown to Israel, Egyptian President Gamal Abdel Nasser actually accepted the Israeli Prime Minister and Minister of Defense's invitation and ordered Egyptian armed forces to advance into Sinai as a preparatory action prior to actual attack. Forward deployment of Egyptian forces in Sinai started on 17 February 1960, and Israel was unaware of this activity until the afternoon hours of 22 February 1960, when the US notified Israel that Egyptian forces were fully deployed to Sinai and ready to attack Israel.

On 23 and 24 February 1960, ILAF reconnaissance missions over Egypt verified the US tip, so Israel mobilized reserves and moved forces south to face Egypt in line with OPOR RETAMA, while the ILAF switched to Readiness State C from 16:30 on 24 February 1960. Squadron 109 was tasked to maintain two pairs on QRA during daytime, while twelve more Mystères were to be ready for air-to-ground operations armed with two 250 kilogram (550 lb) bombs and loaded with two fuel tanks. In addition to readiness to attack Egyptian forces and to defend Israeli territory in case of an Egyptian offensive, Squadron 109 was also ready to take part in an ILAF air superiority campaign in case Israel decided to strike first.

The crisis ended almost as abruptly as it started, but a return to normalcy was accomplished in two strokes: the first was on 1 March 1960, when the discharge of ILDF reserves started and the ILAF relaxed to Readiness State B; the second was on 1 April 1960, when the readiness state was returned to normal.

SQUADRON 109 RESERVE PILOTS

Until now, Squadron 109's pilot population was composed only of regulars and EPs, primarily because only three years had elapsed

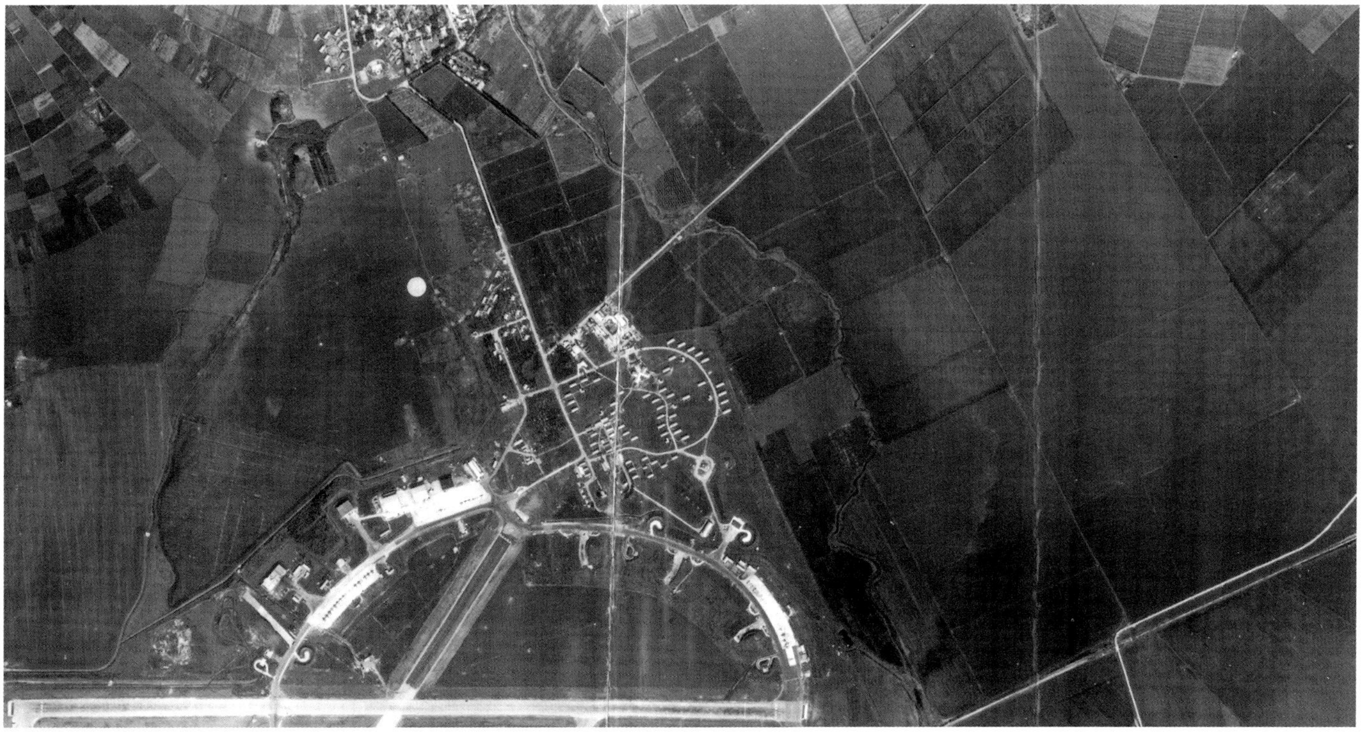

The Squadron 109 complex at Ramat David near the start of runway 11 (on the right in this view) in February 1960, with the squadron buildings northwest of the crescent shaped line with a pair of QRA aircraft parked on the line closer to the squadron buildings and one Mystère visible at a HAS taxiway. (PC)

On 6 February 1960, Asaf Ben-Nun was scrambled at night in Mystère 15 to the Israeli Syrian border. This photo of Mystère 15 during take off from Ramat David was taken between painting of the fuselage flash in 1959 and installation of the parachute pack in 1961. (PC)

since its activation as a Mystère outfit in December 1956. A sign of a squadron's maturity was a change in its squadron pilot population from two groups to three groups: regulars, EPs, and reservists.

The challenge was to preserve the combat qualifications of reserve pilots. The ILAF's initial attitude was to summon reserve pilots for two weeks of active duty every training term, but such a gap between flights resulted in "rusty" pilots; the attitude changed ideally to one day of flying per week, plus participation in the end of term combat day exercise. At the time, the ILAF's standard flight hours allocation per year was 150 flight hours per regular pilot and sixty flight hours per EP, with reserve pilots with superior experience over the EP and reserve pilots making up fewer flight hours. Additionally, EP and reserve pilots were required to preserve operational qualifications, while the flight hour allocation for regular pilots also covered the accomplishment of qualifications.

The first three Squadron 109 reserve pilots were Asaf Ben-Nun and Arie Dagan—assigned to Squadron 109 from March 1957—and

Mystère 06 landing at Ramat David; the aircraft has been camouflaged but not yet fitted with its braking parachute. Reserve pilot Asaf Ben-Nun flew two sorties in 4506 out of twenty-eight he flew during ILAF Year 1960 Term 1. (PC)

Jacob Yariv, who was assigned to Squadron 109 from August 1957. Arie Dagan recalled:

> There were no reserve pilots in the squadron when we discharged from active service. There were regular pilots and EP pilots who were [mostly] flying school instructors. In the past, in Mosquito and Mustang squadrons, reserve pilots were called for active service once every several months for a compressed time frame of training for the refreshment of flying skills and to preserve flying standards. This seemed impossible in jet squadrons that operated cutting edge equipment with constantly and rapidly updated tactics.
>
> The ILAF was thus willing to give up our services as fighter pilots, but we did not give up; we foresaw a way of life that would combine combat flying with civil conduct. We lived and worked not far from Ramat David. We loved flying. We knew the importance of service as fighters. Therefore, we suggested to Squadron [109] Commander [Samuel] Sheffer that we would report to flying in the same manner as EP pilots did, that we would fly one day every week or fortnight, that we would preserve our standard of flying, that we would maintain contact with what was going on in the squadron, and that we would share readiness shifts. Our offer was accepted and a new standard for reserve pilots was set.
>
> It was not simple. At the time, ILDF orders forbade calling reservists to a split service on an unlimited number of days, but mutual trust overcame all difficulties. We reported to the squadron as needed; we flew every week in line with the allocation of flight hours; we reported to exercises; and we shared readiness. The squadron treated us fairly and made us feel like we belonged, that we were "one of the family." Throughout the years I flew as a Squadron 109 reserve pilot, I never felt someone was trying to force us out; we were assigned to fly operational missions, we were tasked to lead formations, and we were allocated flight hours even when budgets were tight and flight hour allocations were scarce.
>
> Every day in reserve service was an experience—a meeting with friends—and the bond between reserve pilots tightened over the years. A special cultural pattern developed during combat day exercises when we erected tents, with every tent populated by eight pilots: a senior leader, a four-ship formation leader, two pair leaders, and four wingmen. We the veterans—actually anyone more than twenty-five years old—were called "old," and over the years dozens of young pilots were posted to the squadron, but most of them trained in the squadron for a few terms and only a few of them remained in the squadron. The really regular pilots in the squadron were the reservists.

EXERCISE MICHAL

ILAF Year 1959 Term 3 Wing 1's combat day was Exercise MICHAL, from 30 to 31 March 1960. Regular pilot Isaac Golan flew four

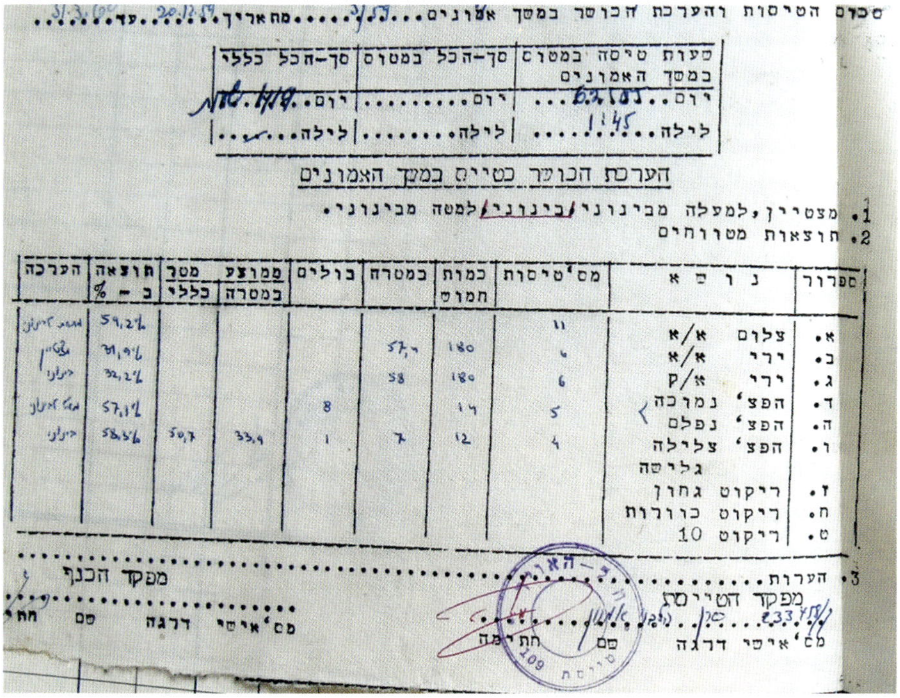

סכום הטיסות והערכת הכושר במשך אמונים ... מתאריך ... עד ...

שעות טיסה במטוס במשך האמונים	סך-הכל במטוס	סך-הכל כללי
יום ... 62.55	יום ...	יום ...
לילה ... 1:45	לילה ...	לילה ...

הערכת הכושר כטייס במשך האמונים

1. מצטיין, למעלה מבינוני/בינוני/למטה מבינוני.
2. תוצאות מטווחים

מספור	נושא	מס' טיסות	כמות תחמושת	במטרה	בולים	ממוצע במטרה	מטר כללי	תוצאה %	הערכה
א.	צלום א/א	11						59.2%	[illegible]
ב.	ירי א/א	6	180	57.?				31.9%	[illegible]
ג.	ירי ק/א	6	180	58				32.2%	[illegible]
ד.	הפצ' נמוכה	5	14		8			57.1%	[illegible]
ה.	הפצ' נפלם								
ו.	הפצ' צלילה גלישה	4	12	7	1	33.9	50.7	58.3%	[illegible]
ז.	ריקוט גחון								
ח.	ריקוט כוורות								
ט.	ריקוט 10								

3. הערות ...

מפקד הטייסת — מס' אישי, דרגה, שם, חתימה

מפקד הכנף — מס' אישי, דרגה, שם, חתימה

A typical end of term Squadron 109 pilot evaluation form—for ILAF Year 1959 Term 3 from 20 December 1959 until 31 March 1960—included the number of flight hours (62:55 daytime and 1:45 nighttime) and training results: air-to-air photography 59.2% (Grade D, lower than average); air-to-air gunnery 31.9% (Grade A, excellent); air-to-ground gunnery 32.2% (Grade C, average); low altitude bombing and napalm attack 57.1% (Grade B, higher than average); and dive bombing 58.3% (Grade C, average). Belly rocketry, pod rocketry, and T-10 rocketry were not practiced during ILAF Year 1959 Term 3. (PC)

MICHAL sorties on 30 March 1960 and two MICHAL sorties on 31 March 1960 that totaled 5:00 flight hours, or an average of 0:50 flight hours per sortie. Reserve pilot Asaf Ben-Nun flew four MICHAL sorties on 30 March 1960 and four MICHAL sorties on 31 March 1960 totaling 5:50 flight hours, or an average of 0:44 flight hours per sortie.

The total figures for Squadron 109 during Exercise MICHAL were 149 sorties, 101:00 flight hours, and an average of 0:41 flight hours per sortie.

REPORT FOR ILAF YEAR 1959 TERM 3

Flying School Class 29 graduates and Squadron 113 Ouragan ILAF Year 1959 Term 3 OTU Course 11 graduates Uri Margalit and Pesach Shraga were posted to Squadron 109.

1 April 1960 ORBAT included forty-nine Mystères—down two from the previous year's report—and Mystère fleet utilization during the year ending 1 April 1960 was 5,465 flight hours—down 772 flight hours comparison to the ILAF Mystère's all time record utilization of 6,237 flight hours during ILAF Year 1958.

The ILAF's Year 1959 Term 3 report was issued on 15 April 1960. Squadron 109 accumulated 861 flight hours, including 120 flight hours during December 1959, 222 flight hours during January 1960, 212 flight hours during February 1960, and 307 flight hours during March 1960.

MIOR sorties numbered forty-three, including twenty-three training, twelve tests, four demonstrations, and four operations. The overall impression of Squadron 109 during ILAF Year 1959 term 3 was:

The squadron conducted the training term with seven regular pilots, sixteen EP pilots, and three reserve pilots. The standard of junior pilots was good and the standard of EP pilots and reserve pilots was satisfactory. The air-to-air gunnery standard was improved, but air-to-ground gunnery results did not improve. Weather conditions limited the squadron's training over ranges. Maintenance standards and the maintainers' professionalism has improved.

NOTORIOUS MYSTÈRES

Aircraft are personified machines; the same types of aircraft tend to have different qualities, some imaginative, some real. Specific aircraft were known to be more powerful, faster, and as such more friendly to pilots. A few aircraft were famed for harmonized weapons system, while others were known as prone to miss. Rarely, an aircraft acquired a reputation of a savior; an aircraft that no matter what would always return to base. Other aircraft tended to be less powerful, slower, or exhibited bizarre tendencies that made pilots treat them as notorious. In extreme cases, very few aircraft acquired the label of "jinxed jet"—an aircraft that was involved in accidents more than other similar aircraft and an aircraft that was evidently unfriendly to pilots.

By the summer of 1960, two of Squadron 109's Mystères had acquired a notorious reputation: Mystère 32, which had flown with Squadron 109 since activation in December 1956; and Mystère 47, which was reassigned from Squadron 101 to Squadron 109 in late 1958.

Mystère 32 was among Squadron 109's notoriously known aircraft; it was claimed that it was unable to climb the HAS taxiway and that the Ramat David runways were not long enough to enable 4532 to take off safely. (PC)

SENIOR LEADERS COURSE 2

Squadron 101 ran Senior Leaders Course 2 during ILAF Year 1960 Term 2; the six students included three from Hatzor "Air Force South" (two from Squadron 101 Mystère and one from Squadron 105 SMB2) and three from Ramat David "Air Force North": Shy Egozi and Amihy Shmueli from Squadron 109 and Maoz Poraz from Squadron 110 Vautour.

No new pilots were assigned to Mystère squadrons during ILAF Year 1960 Term 2 because no Squadron 113 Ouragan OTU course ran during ILAF Year 1960 Term 1; Flying School Class 30's output included only one fast jet pilot, so he was delayed a term to join the ILAF's Year 1960 Term 2 Squadron 113 OTU course for Class 31 graduates.

SHAHAK SETUP TEAM SELECTION

Back in November 1959, the ILAF Commander recommended Squadron 109 should convert to the Shahak during ILAF Year 1961. A significant step forward was the selection of the Shahak setup team in August 1960.

The activation of two Shahak squadrons was planned: one at Hatzor and one at Ramat David. The setup team for the Ramat David-based Shahak squadron was Squadron 109 Commander Samuel Sheffer as commander, Squadron 109 Deputy B Dror Avneri as deputy, and David Ivry from Squadron 105 SMB2. The setup team for the Hatzor-based Shahak squadron was Squadron 101 Commander Joe Alon as commander, Squadron 101 Deputy B Ezra Aharon as deputy, and Amos Lapidot from Squadron 113 Ouragan.

The selection of Shahak squadron setup teams most impacted the two Mystère squadrons, but the actual impact was not expected to be felt until the departure of the Shahak squadron setup teams to France for a Mirage conversion course.

MYSTÈRE 26

Eliezer Prigat experienced a hydraulic malfunction while flying Mystère 26 on 10 August 1960. At the time, Eliezer Prigat recalled:

> It was on Friday at 10:00. We were returning to base in formation at the end of a training flight, descending from 15,000 feet with deployed air brakes. When we leveled I tried to close air brakes, but a red light indicating deployed air brakes was still on. I tried again, but the deployed air brakes light was still on, so I had a look at the hydraulic pressure gauge that read zero; the hydraulic system that operated the landing gear, flaps, and air brakes had malfunctioned.
>
> By then, we had arrived over base and it was time to break prior to landing. The formation broke, but I pulled up and reported to the formation leader that I had experienced a malfunction and that I had pulled up.
>
> I then had to activate the emergency system; a handle normally stored in the right side of the cockpit that had to be attached to an axle and then used to pump with the right hand. I sensed that pumping was not building up pressure and the landing gear doors did not open and the landing gear did not detract.
>
> I had never heard of a similar incident when both systems malfunctioned, so I tried again [but to no avail]. Meanwhile, the squadron commander [Samuel Sheffer] had arrived at the control tower, so I explained what happened and asked what to do. By then I was flying at 12,000 feet over base with only five minutes of fuel.
>
> The squadron commander's advice was to try and detract the landing gear in pull up and accelerations.

Mystère 26 taxiing at Ramat David in late 1960; the aircraft is not yet camouflaged and not yet fitted with its braking parachute. Eliezer Prigat saved this aircraft on 10 August 1960. (PC)

Two landing gear doors opened, but the landing gear remained retracted.

The squadron commander then asked if I was ready to land on the external fuel tanks on a secondary, shorter runway. I replied affirmative and turned in to land. Since the air brakes and flaps did not deploy, my approach to the runway was different than usual. I flew a wide circuit at low altitude and slow speed, and I did not switch off the engine so I could go around in case of a missed approach.

During my first approach, I arrived over the runway's edge too high and too fast, so I went around. The fuel gauge indicated I only had fuel for one more approach, so I came in lower and slower. I arrived over the runway's edge at not higher than one meter [three feet], switched off the engine and electrical systems, fastened my seat belts and started sliding along the runway. At first I used rudder to control my heading, but as the aircraft slowed down I was no longer in control; the aircraft skidded straight ahead, veering a little to the left until it stopped.

Before the aircraft stopped I had unlocked harnesses and tried to open the canopy, but it was impossible due to deceleration. The moment the aircraft stopped [I opened the canopy] and jumped out. Firefighting and rescue vehicles were already nearby, and as I realized the aircraft was not on fire, I returned to the aircraft and inserted the ejection seat and open canopy safety pins.

The squadron commander arrived within a few minutes and it was obvious he was pleased. The fuel tanks were ruined, but the aircraft was not damaged, except for superficial damage to the lower rear fuselage. An examination of the runway revealed that the two fuel tanks touched the surface at even distances from the runway's centerline.

Only five minutes afterward I started to get excited, and when I arrived at the squadron, a bottle of champagne awaited me.

Repair work included inspection of the systems that malfunctioned and a few hours of body work to fix the empennage. Three days later I again flew this aircraft.

CHUTE AND RATO

The ongoing effort to tackle the Mystère's weaknesses as an attack aircraft was accelerated in anticipation of the Shahak's introduction and the planned post-Shahak introduction shift of the Mystère's primary tasking from air-to-air to air-to-ground. Two potential modifications were tested: a chute and RATO.

The first thus far unearthed flight of an ILAF Mystère with a braking parachute is dated 22 August 1960, when a chute helped Squadron 101 Commander Joe Alon to stop during a landing ground run of Mystère 51.

Squadron 101 Commander Joe Alon was also assigned as Mystère RATO test pilot after the ILAF acquired ten Aerojet General RATO bottles with 0.5 tons thrust. This was also after MAT4 designed the Mystère modification mechanical system, after MAT5 designed the Mystère modification electrical system, and after AMU22 modified Mystère 30. Three test flights were flown in line with AIR3's MIOR Heth165 on 22 December 1960, 29 December 1960, and 4 January

The ILAF Firefighting Course graduation parade in October 1960 included a demonstration of a drill to rescue a pilot from an aircraft; the aircraft used in the demonstration was Squadron 109 Mystère 47. (PC)

1961; the objectives of this initial series of test flights were:

- To quantify RATO's impact on take-off distance
- To test jettisoning used rockets
- To examine the impact of rocket flames on the runway and airframe
- To check whether the system was reusable.

The first flight tested jettisoning the system with four dummy rockets. Take-off weight was 8.5 tons and the jettison was at 200 feet and 190 knots, with full flaps and on maximum throttle setting. The structure—with four attached dummy rockets—released from the aircraft, but hit under fuselage during separation. The electrical plug and socket did not disconnect. The structure was damaged to the point it was not reusable.

Ramat David Wing 1 celebrated Suez War Day on 27 October 1961 with a turnaround competition and a flyover; the participating Squadron 109 Mystères were all still in metal finish and included 4509, 4505, 4511, 4516, 4525, and 4547. (PC)

The second flight tested take-off with two rockets. Take-off weight was 8.5 tons and the temperature was 18°C (64°F). The rockets were ignited at eighty knots and the take-off distance was 1,050 meters (3,444 ft). The runway was not damaged and the maximum lower airframe temperature was estimated at 120°C (248°F).

The third flight tested take-off with four rockets. Take-off weight was 9.5 tons and the temperature was 19°C (66°F). The rockets were ignited at sixty-six knots and the take-off distance was 900 meters (2,952 ft). The runway was not damaged and the maximum lower airframe temperature was estimated at 120°C (248°F).

The conclusion was the system design was not satisfactory, while actual take-off distances were better than predicted.

Recommendations were to redesign the system and to fit the redesigned system to an aircraft during the planned twenty-day down time at AMU22 (for installation of a braking parachute) and to retest jettisoning of the system, but to discontinue take-off tests because take-off distances were more than verified:

Weight	Distance	Rockets	Calculated	Actual	Notes
8.5 tons	1,500 m (4,934 ft)	2	1,100 m (3,618 ft)	1,050 m (3,454 ft)	second test flight
9.5 tons	1,900 m (6,250 ft)	2	1,400 m (4,605 ft)	-	-
9.5 tons	1,900 m (6,250 ft)	4	1,050 m (3,454 ft)	900 m (2,953 ft)	third test flight
10.5 tons	2,150 m (7,072 ft)	2	1,650 m (5,428 ft)	-	-
10.5 tons	2,150 m (7,072 ft)	4	1,250 m (4,112 ft)	-	-

While the data referred to take-off parameters and performance at 18°C (64°F), it was calculated that an increase of one degree Celsius added 1.2% to the take-off distance, so at 40°C (104°F) the relevant data was:

Weight	Distance	Rockets	Calculated	Actual	Notes
10.5 tons	2,700 m (8,882 ft)	2	2,050 m (6,743 ft)	-	-
10.5 tons	2,700 m (8,882 ft)	4	1,550 m (5,099 ft)	-	-

TWO-SEAT MYSTÈRE FEASIBLITY STUDY

On 9 January 1961, AIR2 ordered a MAT4 feasibility study concerning a Mystère with two seats. AIR2 asked MAT4 to conclude if a two-seat Mystère modification was possible. If it was, then AIR2 also asked MAT4 to estimate the cost and a schedule.

MAT4 replied on 22 January 1961 that a two-seat Mystère modification was possible.

TAKE-OFF WITH FLAPS

A less radical proposition than RATO for shortening the Mystère's take-off distance was to take-off with flaps, since until that time ILAF Mystères took off with flaps at zero degrees deflection.

On 27 January 1961, MAT4 presented calculated take-off runs for combinations of three configurations, two temperatures, two power settings, and four flap deflections:

The winter of 1960 to 1961 surfaced HAS construction drainage issues that were not foreseen at the time of HAS planning. HASs at Ramat David were flooded during December 1960 and aircraft were damaged, including Mystère 07. (PC)

Weight	Thrust	Temp	0 Deg	15 Deg	30 Deg	45 Deg FLAPS
9,292 kilograms	100%	27 Celsius	1,750 m (5,757 ft)	1,570 m (5,164 ft)	1,660 m (5,461 ft)	1,980 m (6,513 ft)
9,292 kilograms	86%	27 Celsius	2,140 m (7,039 ft)	2,000 m (6,579 ft)	2,590 m (8,520 ft)	3,310 m (10,888 ft)
9,292 kilograms	100%	41 Celsius	1,940 m (6,365 ft)	1,780 m (5,840 ft)	1,870 m (6,135ft)	2,400 m (7,874 ft)
9,292 kilograms	86%	41 Celsius	2,390 m (7,862ft)	2,340 m (7,697 ft)	3,770 m (12,401 ft)	4,020 m (13,224 ft)
9,890 kilograms	100%	27 Celsius	2,050 m (6,743 ft)	1,900 m (6,250 ft)	2,020 m (6,645 ft)	3,040 m (10,000 ft)
9,890 kilograms	86%	27 Celsius	2,560 m (8,421 ft)	2,490 m (8,191 ft)	3,800 m (12,500 ft)	4,540 m (14,934 ft)
9,890 kilograms	100%	41 Celsius	2,310 m (7,599 ft)	2,160 m (7,105 ft)	2,510 m (8,257 ft)	3,360 m (11,053 ft)
9,890 kilograms	86%	41 Celsius	2,890 m (9,507 ft)	3,190 m (10,493 ft)	4,650 m (15,296 ft)	5,380 m (17,697 ft)
10,362 kilograms	100%	27 Celsius	2,250 m (7,401 ft)	2,120 m (6,974 ft)	2,430 m (7,993 ft)	3,590 m (11,809 ft)
10,362 kilograms	86%	27 Celsius	2,790 m (9,178 ft)	2,960 m (9,737 ft)	4,540 m (14,934 ft)	5,390 m (17,730 ft)
10,362 kilograms	100%	41 Celsius	2,500 m (8,224 ft)	2,440 m (8,026 ft)	3,360 m (11,053 ft)	4,250 m (13,980 ft)
10,362 kilograms	86%	41 Celsius	3,200 m (10,526 ft)	3,780 m (12,434 ft)	5,270 m (17,336 ft)	7,310 m (24,046 ft)

In case of an engine with 100% thrust, the shortest calculated take-off distances were with flaps deflected to 15 degrees, but for aircraft with an engine delivering 86% power the results were less unequivocal.

MIXED EXTERNAL ORDNANCE

The Mystère was limited to a single type of external ordnance — bombs, napalm canisters, or rockets—that was mostly limited to the outer wing stations, as the inner wing stations were almost invariably used to lift two 625 liter (165 gallon) fuel tanks to boost endurance.

To enhance the Mystère's punch for short range operations, such as Squadron 109 flying air-to-ground missions from Ramat David to the Israeli-Syrian border—a mere fifty to eighty kilometers (thirty-one to fifty miles)—on 9 February 1961 MAT5 issued a requirement to test the Mystère with bombs and rockets. The Mystère's configuration with bombs and rockets was only possible for aircraft with higher stress wings (a French modification) and with all four hard points wired for bombs (an ILAF modification). At the time, all ILAF Mystères except 4576 had higher stress wings, while only nine Mystères—seven assigned to Squadron 101 and two assigned to Squadron 109—were not wired for bomb attachment to the inner wing stations.

The proposed configuration—two 250 kilogram (550 lb) bombs on the inner wing stations and twelve T-10 rockets on the outer wing stations, for an aircraft weight of 9.15 tons—still required an electrical wiring modification so that the inner bombs would be dropped first.

Squadron 101 tested the mixed ordnance configuration on 1 March 1961; the test pilot first bombed and then flew four rocketry passes. MAT5 considered the test a success and on 7 March 1961 recommended accepting the mixed ordnance configuration as standard.

AIR2 then qualified the Mystère mixed ordnance configuration as standard and ordered to modify all Mystères accordingly.

END OF ILAF YEAR 1960

Flying School Class 32 graduates and Squadron 113 Ouragan ILAF Year 1960 Term 3 OTU Course 13 graduates Jacob Gal, Shlomo Keren, and Iftach Zemmer were posted to Squadron 109; Gal and Keren would remain in Squadron 109 service for a single term prior to posting to Squadron 110 Vautour. Class 10 graduate Nahum Yahalom—at the time an AIR5 staff officer—also converted to the Mystère and flew his Mystère "solo" flight on 10 April 1961 in 4571.

Squadron 109 Day was celebrated on 26 January 1961. Mystère 16 took part in the traditional turnaround competition and Mystère 10 has already been modified with a braking parachute. (PC)

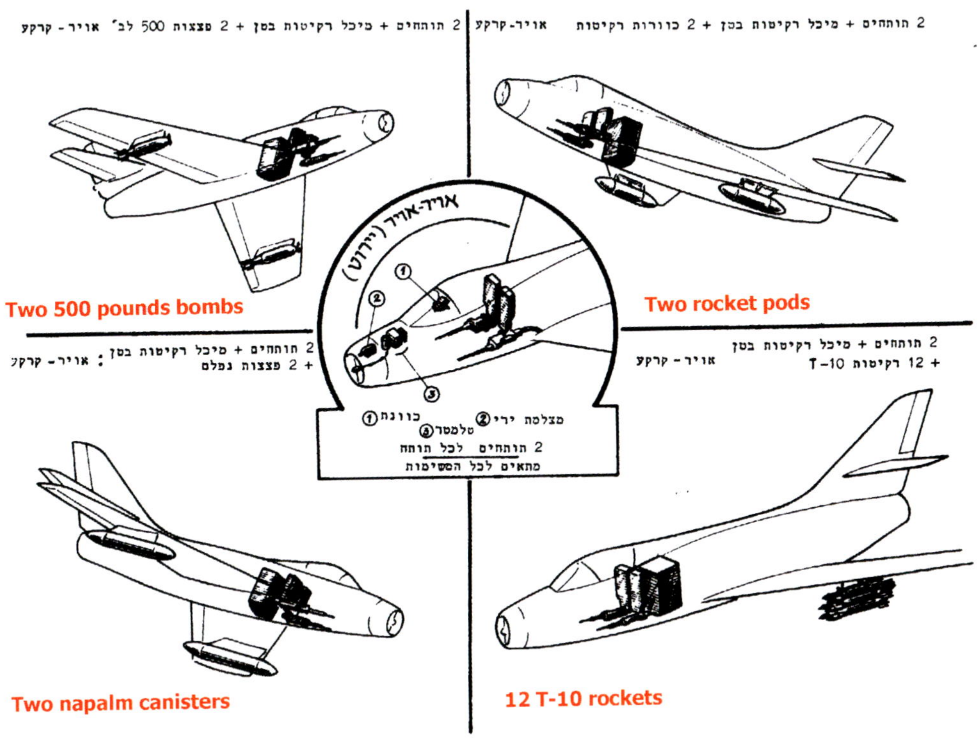

The original Mystère external ordnance options—as extracted from the Mystère manual—all involved weapons attached to its outer wing stations. ILAF modifications enabling the Mystère to fly air-to-ground operations with weapons attached to all four wing stations severely compromised its endurance, but was of special relevance for Squadron 109, flying short range air-to-ground missions from Ramat David to the Golan Heights or to the West Bank; in both cases the radius of action was less than 100 kilometers (sixty-two miles). (PC)

Flying School Class 32 graduate Iftach Zemmer in the cockpit of Mystère 10 sometime after assignment to Squadron 109 in March 1961; Mystère 10 has been camouflaged and modified with a braking chute. (PC)

The 1 April 1961 ORBAT included forty-seven Mystères—down two from the previous year's report—and Mystère fleet utilization during ILAF Year 1960, ending on 31 March 1961, was 4,993 flight hours—down 472 flight hours compared to 5,465 flight hours during ILAF Year 1959.

COMMAND HANDOVER SHEFFER HALVINI

The departure of Shahak squadron setup teams to France for the Mirage conversion course was planned during ILAF Year 1961 Term 1, but actually took place during ILAF Year 1961 Term 2, so it was time for Samuel Sheffer—who flew his last Squadron 109 Mystère flight on 1 April 1961—to hand over command of Squadron 109.

Following in the footsteps of Menahem Bar—a moshav native from Kfar Joshua—and Samuel Sheffer—a moshav native from Beer Tuvya—Amnon Halivni was a moshav native from En Vered. Born in 1935, Amnon Halivni graduated from Flying School Class 11 in August 1953; served as a flying school instructor; attended a Squadron 105 Spitfire OTU course from June 1954; served as a Squadron 101 Mustang pilot until July 1955, when he was posted to a Squadron 117 Meteor conversion course; was assigned to Squadron 117 Sabre's setup team; hastily converted to the Ouragan and Mystère during September 1956, prior to departure to Canada for the Sabre conversion course; was called back to Israel on temporary assignment to Squadron 113 Ouragan during the Suez War; was posted to the Squadron 109 Mystère setup team; and served as deputy commander until Samuel Sheffer formally handed over command of Squadron 109 to him on 18 April 1961, at which point Amnon Halivni was twenty-six.

MYSTÈRE TAKE-OFF DISTANCE

The ILAF had evaluated Mystère take-off issues for quite some time, but no new insights filtered down to field level. Wing 1 Maintenance Squadron's Ben-Ami Gov addressed MAT2 and MAT4 on 14 May 1961 with a request for guidelines:

> There is no authorized and precise data concerning the Mystère's take-off distance at various weights and temperatures. This data is crucial to determine the maximum weight at different temperatures for safe take-off from available runways.
>
> The Mystère manual does include a graph that generates required runway length for take-off in all configurations, but this graph only refers to 15 and 35°C [59 and 86°F], while the Squadron 109 commander claims this graph no longer represents reality, as it was determined during the development of the Mystère. There is a possibility that aircraft weight in different configurations does not fit data in the manual due to many modifications that were implemented since the publication of that data. I suggest weighing a current standard Mystère in all fuel and ordnance combinations specified for the squadron's missions.

MYSTÈRE TARGET TUG

The air-to-air gunnery target towing platform was the Mustang until the Meteor and Ouragan took over this mission. Retirement of the Meteor was scheduled during ILAF Year 1962 and retirement of the Ouragan was scheduled during ILAF Year 1963. Additionally,

Amnon Halivni (center, sitting on the wheel) took over from Samuel Sheffer as Squadron 109 Commander in April 1961. (PC)

Squadron 101 celebrated its thirteenth anniversary on 23 May 1961, so Squadron 109 deployed a team to Hatzor for the traditional turnaround contest between rival sister squadrons; Mystères 05 and 11 were already camouflaged when photographed at Hatzor during that turnaround contest. Mystère 05 had already been modified with a landing parachute. (PC)

Meteors and Ouragans fit for target towing suffered serviceability issues that impacted ILAF air-to-air gunnery training.

The next aircraft type in the queue was the Mystère, so it seemed natural to explore it for air-to-air gunnery target towing to back up the Meteor and Ouragan target tugs and succeed them in due time. However, logic seemed to have overlooked the Mystère's take-off issues that were under ILAF discussion for quite some time prior to the Mystère target tug proposal.

As often happened—perhaps simply because Hatzor was closer than Ramat David to ILAF HQ in Tel Aviv and to AMU22 at Tel Nof—Squadron 101 was tasked to test the new Mystère innovation.

The test was a complete failure. During the take-off run on 17 May 1961, the Mystère failed to accelerate to 155 knots, so the target was released when the Mystère was 600 meters (1,968 ft) from the end of the runway. Only in hindsight was it realized that the Mystère in question (4595) was well known as a "weak" Mystère—an aircraft with lower-than-average thrust.

The AIR2 forum—a member of the forum was AIR5 staff officer Nahum Yahalom—discussed the Mystère target tug in wake of the failed test on 24 May 1961. Since the Mystère was already modified for the target tug mission, the forum ordered MAT3 and MAT4 to test the performance of 4595 and to retest the target tug, but at Lod, where the runway was longer than at Hatzor. Additionally, and perhaps sensing the Mystère target tug proposal was shaky, the AIR2 forum ordered MAT3 to improve the availability of Meteor and Ouragan target tugs.

The issue of the Mystère target tug made it to the ILAF Commander who, by 26 May 1961, had ordered AIR2 to discontinue development of the Mystère target tug and to seek alternative solutions.

DETERIORATION IN PERFORMANCE

The target tug test surfaced the issue of Mystère performance deterioration and differences in performance between specific aircraft. A MAT4 forum—with Squadron 109 Commander Amnon Halivni present—convened on 31 May 1961 and divided the discussion into take-off in particular and performance in general.

Take-off issues impacted Squadron 109 more than Squadron 101, because Ramat David's runways were shorter and inclined. As a result, during hot days, not all of Squadron 109's Mystères were able to take-off with a normal load of two 625 liter (165 gallon) tanks and two 250 kilogram (550 lb) bombs. An issue that impacted both squadrons was the lack of take-off tables. The only suggested solution to the Mystère's take-off woes was to paint a Mystère stop line on runways so it would be crystal clear for pilots when and where to abort take-off.

Performance problems highlighted differences between aircraft. Squadron 101's Mystère 44 was considered a "weak" aircraft that climbed slowly or had to set power at 11,100 RPM in order to keep up with Mystères that climbed at 10,550 RPM. Squadron 101's 4548, 4560, 4562, and 4563 were known to have powerful engines and were thus performing better than most Mystères. In order to make up for differences, engine take-off temperature was increased from 690 to 710°C (1,274 to 1,310°F), but this change caused engine temperatures to reach 755°C (1,391°F) at 10,000 feet, so pilots had to close throttle at 10,000 feet. There were also concerns that implemented modifications degraded engine thrust, and an opinion was expressed that standard IAI engine overhaul should have been improved. The forum's recommendations were to overhaul engines every 225 flight hours, to accept overhauled engines that generated required thrust at temperatures not higher than 700°C (1,292°F), to explore the impact of modifications, and to try to find out why the engines of 4548, 4560, 4562, and 4563 performed so well.

MYSTÈRE 70

Josef Henkin flew lead in a four-ship formation on 12 July 1961 when Mystère 70 experienced an engine cut. Henkin attempted to land at En Shemer—the Mystère finished runway—but stopped in a field and the external fuel tanks caught fire, but managed to evacuate the cockpit in time. MAT2 subsequently reported:

> 4570's accident investigation revealed a major fault in the maintenance of Squadron 109 aircraft: adjustment of the engines without external measurement equipment stipulated by the manufacturer.
>
> Mystère 70 underwent three incorrect engine adjustments between 16 and 25 June [1961], and who knows in which true RPM and temperatures it actually functioned in the end.
>
> This fault—that probably became normal practice in the squadron—was reported after a [MAT2] visit to the squadron on 31 October 1960, but continued.
>
> In order to avoid malfunctions, and even accidents as a result of engines operating at higher RPM and temperatures than allowed, technical orders should be followed.

On 8 August 1961, AIR Department Chief Moti Hod issued a list of lessons that were divided into technical troubles and procedural problems.

The cause of the engine cut was reported as a failure of a main bearing, but two similar failures were experienced during 1960 while a modification that specifically addressed this issue was not implemented in these three engines due to a shortage in modification kits. A technical order that may have signaled a warning was to stop the use of aircraft that did not consume oil in twenty flight hours, thus suggesting a leak of fuel into the oil system, but this technical order was not followed and the engine of 4570 did not consume oil during at least 21:35 flight hours prior to the accident. During these 21:35 flight hours there were three complaints concerning engine RPM and temperature, but the engine was then adjusted without external measurement equipment. During this time the turbine stop time frame dropped from fifty to forty-three seconds measured in twelve flights, while at the end of the last three flights prior to the accident the turbine stop time frame was not measured. The turbine blade clearance was also not measured during five daily inspections that preceded the accident.

As for procedural problems, in the wake of the accident, ILAF Comptroller Branch recommended issuing an order to eject from aircraft that cannot be landed at Hatzor, Tel Nof, Lod, or Ramat David.

EXERCISE PORCUPINE

ILAF Year 1961 Term 1 ended with an ILAF level "combat day" maneuver from 24 to 26 July 1961 that involved all ILAF bases, squadrons, and regular units, as well as some ILAF reserve units.

PORCUPINE's objective was to exercise the ILAF in a simulated combat environment. The exercise examined:

- Deployment of squadrons to alternative air bases
- Dispersal of aircraft in bases and high tempo operations
- Diversion of formations to land at alternative bases where they would be turned around for their next mission.
- Attack at night with illumination.
- Scrambling of formations to holding patterns without pre-departure MIOR issuing the mission in midair.

The ILAF generated 638 combat aircraft sorties during PORCUPINE for an average of 5.3 sorties per pilot and 5.0 sorties per aircraft. Squadron 109 generated 119 sorties, with an average

Squadron 109 reservists preparing Mystère 16 for its next flight inside HAS, most likely during Exercise PORCUPINE (July 1961). (PC)

Squadron 109 service persons push Mystère 16—loaded with two 250 kilogram (550 lb) bombs and two fuel tanks—out of HAS prior to a combat day mission, most likely during Exercise PORCUPINE (July 1961). (PC)

of 5.1 sorties per pilot and 5.2 sorties per aircraft. Squadron 109 reserve pilot Asaf Ben-Nun flew four daytime and one nighttime PORCUPINE missions on 25 July 1961 and one daytime PORCUPINE mission on 26 July 1961; at the end of the latter, Ben-Nun's formation landed at Tel Nof, where the Mystères were turned around for another daytime PORCUPINE mission, after which they returned to Ramat David.

MYSTÈRE TAKE OFF SAFETY

To define where to paint the "abort take-off" line for the Mystère on runways, MAT4 tested the Mystère's take-off performance in a single configuration: two 625 liter (165 gallon) fuel tanks and two 250 kilogram (550 lb) bombs. By then, it was well known that most Mystères were powered by engines that did not deliver maximum thrust.

A MAT5 forum discussed MAT4's data on 20 August 1961 and issued the following recommendations:

- Position the "abort take-off" mark 650 meters (2,132 ft) from the start of runway, so that if a Mystère in the common configuration, with two tanks and two bombs, did not accelerate to 100 knots by the time it reached the line, then the pilot must abort the take-off.
- The definition of a "weak" engine is an engine delivering 85% standard thrust.
- Classification of all Mystères in line with actual engine thrust.
- Preparation of take-off options—based on the definition of a "weak" engine and the classification of all Mystères—at 15, 27, and 41°C (59, 81, and 106°F).

TWO-SEAT MYSTÈRE REQUEST FOR PROPOSAL

The ILAF's examination of a two-seat Mystère conversion was still ongoing. On 22 August 1961, AIR2 informed MAT3 of an ILAF Commander directive to deliver a Mystère to IAI for thirty days, so that IAI would be able to issue the ILAF a proposition concerning the conversion of a Mystère with two cockpits.

Ramat David Wing's Suez War Day was marked on 24 October 1961; Squadron 109 Mystères that took part in the turnaround competition included 4531, 4547, and 4575. 4531 and 4547 were still in metal finish but already equipped with a braking chute and 4575 was already camouflaged but not yet equipped with a braking chute. A team of pilots usually participated in turnaround contests, and in this competition the pilot team's turnaround aircraft was Mystère 47; the turnaround configuration was gun rounds, fuel tanks, and two bombs. (PC)

Squadron 109 service persons, including three pilots ((left to right): Iftach Zemmer, Eliezer Prigat, and Uri Dekel) in front of Mystère 16 during Ramat David Wing's Suez War Day on 24 October 1961, only thirteen days before Mystère 16 was lost in a fatal accident. (PC)

SHY EGOZI

The Shahak set-up team attended the Mirage conversion course in France from August to September 1961. Shortly after their return, a second group of six pilots was selected to bolster the Shahak squadron set-up teams.

Pilots selected for assignment to the Hatzor Shahak squadron were Ran Ronen from Squadron 101 Mystère, Josef Henkin from Squadron 109 Mystère, and Maoz Poraz from Squadron 110 Vautour.

Pilots selected for assignment to Ramat David's Shahak squadron were Shy Egozi from Squadron 109 Mystère, Uri Dekel from Squadron 109 Mystère, and Amnon Arad from Squadron 109 Mystère.

Shy Egozi's final flight was in Squadron 109's Mystère 16 on 6 November 1961. Eliezer Prigat recalled:

I was a flying school instructor and a Squadron 109 EP when we practiced instrument flying. The pilot practicing instrument flying placed a brown cardboard on his helmet's visor—blocking his vision so he would not see the horizon in particular nor the outside view in general—and lowered his seat to the lowest possible setting so that he flew the aircraft with instruments only, without looking outside. I was wingman, and the task of Number 2 was to escort in trail because [the practicing pilot] could not see where he was flying.

We took off from Ramat David, and after a short while I saw that his aircraft was rocking, so I asked "Number 1, what is going on?" and he replied that he had just put on the cardboard. We then practiced. I followed him and we arrived over Megiddo airfield, from where we headed to Ramat David for GCA. Normal procedure at the end of practice was to remove the cardboard, reposition the seat, change the radio channel and land visually. He descended and then he was ordered to change the radio channel to the channel of the control tower, because practice was over. It was then that I saw him diving in the direction of the base.

I tried to say "1, pull up" but it was too late; he crashed inside the base perimeter.

ATAR 8 AGAIN

In October 1958, the ILAF evaluated and rejected the proposition of replacing the Verdon 350 with the Atar 8 so that thrust would increase from 3.5 tons to 4.4 tons. In light of Mystère engine issues, interest in an Atar 8 powered Mystère was renewed.

An initial investigation addressed three basic aspects: the fit of the Atar 8 inside a Mystère airframe, center of gravity impact, and air inlet compatibility.

ILAF data of the Atar 8's dimensions was not conclusive, but available dimensions indicated it would be possible to fit the Atar 8 inside the Mystère's engine bay. However, the Atar 8 attachment points were not compatible, and there was no space in the Mystère's engine bay to fit new attachment points, so the only possible path to enable fitting the Atar 8 inside the Mystère would have been to modify the existing engine attachment points.

The Atar 8 was thirty kilograms (sixty-six pounds) lighter than the Verdon 350, so aircraft center of gravity moved aft beyond the rear limits. It proved impossible to move the Atar 8 forward, so in order to restore the center of gravity to safe limits, a fifty kilogram (110 pound) balance had to be placed in the aircraft's nose section.

The Verdon 350's maximum air consumption was sixty kilograms (312 pounds) per second and the Mystère's air inlet could intake up to sixty-eight kilograms (150 pounds) per second, but the Mystère's air inlet was designed to feed air to a centrifugal compressor, while the Atar 8 had an axial compressor.

MAT4's conclusions, dated 7 November 1961, were that fitting an Atar 8 in the Mystère was feasible, but more information was required, including exact dimensions, weight distribution data, attachment point characteristics, engine parameters, and details of engine accessories to conduct a structural analysis and make performance predictions.

MYSTÈRE 31

Ezra Dotan and Yakir Naveh practiced air combat on 24 November 1961 when Mystère 31 entered a spin and Ezra Dotan was forced to eject.

Mystère 31's crash site on 24 December 1961, including the tail section, cockpit, and ejection seat. (PC)

TWO-SEAT MYSTÈRE MOCK-UP PROPOSAL

On 3 December 1961, the IAI suggested progressing with two-seat Mystères with the preparation of a mock-up. The ILAF was only willing to spare nonstandard Mystère 76, so the IAI proposed using 4576 for the mock-up and, if approved, to convert it to a two-seat Mystère, as well as modifying it to the ILAF Mystère standard.

On 4 December 1961, AIR2 issued an operational requirement for a two-seat Mystère aimed at bridging the gap between Fouga training aircraft and operational types, such as the SMB2, Vautour, and Shahak:

- The aircraft will be used only for conversion, while type training will use the regular Mystère aircraft.
- The aircraft will have two seats in tandem, with all control systems in both cockpits.
- The aircraft will enable training students with servo control systems.
- The aircraft will enable instrument flying and controlled landing with a radio compass.
- The aircraft will be restricted to external ordnance only and will not be equipped with guns or a belly fuel tank.
- The aircraft center of gravity [limits] will enable flight by a single pilot.

While the IAI suggested converting and modifying Mystère 76, the ILAF explored getting rid of 4576, as the Material Department Chief informed the ILMD on 14 December 1961:

> The ILAF Commander asks to check if France would be willing to trade Mystère 76 for two Ouragans. This Mystère was loaned to us with equipment for high altitude photography and was then sold to us. Our pilots refuse to fly it, since it is an early production Mystère that differs a lot from our aircraft.

PROBLEMATIC PASSABILITY

Squadron 109's first aircraft modified for RATO was Mystère 09; the RATO modification was completed by November 1961, and on 15 December 1961, Mystère 09 was involved in an accident during landing. The Mystère landing continued past the end of runway 15 until it stopped in mud. Wing 1 Operations Officer Amihy Shmueli reported:

> We operated the big crane with a special device for extricating a Mystère to retrieve the aircraft. To our surprise, the crane was unable to move in mud, as it entrenched and did not move. Even after we paved a way with PSP, the crane was still unable to move.
>
> Extrication of the aircraft lasted ten hours, during which the runway was closed. I therefore recommend evaluating the possibility of fitting chains to the crane's wheels so it can move in mud.

LARGEST NEW PILOT INTAKE

Eight Flying School Class 34 graduates were assigned to Squadron 109 at the end of ILAF Year 1961 Term 2 Squadron 113 Ouragan OTU Course 15: Irik Bester, Michael Barzam, Zvika Hess, Uri Lis, Arnon Livnat, Menahem Nehushtan, Shlomo Nir, and David Porat. Solo day was on 17 December 1961; Michael Barzam first flew Mystère 4510; Zvika Hess first flew Mystère 4510; and Uri Lis first flew Mystère 4511.

On 15 December 1961, Mystère 09 was involved in a landing accident that closed Ramat David's runway for ten hours because the available crane was unable to travel in mud. (PC)

Flying School Class 34 graduate Uri Lis in a Mystère cockpit; Lis first flew the Mystère on 17 December 1961. The sunshade sheltered the cockpits of QRA aircraft until the construction of QRA sheds. (PC)

CHAPTER 4

WATER WAR START

1962-1964

By 1962, the dispute concerning regional water resources had evolved into the Water War; a series of occasional armed clashes—mostly between Israel and Syria—that escalated towards the activation of the Israel National Pipeline, an Israeli national enterprise to pipe water from the Sea of Galilee to the Negev Desert that was launched in 1953 and was scheduled for activation in late 1962, but was actually inaugurated on 10 June 1964. As work progressed towards activation tension between Israel and Syria soared, but from 1962 until 1964, the ILAF's participation in Water War clashes was mostly minor.

Also, from 1962 until 1964, the ILAF introduced three Shahak squadrons: Squadron 101 Shahak was activated at Hatzor in April 1962, Squadron 117 Shahak was activated at Ramat David in July 1962, and Squadron 119 Shahak was activated at Tel Nof in March 1964. In preparation for the Shahak's introduction, Squadron 101 Mystère moved from Hatzor to Tel Nof on 29 November 1961 and transformed into Squadron 116 Mystère. All of these changes impacted Squadron 109: the squadron was not converted to the Shahak as originally planned; the Mystère was no longer a first-line backup interceptor, but a second line attack aircraft; the Mystère community changed from Squadron 109 at Ramat David and Squadron 101 at Hatzor to Squadron 109 at Ramat David and Squadron 116 at Tel Nof; and the traditional division between Hatzor "Air Force South" and Ramat David "Air Force North" was no longer unequivocal, as Squadron 116 Mystère and Squadron 119 Shahak operated from midland Tel Nof.

Squadron 109 pilot Uri Lis was attached to Command North as ALO for Operation SWALLOW 1; this photo, along Squadron 109's veranda, was taken during the tense time in the wake of Operation SWALLOW 1. (PC)

OPERATION SWALLOW 1

On 1 March 1962, the Syrian Prime Minister stated that Syria would react against the Israel National Pipeline in due time. On 3 March 1962, Syria filed a complaint to the UN concerning the Israel National Pipeline. Actions followed words on 8 March 1962, when Syrian soldiers engaged Israeli boats in the Sea of Galilee with machine guns and recoilless guns.

The ILDF prepared Operation SWALLOW 1 as a potential reprisal action against Syrian fortifications, but the Israeli government decided to refrain for the time being, as well as to authorize Prime Minister and Minister of Defense David Ben-Gurion to order reaction. Therefore, after Syrian soldiers again opened fire at Israeli boats in the Sea of Galilee on 15 March 1962, Prime Minister and Minister of Defense David Ben-Gurion ordered the ILDF to activate Operation SWALLOW 1.

ILDF Brigade 1 was tasked to launch Operation SWALLOW 1 during the night of 16 to 17 March 1962. In preparation for Operation SWALLOW 1, two Squadron 109 pilots—Irik Bester and Uri Lis—were attached to Brigade 1 as ALOs. The pilots were at their homes for weekend leave, so on Friday, 16 March 1962, Dror Avneri flew a Piper from Ramat David to En Shemer airfield to retrieve Uri Lis from his home at nearby kibbutz En Shemer.

The ILAF was on readiness to support ILDF forces during Operation SWALLOW 1 and to contain potential Syrian reaction after Operation SWALLOW 1. Syrian artillery fire harassed ILDF troops during disengagement and slowed down the evacuation of casualties, so at 04:05 on 17 March 1962, the ILDF ordered the ILAF to scramble support aircraft to silence Syrian artillery batteries.

Squadron 110 Vautours departed Ramat David at 04:10 and Squadron 109 Mystères followed at 04:30. In line with the previous readiness order, the Squadron 109 Mystères were armed with rockets, but weather conditions at the time—low clouds and poor visibility—were unfavorable for rocketry. Squadron 109 was thus ordered to change the configuration of its readiness aircraft from rockets to two 250 kilogram (550 lb) bombs in case more Mystères were scrambled, while the four aircraft that were already in the air—pilots Amnon Halivni, Jacob Terner, Dror Avneri, and Haggai Ronen—were ordered to hold while the Vautours bombed. However, the ILDF concluded that ILAF bombing was inaccurate and that the ILAF's action did not silence Syrian artillery fire, so the ILDF ordered the ILAF to suspend support. Meanwhile, the retreat of ILDF forces was completed by 05:00 and Syrian artillery fire ceased, so ILAF support was no longer required and the Squadron 109 Mystères returned to Ramat David.

As usual, a tense time followed the ILDF's reprisal action. EP and reserve pilots remained in squadrons while limited action over the Israeli-Syrian border continued. On 18 March 1962, Eliezer Prigat and Yakir Naveh escorted a Noratlas flying a LOROP mission west of the Israeli-Syrian border.

Prime Minister and Minister of Defense David Ben-Gurion's statement that the objective of the ILDF's reprisal action was to deter Syria was answered on 20 March 1962, when Syrian soldiers again opened fire at Israeli boats in the Sea of Galilee.

Squadron 109 reserve pilot Asaf Ben-Nun was scrambled in Mystère 90 on 20 March 1962, in Mystère 90 on 21 March 1962, and in Mystère 05 on 22 March 1962, but although Squadron 105 SMB2s inconclusively clashed with Syrian MiG-17s on 21 March 1962, Squadron 109 Mystères did not engage Syrian MiGs before tensions faded around 25 March 1962.

RELOCATION

The 1 April 1962 ORBAT included forty-three Mystères—down four from the previous year's report—and Mystère fleet utilization during the year ending 1 April 1962 was 5,423 flight hours, which was up 430 flight hours compared to ILAF Mystère utilization of 4,993 flight hours during ILAF Year 1960.

Ramat David Wing 1 Maintenance Squadron Ordnance Flight service persons prepared Mystère 11 for display at Ramat David (probably in 1962) with an array of weapons: bombs and rockets, napalm canisters, and gun rounds. (PC)

Ramat David Wing 1 Maintenance Squadron Ordnance Flight service persons prepared Mystère 11 for display at Ramat David (probably in 1962) with an array of weapons: bombs and rockets, napalm canisters, and gun rounds. (PC)

Also during April 1962, Squadron 101 opened at Hatzor as the ILAF's first Shahak squadron. In preparation for activation of Squadron 117 as Ramat David's Shahak squadron, Squadron 117 Shahak's setup team took over Squadron 109 Mystère's facilities—from 1953 until 1956 originally the Squadron 117 Meteor facilities—as these were more suitable for an interception squadron, while Squadron 109 moved into facilities that Squadron 117 Meteor used from 1956 until 1962 that were appropriate for an attack squadron. Squadron 117 Meteor transformed into Squadron 107 Meteor and relocated to facilities that served Squadron 107 Spitfire and Squadron 107 Mustang from 1953 until 1956.

INDEPENDENCE DAY 1962

The ILAF's participation in Israel Independence Day 14 on 9 May 1962 included a "train" of formations flying over the main stage at Haifa Road in Tel Aviv in line with AIR3 OPOR 27/62 issued on 12 April 1962.

The flyover plan was a Flying School Aerobatic Team in a "rose maneuver" right over the main stage, a Flying School Fouga formation shaped "14," and then a "train" of formations from old to new: twenty Meteors, sixteen Ouragans, sixteen Squadron 116 Mystères, sixteen Squadron 109 Mystères, twelve Vautours, twenty-four SMB2s, seven Shahaks, nine Nords, and two Alouettes, with the seven Shahaks flying a tight circuit for a second flyover of the main stage right after the Alouettes that ended in a zoom climb with afterburners.

AIR3 defined the shape of the formations: the Squadron 109 Mystères were to fly in four diamond shaped four-ship formations, with one four-ship formation leading three arrowhead shaped four-ship formations.

The Shahak—the star of the flyover—was not yet operational, so SMB2s and Mystères were tasked to defend the flyover. Two fully armed SMB2s flew patrol at high altitude over Tel Aviv, while all SMB2s and Mystères taking part in the flyover flew with armed and cocked guns fully loaded with operational rounds.

Among the Squadron 109 pilots participating in the Israel Independence Day 14 flyover of Tel Aviv on 9 May 1962 were Levy Zur in Mystère 82 and Uri Lis in Mystère 90.

OPERATION BIND

The ILAF's plan to retire the Ouragan during ILAF Year 1963 was also reversed, and Israel acquired additional Ouragans from France with a partial payment of three Mystères, even though the ILAF's Mystère ORBAT numbered forty-three aircraft, which was well below the ILAF standard for two combat aircraft squadrons and excluded adequate reserve. Thus, Operation BIND resulted in the shrinkage of the ILAF's Mystère fleet from forty-three to forty.

All three Mystères marked for return to France were Squadron 109 aircraft: 4575, 4581, and 4590. On 21 May 1962, MAT3 ordered Wing 1 to prepare the three Mystères for the ferry flight from Israel to France, including the deletion of all ILAF markings. In order to adjust squadron inventories, Squadron 116 pilot Dan Sever transferred 4544 from Tel Nof to Ramat David on 1 June 1962, so that nineteen aircraft would be assigned to Squadron 109, versus twenty-one aircraft assigned to Squadron 116.

On 5 June 1962, MAT3 informed Wing 1 that FRAF pilots would fly the three Mystères from Ramat David to France from 18 June 1962. Wing 1 was asked to ready four Mystères in case one of the three assigned Mystères failed during the acceptance flights planned to precede the ferry flight. The three Mystères departed Ramat David for the last time on 26 June 1962.

COUNTERBATTERY READINESS ORDER

Israel now prepared for the next clash in the undeclared Water War. In the wake of Operation SWALLOW 1, on 20 March 1962, the Israeli government authorized Prime Minister and Minister of Defense David Ben-Gurion to approve an air strike aimed at silencing Syrian artillery without convening the government for discussion, effectively delegating the ILDF's counterbattery mission to the ILAF due to the geographical, numerical, and quality superiority of Syrian artillery compared with the ILDF's artillery; in fact, the ILDF's

Squadron 109 regular pilots on 10 June 1962: standing (left to right): Rafaeli, Halivni, Zur, and Terner; kneeling (left to right): Nehushtan, Lis, Livnat, and Porat; and sitting (left to right): Hess, Nir, Gadish, Barzam, and Bester. This photo was taken after Squadron 109 relocated from facilities east of the Ramat David Maintenance Squadron complex that Squadron 117 Meteor used from 1953 until 1956 to facilities west of the complex that Squadron 117 Meteor used from 1956 until 1962. (PC)

Squadron 116 pilot Dan Sever ferried Mystère 44 from Tel Nof to Ramat David on 1 June 1962. Mystère 44—in this view still wearing the Squadron 101 badge—was reassigned from Squadron 116 as a partial counterbalance to the delivery to the FRAF of 4575, 4581, and 4590. (PC)

regular deployment of forces did not include any artillery battery along the Israeli-Syrian border, so in case of a clash without prior warning the ILAF was the only ILDF counterbattery option.

At all times, both day and night, the ILAF maintained QRA aircraft mostly in air-to-air configuration, with tight time frame definitions for take-off within minutes from the scramble signal for interception, but also in air-to-ground configuration for attack, though attack configured QRA aircraft were subjected to relatively relaxed scramble time frames.

In order to match the ILAF's regular readiness to the scenario of an ILDF counterbattery request, on 5 July 1962 AIR3 defined Ramat David readiness in conjunction with a clash along the Israeli-Syrian border. Obviously, Ramat David was viewed as the first base from where ILAF aircraft would be scrambled to the Israeli-Syrian border, because Ramat David was the closest ILAF air base to this sector.

In fact, Ramat David readiness was not changed, but adapted. AIR3 stipulated that in case of a clash along the Israeli-Syrian border, the proper chain of command would be an ILDF request for ILAF support, followed by AIR3's order to scramble ready aircraft. Since at the time Squadron 109 Mystère was still in charge of Ramat David's air-to-air QRA—Squadron 117 Shahak would receive its first aircraft on 7 July 1962—the first scrambled was a pair of Squadron 109 Mystères in air-to-air configuration, and were therefore only able to strafe Syrian artillery, effectively acting as a makeshift counterbattery solution until the arrival of Squadron 109 Mystères and Squadron 110 Vautours scrambled from air-to-ground readiness and armed with bombs. Target allocation for Squadron 109 Mystères scrambled from air-to-air QRA would be in the air after take-off, due to the tightly defined scramble time. Target allocation to Squadron 109 Mystères and Squadron 110 Vautours scrambled from air-to-ground QRA would be on the ground prior to take-off.

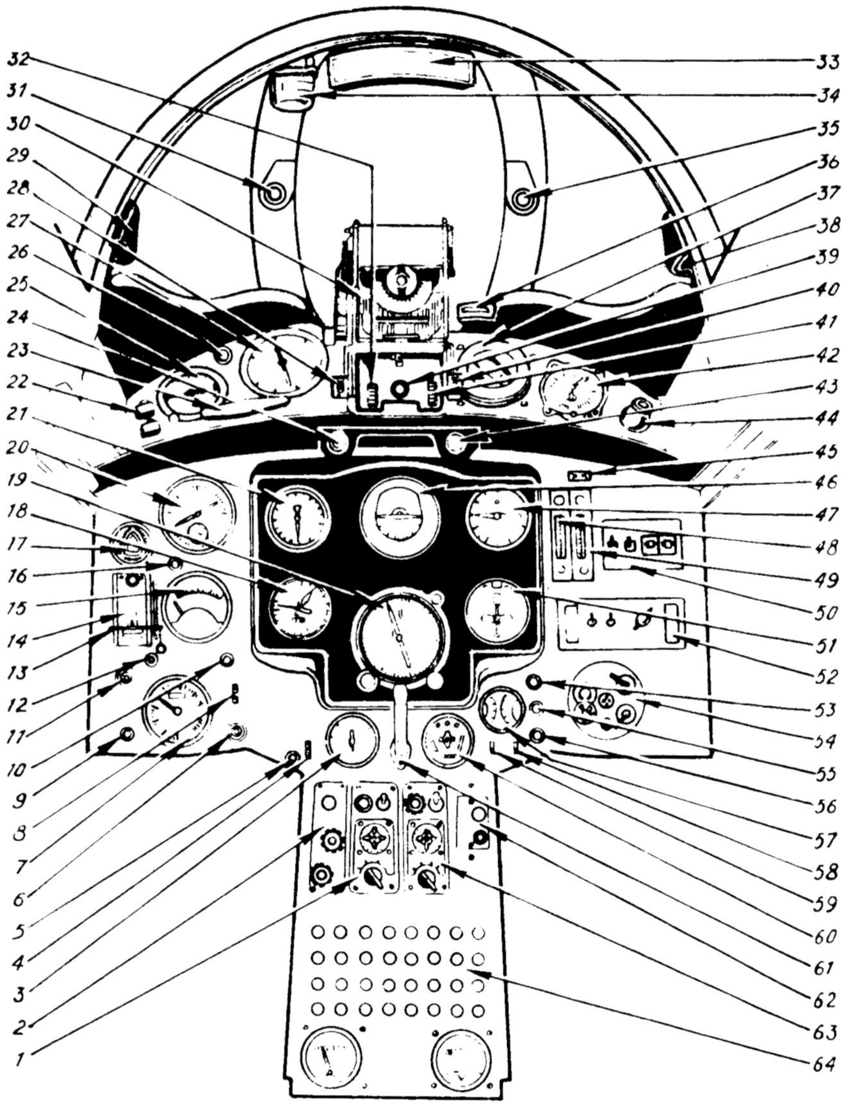

The Mystère's cockpit front panel's original configuration included a VHF1 control box (1) and VHF2 control box (63); VHF2 was replaced with UHF following the Shahak's introduction. (PC)

SHAHAK INTRODUCTION IMPACT

Squadron 117 accepted its first four Shahaks on 7 July 1962, and started work towards the accomplishment of IOC. During this transition period, Squadron 109 continued to sustain Ramat David's air-to-air QRA. The Shahak's introduction impacted Squadron 109's missions, manpower, and maintenance.

The Mystère shift from air-to-air to air-to-ground would no longer be ambiguous, as it was during the period when the ILAF fielded a single SMB2 squadron based at Hatzor.

Migration of pilots and maintainers from the Mystère to the Shahak continued. The third group of Squadron 109 Mystère pilots assigned to the Shahak conversion course—Amihy Shmueli, Jacob Terner, Ezra Dotan, and Uri Even-Nir—departed by August 1962.

The Shahak was equipped with UHF transceivers, while previous ILAF combat aircraft were equipped with VHF radios, so the Mystères had to be modified with one VHF radio and one UHF radio. MAT4 designed the modification and on 21 August 1962, MAT2 asked MAT3 to add a prototype VHF and UHF radio modification to Squadron 116's Mystère 85 AMU 22 PDM program.

MYSTÈRE 50 MIRACLE 1

The ILAF's high attrition during training was not unique; at the time, all modern air forces around the globe suffered high attrition during training, primarily due to the inability to monitor training flight parameters. Safety was breached regularly and pilots who did not breach safety limits—altitude, AOA, speed, and stress —were regarded as "weak." Since safety was not enforced regularly, safety issues only surfaced in the wake of accidents. On 26 October 1962, Flight Safety Branch officer Achikar Eyal reported an accident that happened to Squadron 109's Mystère 50 on 18 October 1962:

> Description of incident: "We departed in Mystère 50 to [practice] attack at Range 53. We strafed in line astern. I entered my fourth strafing pass at an altitude of 5,000 feet. The dive seemed too steep, so I dropped the nose in order to accomplish flatter strafing and opened fire from 500 meters [1,640 ft] or so. I wanted to finish firing all rounds when suddenly the target looked too close, so I started to pull up from strafing when I sensed a strong hit. I noticed something unusual on the left wing and the range control officer reported a fuel leak on my left wing. I switched the fuel selector from wings to fuselage and the fuel gauge indication changed from 350 kilograms [771 pounds] to 600 kilograms [1,322 pounds]. While climbing to 16,000 feet in the direction of Tel Nof, I noted the airspeed indicator reading was 130 knots, so my leader landed me at Tel Nof in line with the landing without airspeed indicator procedure. Apparently I hit the target."
>
> Post landing inspection revealed that both wings were torn so badly that it was necessary to replace them. Accident causes were:
>
> - Strafing pass that breached safety limitations: dive angle, open fire range 450 meters [1,476 ft], end of fire range 200 meters [656 ft].
> - Low flying at an altitude of five meters [16 ft, above ground level] after the end of fire with a radical attempt to avoid getting close [to the target].
> - Erroneous estimate of altitude for pass over target.
> - Strafing in negative G.

ILAF Commander Ezer Weizman sentenced the pilot to thirty-five days in prison, a reduction in rank from 1LT to 2LT, and grounding until decided otherwise. Flight Safety Branch officer Achikar Eyal summarized:

> The pilot's ability to tell his story is a miracle. It is time that pilots stop relying on miracles and start to realize that the breach of flight safety regulations and disrespect of limitations due to overconfidence will necessarily result in accidents. This experience proves this point and smart guys should learn from others' experience.

ILAF YEAR 1963 PLAN

In preparation for the ILDF's General Discussion of ILDF Year 1963 (April 1963 to March 1964) on 29 October 1962, the ILAF's Year 1963 Plan was circulated on 22 October 1962.

The ILAF expected seven major organization changes during ILAF Year 1963, including the closure of Squadron 109 and the assignment of all Mystères to Squadron 116.

Although acquisition of attack aircraft to reequip Squadron 109 was not mentioned in the ILAF's Year 1963 Plan—although inactivation of Squadron 109 during ILAF Year 1963 was explicitly indicated and reactivation of Squadron 109 during ILAF Year 1963 was not mentioned—Squadron 109 was listed in both the start of the year ILAF ORBAT and the end of year ILAF ORBAT with an assignment of twenty-nine pilots (including four reservists) and thirty-two pilots (still including four reservists), respectively.

Additionally, the ILAF's Year 1963 Plan included an extension of one Ramat David runway to 2,400 meters (7,874 ft), an extension that was expected, among other benefits, to solve Ramat David take-off limitations during summertime and hot and heavy Mystère operations.

Therefore, the ILAF forecast that Squadron 109 Mystère would close during ILAF Year 1963 was not unequivocal, but was somewhat ambiguous.

MYSTÈRE DISPOSAL PROPOSAL

High attrition during training as a result of breaching flight safety limitations complicated maintenance and depleted the fleet. By the time Mystère 50 physically hit the target it was attacking at Range 53 on 18 October 1962, only thirty-nine Mystères remained in ILAF inventory. In response to Mystère disposal discussions, on 28 October 1962 Material Department Deputy Chief Israel Roth issued an estimation of the Mystère fleet's value:

Uri Lis first flew lead in a practice SEAB mission on 19 October 1962 in Mystère 15. Mystère 15 is landing at Ramat David sometime between installation of its parachute pack circa 1961 and its camouflage being painted, probably during Level D maintenance in 1964. (PC)

Item	Estimated Value in US Dollars
Aircraft	5,850,000 (39 at 150,000 each)
Engines	1,810,000 (43 at 40,000 to 50,000 each)
Aircraft spares stock	2,000,000 (sufficient stock for 10,000 flight hours)
Engine spares stock	350,000
Aircraft equipment	1,193,500 (racks and tanks at 30,600 per aircraft)
Ground equipment	1,000,000 (ten Level A preflight kits and two Level B maintenance kits)
Ordnance	1,050,000 (stock of 68 millimeter pods and rockets unique to the Mystère)
TOTAL	13,253,500

The real value was either zero, or how much a buyer was willing to pay, but the estimated value was aimed at handing over to the ILMD a starting point for an asking price. Status of aircraft was also an important parameter, so Material Department Deputy Chief Israel Roth indicated thirty-six Mystères were serviceable, with three Mystères grounded for major maintenance. A flight hours table—as of 1 October 1962—was provided for all thirty-nine Mystères, of which the following were assigned to Squadron 109:

Aircraft	**Flight Hours**
4505	822:15
4506	723:00
4507	626:50
4509	679:35
4510	798:10
4511	741:00
4514	750:00
4515	633:55
4525	627:25
4526	784:35
4532	692:40
4544	629:15
4547	900:00
4550	853:40
4571	519:05
4572	696:25
4582	676:00
4583	765:00

So Squadron 109's flight hours ranged from 519:05 to 900:00 and averaged 717:43 flight hours for an average annual utilization of less than 120 flight hours per aircraft.

Ramat David marked Suez War Day 6 on 1 November 1962 for the first time as a four-squadron wing; Mystères that took part in the turnaround competition included 4514, 4515, 4526, and 4532 in metal finish, as well as 4572 and 4582 in camouflage. A flyover was staged in addition to the turnaround competition with Levy Zur flying Mystère 34 and Uri Lis piloting Mystère 15. (PC)

Another potential future path for the ILAF's Mystère force was consolidation of the fleet. AIR1 prepared a staff study to amalgamate the two Mystère squadrons by 1 April 1963.

Both efforts ended in nothing: Israel did not sell the Mystère fleet and the ILAF did not amalgamate the Mystère force.

CLOSE CALLS FOR 4509 AND 4506

Low maintenance standards and poor pilot discipline continued to hamper the Mystère force and nearly cost Squadron 109 two Mystères during November 1962.

The first close call involved 4509 during a routine post Level B maintenance test flight on 9 November 1962, as the pilot reported:

> I returned to land at the end of the test flight, reported [to control tower] "greens" [lights indicating landing gear down] and, at 190 knots, tried to move the stick a little but it did not move backwards. I opened the throttle and leveled the wings so that, with more power and faster speed, and with the same stick setting the maximum possible backwards, the aircraft climbed. I ascended to

Mystère 09 was nearly lost on 9 November 1962 during a post maintenance test flight. (PC)

> [higher] altitude and tried to release the stick but to no avail; the stick only moved forward [all the way] and sideways, but backwards only up to the halfway point. I explored [handling] and noted that with flaps deployed down for a third of a stroke, I was able to maintain 170 [knots] at an acceptable descent rate.
>
> I entered a long [shallow] approach [to runway] with engine power and was over the start of the runway at 170 [knots] and a little bit high. At the same time, I sensed as though something released and the stick started to move backwards and forward as usual. I touched down a little heavy and deployed the [braking] parachute at 130 knots; the parachute detached, but I had no trouble stopping.

Post flight examination revealed that the cylinder of the elevator actuator—a part that was replaced during maintenance —locked as it reached the end of its movement range when the stick was moved backwards.

The second close call involved 4506, which suffered CAT3 damage from ricochets on 26 November 1962. Damage from ricochets during bombing or strafing practice over ranges was commonplace, mostly due to pilots breaching safety regulations due to high motivation to accomplish good results in an environment of competition coupled with an inability to accurately monitor aircraft parameters. Most resulted in CAT2 damage but, from time to time, aircraft also returned to base with CAT3 damage or did not return at all in what were subsequently defined as CAT4 accidents.

OPERATION EAGLE

The Israeli government authorized the Minister of Defense to approve an ILDF request to operate the ILAF against Syrian artillery, but in the next major clash between Israel and Syria on 4 December 1962, Syrian soldiers sprayed Israeli farmers and villages with heavy machine gun fire during a skirmish that lasted from 17:00 until 22:00.

Syria thus challenged Israel, since the Israeli government's authorization to react referred to the ILAF operating in a counterbattery mission, not against machine gun fire. In response to this new Syrian challenge, on 9 December 1962 the Israeli government decided to authorize the Minister of Defense to approve an ILDF request for ILAF support in any scenario during which Syrian soldiers opened fire at Israeli settlements.

AIR3 Chief Jacob Salmon signed OPOR 60/62 Operation EAGLE on 12 December 1962. The OPOR covered three potential levels of escalation:

- Attack Syrian fortifications along the border if Syrian soldiers open fire at Israeli villages.
- Attack Syrian artillery east of the border if Syrian artillery opens fire at any Israeli target.
- Attack SYAF air bases if Syrian artillery opens fire at Israeli towns or cities.

OPOR 60/62 was distributed to squadrons and was stored in safes pending an activation order. Upon activation of Operation EAGLE, the two Mystère squadrons were to field twenty-eight aircraft, each armed with two 250 kilogram (550 lb) bombs, on readiness to attack Syrian targets.

However, the ILDF treated the activation of Operation EAGLE as a reprisal operation against Syria and, at 15:05 on 12 December 1962, ordered the ILAF to activate Operation EAGLE, with D-Day on 13 December 1962 and H-Hour at 10:00. AIR3 distributed the relevant activation orders, EP and reserve pilots reported to squadrons, and Readiness State C was effective from 07:30 on 13

December 1962. The ILDF then ordered the ILAF to reschedule Operation EAGLE to 17 December 1962 due to unfavorable weather conditions, but more likely because there was no exchange of fire along the Israeli-Syrian border and therefore no cause to activate Operation EAGLE as a reprisal action against Syria. The same happened on 17 December 1962, when the ILDF ordered the ILAF to reschedule Operation EAGLE to 23 December 1962, and then again on 23 December 1962, when the ILDF ordered the ILAF to cancel the activation of Operation EAGLE without rescheduling the activation date.

Obviously, activation of Operation EAGLE as a reprisal operation without prior exchange of fire along Israeli-Syrian border was beyond the scope of the Israeli government's authorization to the Minister of Defense, and would have required not only on the spot approval by the Minister of Defense, but an approval after in depth discussion in a government meeting. The Israeli government thus suppressed the ILDF's desire to operate the ILAF and Squadron 109 Mystères did not operate against Syria in December 1962, and would in fact operate against Syria only after the ILAF was activated in line with government guidelines.

MYSTÈRES TO ETHIOPIA?

The ILDF's ambition to sell its Mystères surfaced again on 27 January 1963, when ILDF Deputy Chief of Staff Isaac Rabin wrote to the ILDF's representative in Ethiopia, Emanuel Yardeni:

> The fourth issue concerns Mystères. This issue is much more complicated due to all sorts of reasons. The ILAF and ILAF Commander [Ezer Weizman] firmly objected [to the sale of Mystères to Ethiopia]. ILDF Chief of Staff [Zvi Zur] was also not in favor [of Israel exporting Mystères to Ethiopia], but Deputy Minister of Defense [Simon Peres] forced the ILDF and obtained approval from the Minister of Defense [David Ben-Gurion]. Since it has been decided so, I presume that the ILAF will do whatever it takes. [ILAF AIR Department Chief] Moti [Hod] assured me that he will issue a letter concerning this issue. What worries me is whether the Mystère is indeed the right aircraft for the ETAF and if the introduction of a small number of aircraft different from what they are used to will not get them, and us, into too much trouble. I suggest that you rely on your acquaintance with the ILAF and that you consult this issue with [ILAF advisor to ETAF] Eli Eyal before we get into too much trouble. From what the Deputy Minister of Defense said, we could not understand what they really want, so it would be best to enquire into it with [ETAF Commander] General [Ayene] Asefa.

Similar to so many ideas and plans attributed over the years to Simon Peres, this idea/plan did not bear the hoped for fruits either and ILAF Mystères were not exported to Ethiopia.

RATO REEVALUATION

MAT4's modification to fit four RATO bottles to the Mystère was accepted as standard and eighteen Mystères—seven Squadron 109

Squadron 109 operated a mix of metal-finished and camouflaged Mystères by the time of Operation EAGLE in December 1962. (PC)

Mystère 47 between installation of its parachute pack circa 1961 and application of its camouflage scheme in 1963. (PC)

Mystères and 11 Squadron 116 Mystères—were modified by AMU 22 until February 1963, when modification work was suspended.

The original MAT4 design used 15-KS-1000-A1 RATO bottles that cost 590 US dollars each. Meanwhile, it came to the attention of the ILAF that the cost of one 14-DS-1000-M6 RATO bottle was only 125 US dollars. The drawback of cheaper RATO bottles was the emission of black smoke. In order to evaluate the cheaper RATO bottles, and in order to determine whether the emission of black smoke had any other substantive negative phenomenon, on 4 April 1962 AIR2 directed the Material Department to order ten of the cheaper RATO bottles, as well as to order the IAI to suspend the manufacture of Mystère RATO structures pending final decision, since it was unknown whether the Mystère RATO structure designed for the expensive RATO bottles would also fit the cheaper RATO bottles.

An order for fifteen cheaper RATO bottles was placed on 8 November 1962, but none was accepted by February 1963 and no drawings of cheaper RATO bottles were received, so it was impossible to modify the existing Mystère RATO structure or to design a new Mystère RATO structure. For this reason, it was decided to suspend modification of the Mystère RATO structure until after acceptance of the cheaper RATO bottles and drawings, after design of Mystère RATO structure fit for cheaper RATO bottles, and after testing of the cheaper RATO bottles.

MODIFIED NOZZLE

The continuing quest to improve the Mystère's take-off performance involved replacement of a nozzle, a proposition that surfaced in September 1962, when MAT2 asked Wing 1 Maintenance Squadron Commander Avner Halivni—elder brother of Squadron 109 Commander Amnon Halivni—to prepare for the delivery of a Mystère to the IAI for tests with a modified nozzle.

Mystère 83 was assigned to this project, and IAI evaluation was completed by 16 February 1963. The objective of the nozzle

Levy Zur was scrambled in Mystère 71 on 23 March 1963. Mystère 71—photographed during a scramble drill—was possibly painted in camouflage during Level D maintenance in 1965. (PC)

modification was to improve take-off thrust without exceeding the temperature limit of 730°C (1,346°F) at altitudes up to 30,000 feet. A static test demonstrated a thrust improvement of 130 kilograms (286 lbs) with a temperature increase of only eight degrees celsius (46°F).

Test flights were aimed at verifying calculated data and static test results, as well as to measure temperatures at various altitudes. The test program involved fifteen flights totaling nine flight hours. Six flights were devoted to testing take-off performance only and nine flights involved testing take-off and climb, as well as measurement of temperature during climb. Aircraft configuration during the thirteen test flights was two full 625 liter (165 gallon) external fuel tanks yielding a weight of 9.3 tons. Aircraft configuration during two flights was two external fuel tanks and two 250 kilogram (550 lb) bombs for a total weight of 9.89 tons.

All take-off parameters were normalized to 11,050 RPM, zero velocity wind, and 160 knots lift off speed to enable proper comparison between the test flights, as well as to generate data for general use.

Average take-off distances at 9.3 tons were 1,503 meters (4,931 ft) with the regular nozzle and 1,347 meters (4,419 ft) with the improved nozzle. Average take-off distances at 9.89 tons were 1,631 meters (5,351 ft) with the regular nozzle and 1,573 meters (5,161 ft) with the improved nozzle. Test results varied considerably and were not consistent, and the bottom line average improvement of 156 meters (512 ft) at 9.3 tons was poorer than the predicted improvement of 200 meters (656 ft). When one extraordinary test result—a take-off distance of 1,406 meters (4,612 ft) with a regular nozzle versus 1,470 meters (4,822 ft) with the improved nozzle—was excluded, the average improvement during tests exactly matched the predicted improvement of 200 meters (656 ft).

Take-off distances were within reason primarily because the tests were conducted during winter, with relatively low ambient temperatures. The average improvement of 156 meters (512 ft) was extrapolated to yield an improvement of 204 meters (669 ft) for a take-off weight of 9.89 tons at 30°C (86°F) or an improvement of 263 meters (863 ft) for 10.45 tons at 35°C (95°F).

While the available runway length for ILAF Mystères was 2,300 meters (7,546 ft), it was decided to calculate safe take-off performances from a 2,100 meter (6,890 ft) runway to take into account piloting variances and engine thrust differences. Maximum temperatures for safe take-off from a 2,100 meter (6,890 ft) runway were calculated as follows:

Weight	Configuration	Regular Nozzle	Improved Nozzle
9.89 TONS	two tanks and two 250 kilogram (550 lb) bombs	28°C	39°C
10.1 TONS	two tanks and two napalm canisters	24°C	35°C
10.45 TONS	two tanks and two 500 kilograms bombs	28°C	39°C

Climb performance was tested during six flights—three with the regular nozzle and three with the improved nozzle—in a similar flight profile without exceeding maximum RPM (11,150) and maximum temperature (730°C, 1,346°F). The improved nozzle cut the time to 30,000 feet by one minute, while climb performance between 30,000 and 40,000 feet was the same with the regular nozzle and the improved nozzle; above 40,000 feet the Mystère climbed faster with the regular nozzle. Analysis of the climb tests pointed out that with the improved nozzle engine thrust was up from 0.2 tons at sea level to 0.04 tons at 30,000 feet.

The conclusion was that a Mystère with the improved nozzle and a take-off weight of up to ten tons would not have any limitations during take-off from a 2,100 meter (6,890 ft) runway, while a Mystère with the improved nozzle and a take-off weight of 10.45 tons was limited to an ambient temperature of 39°C (102°F) for safe take-off from a 2,100 meter (6,890 ft) runway.

At the end of IAI testing, the improved nozzle was transferred to Ramat David for ten flight hours to conduct a comparative evaluation in the real world environment of Squadron 109.

COMMAND HANDOVER HALVINI IVRY

On 30 March 1963, David Ivry took over command of Squadron 109 from Amnon Halivni. Ivry graduated Flying School Class 14 in June 1954 and, by the early 1960s, he was identified with Hatzor "Air Force South," even though he started his career as a fighter pilot at Ramat David with "Air Force North," since he attended a Squadron 105 Spitfire OTU course from June 1954 and subsequently served with Squadron 101 Mustang; then, from September 1955, he attended a Squadron 117 Meteor conversion course in preparation for service as a Squadron 113 Ouragan pilot.

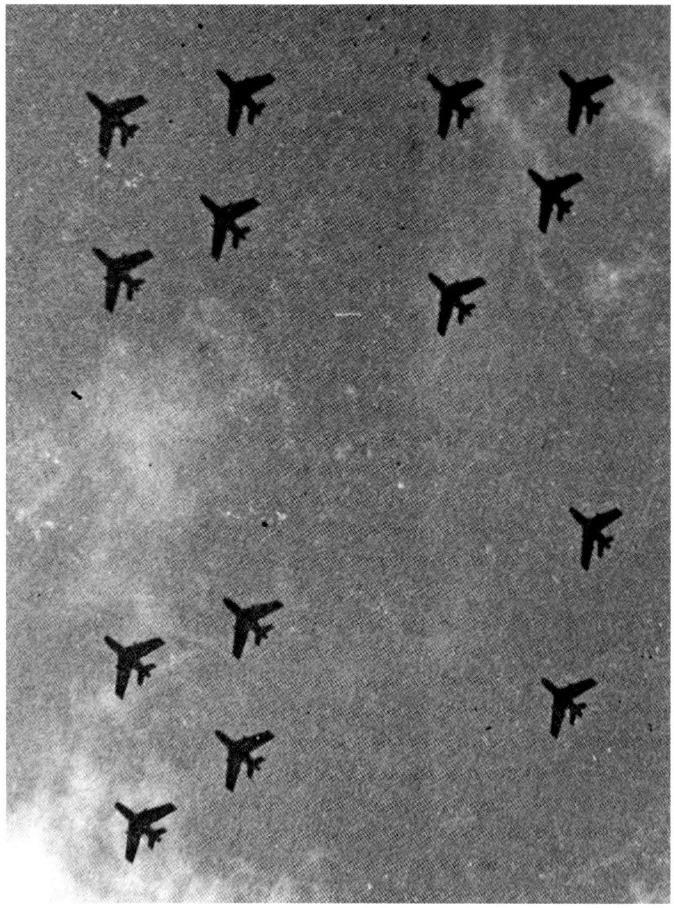

This fourteen-ship formation was reportedly flown at the end of the Squadron 109 command handover parade on 30 March 1963, but no participating pilots have surfaced yet. (PC)

Squadron 109's command handover parade on 30 March 1963 (left to right): David Ivry, Ramat David Wing Commander Menahem Bar, and Amnon Halivni. (PC)

Ivry moved south from Ramat David to Hatzor in November 1955, prior to departure to the UK from March until September 1956 for a PAI course. Upon his return to Israel, Ivry was assigned to the Flying School QFI course while continuing to serve as a Squadron 113 EP pilot, in which capacity he flew nine missions during the October to November 1956 Suez War.

From 1957 until 1958, Ivry served as Squadron 113 Deputy B. Having been selected for assignment to the Squadron 105 SMB2 setup team and subsequent service as Squadron 105 Deputy B, Ivry reported to Squadron 101 Mystère in December 1958 for one term of training in preparation to fly the SMB2 from March 1959.

Ivry then moved to Tel Nof and served as Flying School Basic Training Squadron Commander from 1960. Following graduation from the ILDF Staff School in 1961, Ivry was selected for assignment to the Squadron 117 Shahak setup team and subsequent service as Squadron 117 Deputy A. It was this assignment that returned Ivry to Ramat David, at first as Squadron 117 Deputy A and then, from 30 March 1963, as Squadron 109 Commander.

RATO READINESS REQUEST

One day after entering his office as Squadron 109 Commander, David Ivry addressed AIR3 concerning Mystère RATO readiness:

> As summer draws closer, it is highly likely that high temperatures will prevent the Mystère [from taking off with full ordnance load] or will endanger [Mystère aircraft] taking off with full ordnance load.
>
> In order to accomplish "real" readiness missions for the attack of ground targets in the northern theatre and taking into account the present [combat qualification] possibilities of Shahak aircraft, it seems essential to have RATO bottles in the squadron, at least for four aircraft.
>
> Not least important is training ground crews in the assembly of these rockets; a drill that might possibly be an operational necessity.

ILAF YEAR 1963 TERM 1 CONVERSION

The 1 April 1963 ORBAT included thirty-nine Mystères—down four from the previous year's report—and Mystère fleet utilization during the year ending on 1 April 1963 was 5,611 flight hours, up 188 flight hours compared to the 5,423 flight hours during ILAF Year 1961.

Having graduated Flying School Class 38 in November 1962 and ILAF Year 1962 Term 3 Squadron 113 Ouragan OTU Course 19 in March 1963, four pilots—Uri Bina, Shlomo Milo, Reuben Rosen, and Samuel Yadid—were assigned to Squadron 109. Their Mystère solo day was on 18 April 1963. Reuben Rosen's first flight was in 4507 and lasted 0:35 flight hours. Reuben Rosen recalled:

> At the time, I did not realize what I did in hindsight many years later. I interacted with many squadron commanders during my years in ILAF service, but there was only one [squadron commander]—actually the first, David Ivry—who had no "opposition" [among squadron service persons]; all [squadron service persons] were in his "coalition." At the time I did not realize that this was exceptional, but during subsequent service [as a regular and as a reserve fighter pilot until 1983], this phenomenon was not repeated.

Squadron 109 officers ILAF Year 1963 Term 1 standing (left to right): Mor, Technical Flight Commander, Zur, Ivry, Zemmer, Gadish, and Einav; crouching (left to right): Neeman, Peres, Oren, and Livni; and sitting (left to right): Rosen, Milo, Yadid, and Bina. (PC)

Recently repainted Mystère 47 at IAI in April 1963; IAI test pilot Zeev Tavor is fourth from the left. (PC)

NOZZLE TEST REPORT

MAT2 reported the results of Squadron 109's improved nozzle evaluation on 27 May 1963. The methodology of the comparative test was the selection of two Mystères, a comparison of take-off performance for both with regular nozzles, the installation of the improved nozzle in one of the two Mystères, and then comparison of take-off performance again between the two Mystères.

The Ramat David Maintenance Squadron and Squadron 109 were not professional test establishments, so real world test results were probably less accurate than during the previous IAI test. While the improved nozzle test at IAI resulted in a shorter take-off distance (as mentioned in the February 1963 report of the IAI test and in the May 1963 report of the Squadron 109 test), the Squadron 109 test yielded an improvement of only 50 meters (164 ft).

MAT2 suggested two possible explanations for the difference in take-off distance improvement:

- Engine temperature with the improved nozzle during Squadron 109 use exceeded only 710°C (1,310°F) and not 730°C (1,346°F) as hoped.
- The engine in the comparative aircraft heated 20°C (68°F) above normal temperature, thus generating more thrust than normal.

Again, since Squadron 109 was not a test unit, the aircraft were not tuned to generate accurate normal ratings and the test results were not normalized. MAT2 realized these limitations and recommended viewing the Squadron 109 test results not as quantitative but as qualitative, thus confirming the quantitative results of the IAI test in the field.

At the completion of the Squadron 109 evaluation, the improved nozzle was returned to IAI for the next nozzle replacement project phase, which was a monetary evaluation of manufacturing costs.

Mystère 47—photographed at IAI in April 1963—was the first Squadron 109 Mystère to finish Level D maintenance by June 1963. (PC)

LEVEL D MAINTENANCE SCHEDULE

Seven years had elapsed from the ILAF's introduction of the Mystère during April 1956, and average annual utilization was increasing, as fewer aircraft flew more flight hours; the airframes with the highest number of flight hours were already in need of Level D major maintenance.

Meticulous planning was required to ensure staggered servicing of the Mystères, while at the same time avoiding piling the airframes that finished their flight hour allocation and having them grounded due to a lack of Level D maintenance slots.

Constraints that had to be taken into account were the ILAF's training plan and resultant consumption of flight hours, the Material Department's authorization to allocate an additional seventy-five flight hours per airframe prior to Level D maintenance, six Level D maintenance slots, and an average of five and a half months per Level D maintenance.

While most ILAF aircraft were subjected to in house Level D maintenance at AMU 22 or to outsourced Level D maintenance at IAI, the Mystère fleet's Level D maintenance was entrusted to the Ramat David Wing Maintenance Squadron and Tel Nof Air Base Maintenance Squadron for Squadron 109 aircraft and Squadron 116 aircraft, respectively.

MAT3 processed the Mystère Level D maintenance schedule on 4 June 1963 and the resulting table was issued on 11 June 1963, with Squadron 109's nineteen Mystères scheduled to attend Level D maintenance as follows:

Aircraft	Level D Time Frame	Notes
4547	finished Level D maintenance	
4505	undergoing Level D maintenance until June 1963	
4550	undergoing Level D maintenance until July 1963	
4526	undergoing Level D maintenance until September 1963	
4510	undergoing Level D maintenance until October 1963	
4511	July 1963 to January 1964	
4532	August 1963 to February 1964	
4509	September 1963 to March 1964	
4514	December 1963 to June 1964	75 flight hour extension
4582	January 1964 to July 1964	
4572	March 1964 to September 1964	75 flight hour extension
4515	March 1964 to September 1964	
4583	June 1964 to December 1964	75 flight hour extension
4525	July 1964 to January 1965	
4506	September 1964 to March 1965	75 flight hour extension
4544	November 1964 to May 1965	
4534	February 1965 to August 1965	
4507	April 1965 to October 1965	75 flight hour extension
4571	June 1965 to December 1965	75 flight hour extension

Planning was extremely sensitive to many variables that were difficult to predict, including operational flights that were unaccounted for in the ILAF's training plan, training accidents, and unexpected modifications/repairs, but Squadrons 109 and 116 were urged to plan flight hour consumption in a way that would spread the flight hours and comply with MAT3's plan for the Mystère's Level D schedule.

CONFIGURATION CONSOLIDATION

Mystère configurations were limited in number and variety. To accomplish endurance and range performance adequate for the ILAF's operational requirements, the Mystère was forced to trade internal rockets for an additional internal fuel tank and give up the potential to lift ordnance on two inner wing stations for the carriage of two external fuel tanks.

The inner wing ordnance stations were relevant to the short range attack mission. Since some scenarios, including SEAB, yielded a preference for a larger number of smaller bombs over a smaller number of larger bombs, the ILAF initiated an effort to equip attack aircraft—including the Mystère—with QBR. While the most common configuration for a Mystère with regular racks was two 625 liter (165 gallon) fuel tanks and two 250 kilogram (550 lb) bombs, the planned configuration for Mystères with QBR was two 625 liter (165 gallon) fuel tanks and eight 70, 100, or 120 kilogram (154, 220, or 265 lb) bombs. The overall impact of eight smaller bombs was expected to be better than two larger bombs, while in the days of statistical bombing, the prospects of hitting a target like a runway with an ordnance load of eight bombs per aircraft were much better than hitting a target with two bombs per aircraft.

Unfortunately, QBR development lagged behind schedule. Meanwhile, the ILAF decided to discard the Mystère configuration with ordnance loaded to inner wing stations so the stock of bomb racks reserved for the Mystères was freed for reallocation to the SMB2 that, at the time, transformed from an interceptor to an attack aircraft, with better endurance and range performance than the Mystère.

Mystère 07 in its common configuration—two tanks and two bombs—during turnaround competition probably in July 1963, at a time when the qualified configuration with four bombs was temporarily not in use. (PC)

Ramat David Wing 1's command handover parade in August 1963, with six camouflaged Squadron 109 Mystères on the right. (PC)

On 21 June 1963, MAT5 informed AIR2 that reallocation of the Mystère inner wing bomb racks to the SMB2 would result in a shortage to the point that it would be possible to equip only seventy-five percent of Mystères with four bomb racks or fifty percent of Mystères with four bomb racks, and fifty percent of Mystères with two bomb racks.

On 24 June 1963, AIR2 replied that this situation was well known at the time. AIR2 also clarified its decision to have SMB2s with four ordnance racks over Mystères with four ordnance racks:

- The SMB2 is superior to the Mystère in its ability to lift ordnance on four stations due to higher thrust and a longer radius of action with an identical load.
- The schedule for qualification of the SMB2 with four ordnance points will roughly overlap the start of QBR manufacture for both the Mystère and SMB2.

Thus, during the transition period from SMB2 qualification with four ordnance racks to QBR introduction, the Mystère qualification of a configuration with four ordnance racks was dropped and the Mystère's configurations were limited to fuel tanks attached to its inner wing stations and bombs or napalm canisters loaded on external wing stations.

WING 1 COMMAND HANDOVER BAR SOMECH

Ezekiel Somech took over from Menahem Bar as Wing 1 Commander from August 1963. While Bar was mostly identified with Ramat David interceptor squadrons—having served first as commander of both Squadron 117 Meteor (from 1953) and Squadron 109 Mystère (from 1956)—Somech was mostly associated with attack aircraft, having commanded Squadron 109 Mosquito from 1955 until 1956, Squadron 110 Mosquito during the 1956 Suez War, and Squadron 110 Vautour from 1957 until 1959. Reuben Rosen recalled:

> Ezekiel Somech was [Ramat David] base commander; we flew a one on one air combat training and he defeated me. He landed, called [Squadron 109 Commander David] Ivry, told him that he flew with one of his junior pilots, summarized it as "below standard" and asked to check [in air combat training] the standard of [the squadron] leaders.
>
> Ivry then convened all of the squadron pilots, including junior pilots, in the briefing room and said "there was an unpleasant incident when the base commander defeated Rosen [in air combat practice] and now he has suggested the possibility that the leaders are also not good enough, so he wants to check one of the leaders." The best pilot in our squadron in air-to-air combat was Ami [Gadish] Goldstein (Goldi); he was a wizard in air combat training, but during debrief it was impossible to learn how he managed to bite us, because he said "I see situations and know exactly what to do, but I cannot analyze it on the ground!"
>
> Ivry stated that Goldi would be tasked to fly air combat training with the base commander and defined our mission as the base commander's car would not stop at Squadron 109, but would drive past Squadron 109 on its way to Squadron 110.
>
> Ami Goldstein told us to listen to "00" [the squadron radio channel] ... so we all heard that he indeed accomplished our mission and from then on, we only saw the base commander's car as it drove past [Squadron 109 on its way] to Squadron 110.

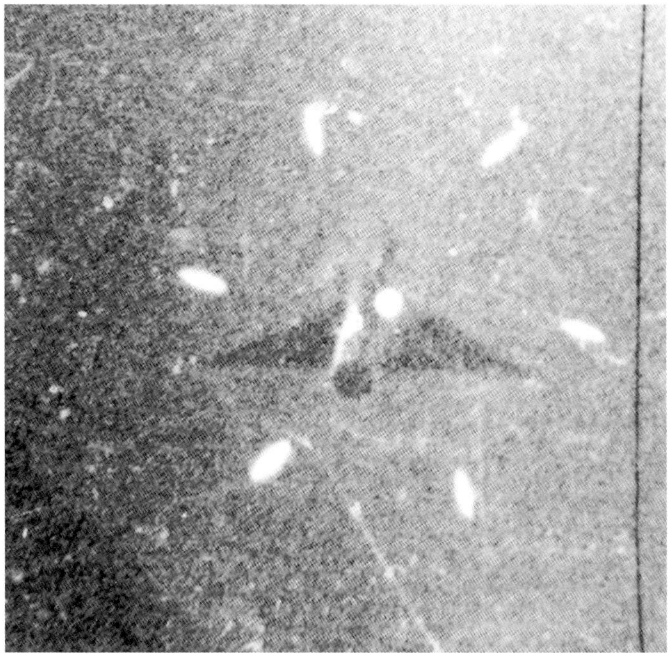

Squadron 117 Shahak assumed Ramat David first line air-to-air QRA from August 1963, but Squadron 109 continued to preserve air-to-air qualification, including in DACT versus Shahak. This Squadron 109 Mystère sight photo was reportedly taken during ILAF Year 1963 Term 2 during DACT; the static aiming point in the center and the dynamic "diamonds" generate a perfect firing solution, since dynamic "diamonds" represented range to target and a proper firing solution was accomplished when the circle that the dynamic "diamonds" created matched the target wing span, while a "kill" in training was awarded if such a scene was maintained for at least one second. (PC)

OPERATION VULTURE

Squadron 117 Shahak accomplished FOR and assumed full responsibility for Ramat David air-to-air QRA duty from August 1963, so Squadron 109 completed transition from air-to-air to air-to-ground, with Mystères no longer assuming Ramat David's first line air-to-air readiness from 15 August 1963, even though Squadron 109's air-to-air qualification was not entirely discarded and occasional scrambles for air-to-air tasking of Squadron 109 Mystères did continue.

Clashes along the Israeli-Syrian border escalated from 19 August 1963. The following day, Squadron 117 Shahaks engaged Syrian MiG-17s, and from 27 August 1963, the ILAF was on readiness to strike Syria in line with OPOR 55/63 Operation EAGLE, which AIR3 distributed on 27 August 1963. EAGLE prepared for three phases:

- Phase 1 was an ILAF attack against up to eight Syrian targets—mostly headquarters and fortifications at the Golan Heights—with three four-ship formations tasked to attack each target and with every aircraft flying two passes: one attack run with external ordnance (bombs or napalm) and one strafing pass.
- Phase 2 covered counterbattery ILAF action if Syria responded to Phase 1 with artillery bombardment against Israel.
- Phase 3 was an air superiority campaign against two Syrian air bases—Dumayr and Mazzeh—that was to be activated in case phases 1 and 2 escalated into large scale or full scale hostilities.

Squadron 109 was tasked to prepare three four-ship formations:

- A formation armed with two 250 kilogram (550 lb) bombs per aircraft would attack one of four targets during phase 1 within fifteen minutes of VULTURE H-Hour.
- A formation armed with two napalm canisters per aircraft would attack one of three targets during phase 1 within fifteen minutes of VULTURE H-Hour.
- A formation armed with two 250 kilogram (550 lb) bombs per aircraft would be on readiness for counterbattery action during Phase 2.

The formations were to be scrambled to one of two holding patterns: one west of the northern sector of the Golan Heights and one west of the southern sector of the Golan Heights. In case of target allocation prior to take-off, the formations tasked to attack in the northern sector would fly to the northern holding pattern and formations tasked to attack in the southern sector would fly to the southern holding pattern. Every squadron was assigned with a different holding altitude—Squadron 109's was 8,000 feet—in order to minimize the risk of collision while holding. Command

Squadron 109 EP and reserve pilots with Squadron 109 Commander David Ivry in August 1963: standing (left to right): Peres, Dagan, Livnat, Ivry, Ben-Nun, and Ran; crouching (left to right): Neeman, Dvir, Hochman, Porat, and Yariv; and sitting (left to right): Oren, Nehushtan, and Hess. (PC)

North ALO would then coordinate attacks through authorization to formations to leave their holding patterns and approach the target area. Routes from the holding patterns to targets and from the targets back to the bases were pre-planned.

The ILAF was on readiness to activate Operation VULTURE from 17 August 1963 until 22 September 1963. Tensions along the Israeli-Syrian border remained high, but no major clashes erupted, so VULTURE was not activated and the ILAF returned to normal peacetime readiness.

MYSTÈRE SWAP

The ILAF's intentions to retire the Mystère as soon as possible were directly linked to the Mystère's transition from air-to-air to air-to-ground—from interception to attack. Having served as the ILAF's interceptor from 1956 to 1959, Squadron 109's air-to-air mission continued from 1959 until 1962 as top interceptor of Ramat David "Air Force North" and from 1962 until 1963 as the backup air-to-air platform pending completion of Squadron 117's Shahak FOR.

While the ILAF never viewed the Mystère as an ideal interceptor—almost right from the start of Mystère service as an interceptor the ILAF evaluated the Mystère as inferior to the MiG-17—it did all the more so as an attack aircraft. The Mystère's switch from air-to-air to air-to-ground was purely by default due to the introduction of superior interceptors; the ILAF did not select the Mystère as an attack aircraft. Poor performance precluded longer range/higher endurance missions with a reasonable load of

ILAF Year 1963 Term 2 Squadron 109 regular pilots: standing (left to right): Gadish, Zur, Ivry, Mor, and Zemmer; crouching (left to right): Livni, Yadid, Bina, Milo, Rosen, and Bester; and sitting (left to right): Goren, Tamir, and Noy. (PC)

Squadron 109's Mystère 50 in the background of a parade in front of Ramat David Wing 1's Maintenance Squadron hangars on 30 August 1963. It is also of interest to compare the October 1963 status report and the June 1963 Level D schedule: the latter scheduled 4510, 4511, 4532, and 4509 to be in Level D maintenance during October 1963, while the former reported 4505, 4509, 4510, 4511, and 4532 in Level D maintenance during October 1963. The schedule for Level D maintenance completion of 4505 was June 1963 and, possibly due to the delay of 4505's Level D maintenance completion, 4509 was delivered to the IAI for Level D maintenance. (PC)

ordnance or shorter range/lower endurance missions with a heavy load of ordnance.

The ILAF tested and qualified Mystère ordnance configurations that included belly rocketry, pod rocketry, T-10 rocketry, four 250 kilogram (550 lb) bombs, and four napalm canisters, but by 1963, the practical Mystère attack configurations for longer range/higher endurance missions were either two 250 kilogram (550 lb) bombs or two napalm canisters, representing a fractional take-off ordnance weight of only five per cent or so. True, the ILAF planned the purchase of QBR, enabling the Mystère to lift up to eight small bombs, but the expected fractional take-off ordnance weight of up to eight per cent was not much of an improvement.

The best solution for the ILAF would have been replacing the Mystère with a true attack aircraft and indeed, during 1963, the ILAF initiated staff studies concerning the acquisition of a new light attack aircraft to replace the Ouragan and Mystère. While at it, the ILMD surfaced the possibility of swapping the ILAF's Mystères for French aircraft that the ILAF considered more suitable for the attack mission: Ouragans, SMB2s, or Vautours. The ILMD noted that the FRAF's Mirage introduction would result in the retirement of these three types, while the FRAF planned to continue use of the Mystère for training combat aircraft pilots, so a swap of ILAF Mystères for a mix of FRAF Ouragans, SMB2s, and Vautours seemed like a win-win situation.

On 27 October 1963, AIR2 Chief Yoash Tsiddon chaired a meeting—in the presence of AIR3 Chief Jacob Nevo, AIR2 staff officer Achikar Eyal, and AIR3 staff officer Meir Livneh—that discussed Mystère swap options. The protocol of this discussion outlined the background, objective, and facts as follows:

> The Mystère has lost status in air-to-air warfare due to service introduction of more modern aircraft. On the other hand, the Mystère as an attack aircraft surfaced several shortcomings that motivated the ILAF to consider its withdrawal from service in return for adequate replacement.
>
> We are being offered a trade transaction in which we will be able to swap Mystères for other French aircraft.
>
> The objective is to recommend the ILAF's minimum requirements in this trade.
>
> Our motivation for this transaction is the performance of the Mystère as an attack aircraft. We would like to obtain aircraft that will add to the ILAF's attack capability through superior load/range performance, development potential (compatibility with new [weapon] systems), and take-off distances.
>
> An increase in [the ILAF's] attack potential is the result of a combination of factors, so it will be possible to accomplish [improvement of the ILAF's attack potential] even if the total load for certain ranges will be smaller.
>
> Nevertheless, the ILAF aspires for a minimum number of aircraft to replace the Mystère; a requirement that results from both operational plans and training considerations.
>
> Aircraft under consideration for trade are the Ouragan, SMB2, and Vautour N; aircraft such as the [A-4] Skyhawk, F-84F [Thunderstreak], and [F-100] Super Sabre are not under consideration.

The issue of a minimum number of aircraft was critical. At the time, ILAF ORBAT included thirty-nine Mystères that equipped two squadrons and were valued at approximately eight million US dollars. For aircraft trade purposes, the value of the ILAF Mystères was set at six million US dollars, thus enabling the ILAF to acquire fifteen Vautours at a unit cost of 400,000 US dollars, thirty SMB2s at a unit cost of 200,000 US dollars, or 120 Ouragans at a unit cost of 50,000 US dollars, or any mix of these three types below the monetary ceiling of six million US dollars. Any acquisition solution that excluded the Ouragan entirely challenged ILAF ORBAT plans and affected the ILAF's strike potential.

Considering minimum ORBAT numbers and minimum strike potential, the forum formulated two recommended trade options:

- Option A was eighteen Ouragans, eighteen SMB2s, and four Vautour Ns.
- Option B was eighteen SMB2s and six Vautour Ns.

Option A was preferable on the grounds of quantity, as it enabled sustaining Squadrons 109 and 116 as Ouragan and SMB2 squadrons while also augmenting Squadron 110 Vautour.

Option B was preferable on the grounds of quality, but it enabled sustaining only Squadron 109 or Squadron 116 as a SMB2 squadron while considerably boosting Squadron 110 Vautour.

AIR2 suggested completing the trade by August 1964, but there were many objections and obstacles among both potential parties along the path to realizing this seemingly win-win transaction. The FRAF was reluctant to release the SMB2 while the ILAF resented the introduction of additional Vautours, so in light of this situation, the only viable option was the Ouragan, which was the most appealing from an economical perspective but the least attractive from an operational point of view.

Meantime, the AIR2 discussion was a good opportunity to present a Mystère fleet status report; data for Squadron 109 was as follows:

Aircraft	Flight Hours	Notes
4505		Level D
4506	903:05	
4507	826:20	
4509	904:00	Level D at IAI
4510		Level D
4511		Level D
4514	954:15	
4515	828:40	
4525	840:40	
4526		flight hours not reported
4532		Level D
4534	799:55	

4544	828:40	
4547		flight hours not reported
4550	946:20	Level B
4571	712:45	
4572	949:55	
4582	847:25	
4583	888:45	

Squadron 109's aircraft flight hours ranged from 712:45 to 954:15 and available flight hours averaged 863:55.

It is also of interest to compare the October 1963 status report and the June 1963 Level D schedule; the latter scheduled 4510, 4511, 4532, and 4509 to be in Level D maintenance during October 1963, while the former reported 4505, 4509, 4510, 4511, and 4532 in Level D maintenance during October 1963. The schedule for Level D maintenance completion of 4505 was June 1963 and, possibly due to the delay of 4505's Level D maintenance completion, 4509 was delivered to the IAI for Level D maintenance.

PRESIDENTIAL VISIT

Zalman Shazar entered office as Israel's third president on 21 May 1963. President Shazar first visited the ILDF and ILAF on 31 October 1963. Prime Minister and Minister of Defense Levy Eshkol, Deputy Minister of Defense Simon Peres, ILDF Chief of Staff Zvi Zur, and ILDF senior officers, including ILAF Commander Ezer Weizman, welcomed the president at ILDF headquarters in Tel Aviv, where the president attended a brief concerning the ILDF prior to flight in a helicopter accompanied by the ILDF Chief of Staff and ILAF Commander from Tel Aviv to Ramat David.

The president reviewed an exhibition of aircraft and ordnance, including a Squadron 109 Mystère; viewed a Squadron 110 Vautour fast turnaround demonstration; lunched in the Ramat David officers mess; and met Ramat David pilots for a dialogue that bolstered the president's confidence in the ILDF as expressed in a formal statement that the president released after the visit.

President Zalman Shazar visited Ramat David on 31 October 1963: he inspected an ordnance exhibition that included a Squadron 109 Mystère (above), viewed a twelve-ship flyover that included four Squadron 109 Mystères (opposite, top), and addressed Ramat David Wing pilots (opposite, bottom). (PC)

Probably the final photo of Mystère 47 prior to its demise on 5 November 1963, during the end of ILAF Year 1963 Term 2's combat day exercise on 1 August 1963. (PC)

MYSTÈRE 47

Less than a fortnight after AIR2 and AIR3 discussed the possibility of a Mystère fleet trade, the number of ILAF Mystères dropped from thirty-nine to thirty-eight, as Squadron 109's inventory decreased from nineteen to eighteen aircraft.

The ILAF staged a major ordnance demonstration on 5 November 1963. Among participating formations was a Squadron 109 four-ship—David Ivry, Eli Mor, Ami Gadish, and Irik Bester in Mystère 47—that strafed. It was during strafing that Mystère 47 was damaged, and the pilot pulled up and ejected.

MYSTÈRE 32

Three days after the crash of Mystère 47, Squadron 109 almost lost Mystère 32. At the time a Squadron 109 reserve pilot, Asaf Ben-Nun, recalled:

> We practiced air base attack over Ramat David and while exiting from [a dummy] strafing pass at low altitude and high speed in the direction of Mount Carmel [general heading west] I experienced an engine cut.
>
> I was at the foot of Mount Carmel and the most common reaction in such an emergency was to pull up and eject, but I decided to save the aircraft. I was fast enough so I managed to pull up, extend the landing gear, and land on the runway; a perfect landing.

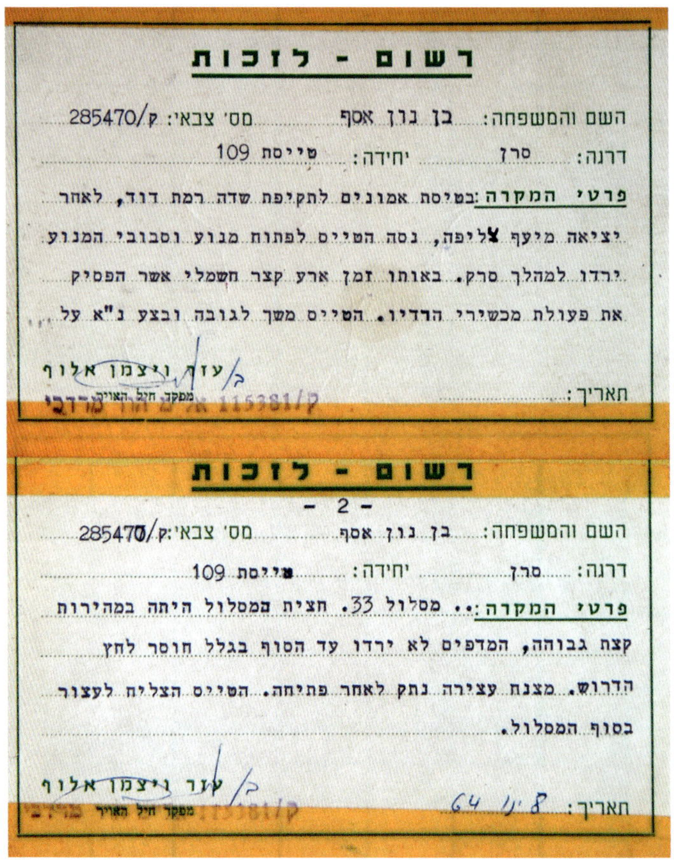

רשום - לזכות

השם והמשפחה: בן נון אסף מס' צבאי: 285470/ק

דרגה: סרן יחידה: טייסת 109

פרטי המקרה: בטיסת אמונים לתקיפת שדה רמת דוד, לאחר
יציאה מיעף צליפה, נסה הטייס לפתוח מנוע וסבובי המנוע
ירדו למהלך סרק. באותו זמן ארע קצר חשמלי אשר הפסיק
את פעולת מכשירי הרדיו. הטייס משך לגובה ובצע נ"א על

עזר ויצמן אלוף
מפקד חיל האויר

תאריך:

רשום - לזכות

- 2 -

השם והמשפחה: בן נון אסף מס' צבאי: 285470/ק

דרגה: סרן יחידה: טייסת 109

פרטי המקרה: .. מסלול 33. חצית המסלול היתה במהירות
קצת גבוהה, המדפים לא ירדו עד הסוף בגלל חוסר לחץ
הדרוש. מצנח עצירה נתק לאחר פתיחה. הטייס הצליח לעצור
בסוף המסלול.

עזר ויצמן אלוף
מפקד חיל האויר

תאריך: 8 ינו' 64

Asaf Ben-Nun saved Mystère 32 on 8 November 1963 and earned an ILAF Commander Green Note Endorsement. (PC)

ILAF Commander Ezer Weizman awarded Asaf Ben-Nun with a Green Endorsement—at the time the ILAF's highest accolade in the best tradition of the British Royal Air Force—that was signed on 8 January 1964:

> During a training flight that practiced air base attack against Ramat David, at the end of a strafing pass the pilot tried to open the throttle but RPM dropped to idle. At the same time an electrical malfunction disabled the radio sets.
>
> The pilot pulled up and performed an emergency landing on runway 33. The landing's initial speed was a little too high, flaps did not fully deploy due to a drop in [hydraulic] pressure, and the braking chute detached after deployment, but the pilot managed to stop at the end of the runway.

The next known flight of Mystère 32 was on 19 April 1964.

SEEMING SKIRMISH

Israel and Syria clashed again on 11 November 1963, when Syrian fortifications at Mound Hamra and Mound Azazyat opened fire at an Israeli agricultural tractor working in the fields of kibbutz Dan. The ILDF returned fire, and the exchange of fire lasted over an hour. On 12 November 1963, Israeli agricultural work was resumed without Syrian interference, perhaps because Syria was preoccupied with internal affairs, as on that day a new Syrian government, with Syria President Amin Hafiz as Prime Minister, entered office in Damascus.

Therefore, the 11 November 1963 clash did not escalate, did not result in ILAF action, and was not followed by any engagement between the ILAF and SYAF. Regardless of this reality, AMV2 (page 165) stated:

> For example, on 12 November 1963, there were a series of clashes with Israeli units along the border on the Jordan River, escalating to a point where IDF/AF fighter-bombers struck several Syrian strongpoints, leaving seven killed and twenty wounded. Skirmishes continued into the following day, with the Israelis flying additional attacks until around 15:30; two SyAAF MiG-21s intercepted one of the attacking formations and claimed a Mystère shot down.

None of this happened on 12 and 13 November 1963: the exchange of fire between Israeli troops and Syrian soldiers was only on 11 November 1963, the exchange of fire was local and short, no ILAF activity followed, no ILAF versus SYAF air combat occurred on any of these three days, and Squadrons 109 and 116 did not lose a Mystère to any cause.

HUMANE COMMANDER

Personnel changes at the start of ILAF Year 1963 Term 3 in December 1963 included Amihy Shmueli, who succeeded Levy Zur as Squadron 109 Deputy A, and the assignment to Squadron 109 of two Flying School Class 41 graduates who had attended Squadron 113 OTU Course 22 during ILAF Year 1963 Term 3: Yaron Golan and Isaac Nir. Reuben Rosen recalled:

Flying School Class 41 graduates Nir and Golan "soloed" in 4506 and 4544, respectively, at the start of ILAF Year 1963 Term 3. (PC)

> [Squadron 109 Commander David] Ivry was a very humane commander; during my third term in the squadron, amidst training as a pair leader, I got into a romantic involvement that left me confused and detached. Ivry summoned me to his office and said "you were OK until recently, but lately it appears as though you are experiencing some kind of crisis; you do not have to confirm or deny it, but I will tell you my evaluation," and his evaluation was indeed correct, and I did not confirm or deny, so he continued: "I suggest that your training as a pair leader be suspended for the time being; when you feel you have sorted out your problems then inform me and we will resume your training as a pair leader . . . ."

ATTACK AIRCRAFT STAFF STUDY

New ILDF Chief of Staff Isaac Rabin entered office on 1 January 1964 and presented his views to senior ILDF commanders on 6 January 1964. The new ILDF Chief of Staff expressed his opinion that an Arab attack against Israel was a remote possibility for as long as Israel preserved military superiority, while the objective of an Israeli attack would be to destroy enemy military power and/or occupy territories. Concerning re-equipment, Rabin stated:

> I would like to present in a few words the center of gravity of this issue; in my opinion, the center of gravity is quality... The problem today is not the number of ILDF brigades, but the quality of the brigades. The problem is not what is the kind of air force or sea force, but the capabilities of this force... I will start with the ILAF.
>
> The first priority for the ILAF is strengthening the attack force. There is no reason in my opinion to increase the number of high quality Shahak aircraft. On the other hand, I am convinced the ILAF lacks aircraft that I define as "workhorses": aircraft that have to operate under the cover of high quality aircraft. If we have an opportunity, then the central focus for improvement will be low quality aircraft, in numbers and in quality.
>
> Also, I see a requirement to develop measures to enable existing aircraft to penetrate air defenses en route to targets.

Flying School Class 41 graduates Nir and Golan "soloed" in 4506 and 4544, respectively, at the start of ILAF Year 1963 Term 3. (PC)

Squadron 109 regular pilots ILAF Year 1963 Term 3: standing (left to right): Zemmer, Gadish, Shmueli, Ivry, Mor, and Bester; kneeling (left to right): Noy, Rosen, and Tamir; and sitting (left to right): Golan and Nir. (PC)

With deliveries of Shahak interceptors drawing to a close, the ILAF was ripe for progress towards the next step in combat aircraft ORBAT modernization: acquisition of attack aircraft.

On 7 January 1964, AIR2 Chief Yoash Tsiddon signed a staff study entitled "Attack Aircraft in ORBAT 1968 to 1970." The staff study's presuppositions were:

- The ILAF would have to field more attack aircraft due to an anticipated increase in the number of ILAF targets: Arab air bases, runways, and SAM and SSM batteries.
- The ILAF would have to win a war through decisive and swift strikes at the start of the conflict.
- The ILAF would continue to operate tactical attack aircraft and would not need strategic attack aircraft.
- The ILAF would face modern AAA and SAM defenses that would dictate low altitude operations and would force the ILAF to field more attack aircraft to sustain a higher number of expected combat losses to enemy AAA and SAM defenses.

In line with presuppositions and in line with ILAF ORBAT issues, the staff study defined two classes of attack aircraft to be acquired:

- Heavy attack aircraft to replace the Vautour.
- Medium attack aircraft to succeed the Mystère and Ouragan.

Both attack aircraft classes were to be operational from short runways and/or serviceable segments of damaged runway, so the AIR2 staff study suggested robust naval aircraft for the two requirements.

Relevant to Squadron 109 was the medium attack aircraft class. AIR2 listed the following contenders for fulfilling the medium attack aircraft class: the American A-4 Skyhawk or F-5 Freedom Fighter, the British Scimitar, the Canadian F-86 Sabre, or the French Etandard.

The AIR2 staff study ranked the F-5 Freedom Fighter as the top contender for the ILAF's medium attack aircraft class requirement, with the A-4 Skyhawk in second place.

ILAF READINESS ORDER

The unique status of the ILAF as Israel's shield and as the only ILDF arm capable of operating almost immediately at maximum power was revalidated in a new AIR3 Readiness Order issued on 13 February 1964. The AIR3 order defined the readiness level of every ILAF unit based on two criteria: daytime or nighttime and working hours or other hours.

Squadron 109 was tasked to maintain two Mystères on air-to-air readiness during daytime and during both working hours and other hours as backup to the Squadron 117 air-to-air QRA tasked to defend northern Israel.

Squadron 109's main readiness was attack with four aircraft on alert during daytime and two aircraft on alert during nighttime. Squadron 109 Mystère's readiness configuration was maximum rounds per gun, two 250 kilogram (550 lb) bombs, and two external fuel tanks. If scrambled during nighttime, the two Squadron 109 Mystère attack aircraft were planned to operate with an illuminating Squadron 110 Vautour.

NIGHTTIME ATTACK

The ILAF in general and Squadron 109 in particular was still mainly geared for daytime operations. Nighttime operations were limited in scale and in practice. The ILAF aspired to improve nighttime qualifications, but progress was slow.

A concentrated nighttime attack effort was staged the evening of 22 March 1964, with senior pilots from several squadrons attacking targets under searchlight illumination. Squadron 109 reserve pilot Asaf Ben-Nun flew Mystère 10, attacking with napalm in line with MIOR Resh34.

SHAFRIR 2 OPERATIONAL REQUIREMENT

The Mystère was the last ILAF interceptor that was not armed—or planned to be armed—with air-to-air missiles. The Shahak was the first ILAF interceptor actually armed with missiles: the French Yahalom SARH and the Israeli Shafrir IR.

The Mystère was retasked from air-to-air to air-to-ground after the ILAF's introduction of the SMB2 and Shahak, so the potential objective of arming the Mystère with air-to-air missiles was to improve its self-defense against hostile interceptors; however, adding air-to-air missiles to the Mystère was not expected to be a straightforward modification, because the Mystère had only four hard points—the inner hard points were almost always used to carry external fuel tanks, thus sparing only two hard points for offensive ordnance—and because the Mystère was already suffering from power and weight issues. The Mystère was at the top of the ILAF's list of attack aircraft planned for replacement as well, so an

Asaf Ben-Nun flew Mystère 10 on the evening of 22 March 1964 during an ILAF concentrated nighttime attack training effort. (PC)

expensive investment in the Mystère to add hard points for air-to-air missiles and to solve its power and weight issues was highly unlikely.

This attitude was expressed on 23 March 1964, when AIR2 issued an operational requirement for a next generation IR air-to-air missile, the Shafrir 2.

The new missile was required to intercept MiG-17, MiG-19, and MiG-21 fighters, as well as Il-28 and Tu-16 bombers, in an engagement envelope that stretched to a 4 G load and 30,000 feet. The Shafrir 2 had planned compatibility with all ILAF combat aircraft types; beyond the top priority to qualify the Shahak with the Shafrir 2 for interception, the operational requirement set a priority for aircraft missile qualification:

- Priority 1: to qualify the Vautour Shafrir 2 for self-defense
- Priority 2: to qualify the SMB2 Shafrir 2 for self-defense
- Priority 3: to qualify the Ouragan Shafrir 2 for self-defense
- Priority 4: to qualify the Mystère Shafrir 2 for self-defense

Obviously, this priority list was directly related to withdrawal from service plans; the Mystère was top priority for ILAF combat aircraft planned for replacement, and as such was at the lowest priority for Shafrir 2 qualification; as a matter of fact, Squadron 109 Mystères were never to be armed with air-to-air missiles.

COMMAND HANDOVER IVRY SHADMI

ILAF ORBAT was down to thirty-seven Mystères by 1 April 1964, and the fleet accumulated 5,553 flight hours during ILAF Year 1963 for an average of 231 flight hours per month per squadron. ILAF ORBAT on 1 April 1964—just prior to the Water War escalation—was as follows:

Base	Wing	Squadron	Type
Ramat David	1	109	Mystère
Ramat David	1	110	Vautour
Ramat David	1	117	Shahak
Hatzor	4	101	Shahak
Hatzor	4	105	SMB2
Hatzor	4	113	Ouragan
Tel Nof	-	103	transport (medium)
Tel Nof	-	116	Mystère
Tel Nof	-	119	Shahak
Tel Nof	-	124	helicopters
Dov Field	-	100	transport (light)
Lod	-	120	transport (heavy)

The constantly depleted Mystère fleet was again tasked to stage a maximum effort as an element of the Israel Independence Day 16 flyover on 16 April 1964: reserve pilot Asaf Ben-Nun flew Mystère 50; Flying School instructor and EP pilot Reuben Rosen flew Mystère 83; former regular pilot Isaac Nir—at the time undergoing a Squadron 110 Vautour Conversion Course and thus not yet Vautour qualified, but still Mystère qualified—flew Mystère 44; and Ohad Shadmi flew Mystère 34.

After only a year in command of Squadron 109 Mystère, David Ivry was promoted to command Squadron 117 Shahak and Ohad Shadmi took over as Squadron 109 Commander from 26 April 1964.

Ohad Shadmi graduated Flying School Class 17 in May 1955 and the Squadron 105 Spitfire OTU course in August 1955, prior to successive assignments to Squadron 101 Mustang at Ramat David

Squadron 109's command handover parade on 26 April 1964 (left to right): Ramat David Wing 1 Commander Ezekiel Somech, Ohad Shadmi, and David Ivry. The view is generally northeast, with Squadron 109's building and parking in the background. (PC)

Squadron 109's command handover parade on 26 April 1964 from a generally northern direction. (PC)

Pilots present during Squadron 109's command handover parade on 26 April 1964 (left to right): Shmueli, Tamir, Porat, Shadmi, Ivry, Gadish, and Bester. (PC)

Squadron 109 service persons (Flying and Technical Flights) in front of Mystère 09 the day of command handover, 26 April 1964. (PC)

from August 1955, to Squadron 117 Meteor at Ramat David from November 1955, to Squadron 113 Ouragan at Hatzor from April 1956, and to Squadron 101 Mystère at Hatzor from June 1956. It was during assignment to flying school as an instructor from 1957 until 1958—and more specifically while serving as a Squadron 117 Meteor instructor at Ramat David—that Shadmi was acquainted with Squadron 109 as an EP pilot prior to his return south to Hatzor for service as a Squadron 105 SMB2 pilot, Deputy B, Deputy A, and Acting Commander; then back north to Ramat David as Squadron 109 Commander.

CHAPTER 5

WATER WAR ESCALATION

1964-1967

Israel inaugurated the National Water Carrier on 10 June 1964. The Israeli National Water Carrier diverted water from the Sea of Galilee in northern Israel to the arid Negev Desert in southern Israel, but the largest scale Israeli development project of its time was inaugurated in a deliberately austere and played-down ceremony to avoid expected escalation in the ongoing Water War.

In retaliation, Syria started to drill a canal to divert Stream Hermon/Banias from feeding water to the River Jordan—and then the Sea of Galilee—by flowing water to the River Yarmouk, thus depriving the Sea of Galilee and the Israeli National Water Carrier up to fifty percent of its feeding waters. Israel was determined to disrupt the Syrian water diversion project and escalation in the intermittent Water War seemed inevitable.

SURPRISING SCRAMBLE

Irik Bester was in charge of Squadron 109's sports day on 27 May 1964; a sports day that included a turnaround competition between three Technical Flight teams and one Flying Flight team.

Squadron 109's sports day on 27 May 1964 included a turnaround competition between four teams; Flying Flight's team mount was Mystère 09. (PC)

Squadron 109's sports day on 27 May 1964 included a turnaround competition between four teams; Flying Flight's team mount was Mystère 09. (PC)

Squadron 109 officers in a group photo during Exercise PURSUIT, the combat day exercise that ended ILAF Year 1964 Term 1: standing (left to right): Shadmi, Gadish, Oren, Yadid, Dvir, Shmueli, Ran, Neeman, Livnat, Rosen, Dagan, Ben-Nun, and Niv; and sitting (left to right): Technical Flight Commander Zohar Ben-Haim, Tamir, Hochman, and Bester. The painting of two pilots absent from this scene (Porat and Yariv) was added to complete the picture. (PC)

Squadron 117 Shahak assumed Ramat David air-to-air QRA duty from August 1963, but Squadron 109 continued to back them up with a daytime readiness pair. Surprisingly, the Squadron 109 air-to-air readiness pair was scrambled on 8 June 1964. Irik Bester and Hanan Tamir were tasked to intercept a Lebanese airliner that reportedly violated Israeli air space over the Mediterranean Sea, opposite the southern sector of Israel's coastline.

By the time the Squadron 109 pair made contact with the Arab airliner it was still flying over the Mediterranean Sea, but opposite Tyre, Lebanon. The two Mystères flew one pass along the airliner and returned to Ramat David.

MYSTÈRE REPLACEMENT

The ILAF requirement for an influx of modern attack aircraft was redefined on 25 June 1964 to include eight to twelve Mirage IV aircraft, fifty to sixty heavy attack aircraft, and 100 to 120 medium attack aircraft.

The Mystère replacement—the future ILAF medium attack aircraft—was to be capable of flying an offensive mission against a target some 450 kilometers (280 miles) from its base with an offensive load of 1,000 kilograms (2,200 lbs) and with a price tag of circa one million US dollars.

The preferred types for the ILAF's medium attack requirement were the American Skyhawk and the French Cavalier; however, the Skyhawk was not yet available for Israel, while the Dassault Cavalier was still a paper project in competition with the Breguet 121 for the FRAF's Mystère replacement requirement.

OPERATION SMALL EAGLE 1

A new series of occasional clashes along the Israeli-Syrian border started on 2 July 1964. These clashes concerned cartographic disputes—where exactly was the border line between Israel and Syria—and were not directly related to Water War issues.

Israel was determined to exercise control over territory that, from the Israeli perspective, was cultivated fields west of the border and up to the Israeli-figured border line and through patrols along a border track next to that border. Syria sometimes opened fire at Israeli tractors working in the fields or at Israeli patrols along the border track. The exchange of fire was primarily local and mostly ended after UNTSO intervention, but each small scale clash could potentially inflame a large scale clash that could get out of control and result in full scale war.

Therefore, Israel's dilemma was how much power to exert to silence Syrian fire and to deter Syria from opening fire again while avoiding deterioration into full scale war. Since the ILAF's intervention in a small scale border clash was viewed as an escalating step that would result in a large scale border clash and may lead to war, Israel formulated a guideline for the ILDF to operate the ILAF against Syria if Syrian artillery bombarded Israeli cities, towns, and villages. Additionally, the ILAF was expected to support the ILDF when needed, so to cover these two scenarios, AIR3 issued OPOR SMALL EAGLE 1 on 12 July 1964.

OPOR SMALL EAGLE 1 was actually the preparatory phase for OPOR EAGLE. In case of ILAF activation against Syria, Ramat David readiness aircraft would be scrambled first with readiness aircraft from other bases following, and would be tasked to attack any of six OPOR SMALL EAGLE 1 targets (one brigade headquarters, one battalion headquarters, and four fortifications along the border) in retaliation of Syrian fire against an ILDF border patrol. If the clash escalated to include Syrian artillery bombardments against Israeli cities, towns, and villages, then the ILDF would, or would not, order the ILAF to activate OPOR EAGLE.

The ILAF, including Squadron 109, was therefore on readiness to return fire at Syrian positions engaging patrols or tractors, but OPOR SMALL EAGLE 1 was not activated during the summer of 1964.

MYSTÈRE 50 MIRACLE 2

Dissimilar air combat training was emphasized during July 1964, when Squadron 109 pilots trained against Squadron 105 SMB2 and Squadron 117 Shahak pilots. It was during this series of dissimilar air combat training that Irik Bester and Jacob Yariv practiced air combat against Squadron 117 Shahak pilots on 15 July 1964. Irik Bester, in Mystère 50, reported a malfunction, aborted training, and returned to Ramat David.

While roughly over Megiddo, Mystère 50 experienced an engine cut, but was already within reach of Ramat David and Irik Bester managed a dead stick landing.

MYSTÈRE 50 MIRACLE 3

Three pilots—Daniel Ilan, Daniel Lanis, and Elisha Friedman (Perry)—graduated Flying School Class 43 in March 1964 and ILAF Year 1964 Term 1 Squadron 113 Ouragan OTU Course 23 in July 1964 prior to assignment to Squadron 109 at the start of ILAF Year 1964 Term 2. Elisha Friedman's (Perry) first Mystère flight was in 4509 on 17 September 1964.

Midterm, they were joined by Isaac Barzilai, who graduated Flying School Class 35 in November 1961 and then attended ILAF

Ramat David marked Suez War Day 8 on 29 October 1964 with a turnaround competition and flyover, during which Ohad Shadmi flew Mystère 09. (PC)

Squadron 109 pilots of ILAF Year 1964 Term 2 with Ramat David Wing 1 Commander Ezekiel Somech in front of Mystère 72: standing (left to right): Porat, Bester, Shmueli, Shadmi, Somech, Nehushtan, Even-Nir, Gadish, and Tamir; and crouching (left to right): Ilan, Lanis, Friedman (Perry), and Barzilai. (PC)

Mystère 50 after an accident on 2 November 1964. Mystère 50 was eventually repaired, but would return to service after Squadron 109 ceased flying Mystères. (PC)

Year 1961 Term 3 Squadron 113 Ouragan OTU Course 16. At the end of OTU Course 16, Barzilai was assigned to Squadron 113 Ouragan as an OTU instructor aide and was slated for the ILAF's Year 1964 Term 3 Squadron 101 Shahak Conversion Course. However, transition from the subsonic Ouragan to the Mach 2 Shahak was considered too big a jump, so Barzilai was assigned to Squadron 109 for a brief conversion to the transonic Mystère to accumulate some experience in high performance, sensitive servo control aircraft prior to flying the Shahak. Barzilai first flew the Mystère (4550) on 17 October 1964.

On 2 November 1964, while flying Mystère 50 as Uri Even-Nir's wingman during SEAB practice over Ramat David, Isaac Barzilai experienced an engine malfunction:

> We were practicing air base attack and our target was Ramat David. While flying a strafing pass from east to west at low altitude and 500 knots, I experienced an engine cut.
>
> I pulled up for an emergency landing on runway 09, but I crossed the start of the runway at high speed. I released the braking chute immediately after touch down, but the chute was torn off and I finished the runway at 100 knots or faster.
>
> The undercarriage legs were torn off and when the aircraft finally stopped and the cloud of dust settled, I found myself surrounded by female underwear and bras! I thought I was in heaven, but it turned out the aircraft stopped amidst the female dormitories of the base.
>
> The Accident Investigation Board concluded that the main axis of the engine accessories box was sheared, resulting in an engine cut and the loss of hydraulic pressure.

Mystère 50 was saved, but the damage was deemed too extensive to warrant repair, while a lengthy rebuild seemed pointless at the time, when it was still hoped that Mystère replacement was going to be accomplished within a short time. In due time and under different circumstances Mystère 50 would be repaired, but not in time to return to Squadron 109 service.

The engine-related accident of Mystère 50 pointed out the poor power conditions that characterized many Squadron 109 Mystères:

4510 sounded an alarming chirp between 7,000 and 9,800 RPM;
the engine was replaced but the alarming chirp persisted
4526 sounded horrible noises at RPM higher than 10,500; when

the engine was removed, it transpired that the rear section of the compressor was missing
4543 was known to have the weakest engine that resulted in the longest take-off runs; as a result, 4543 was only assigned to formation leaders.

And these were the worst case examples. The general technical situation of the dwindling Mystère fleet—already too small to support two standard squadrons—was not bright, and the view among the Ramat David and Squadron 109 maintenance echelons was that the Mystères were in poor shape and that Squadron 109 would have to be reequipped with a new type of aircraft.

This field level view saw eye to eye with previous staff studies and with then-current ILDF plans, yet as always, it was an issue of available budget and aircraft availability. At the time, it seemed the SMB2 would be the "new" ILAF medium attack aircraft and Squadron 109 Commander Ohad Shadmi informed squadron service persons the SMB2 might replace the Mystère during ILAF Year 1965 Term 1.

TILLAGE TIME

On 29 September 1964, the Israeli cabinet approved the start of tillage in fields adjacent to the Israeli-Syrian border and renewed the March 1962 authorization of the Prime Minister and Minister of Defense to approving the ILDF's request for ILAF support in case of Syrian military action without first convening the cabinet for discussion, since it was feared the time required to convene to discuss reaction would be longer than that of the clash and would close the window of opportunity for ILAF intervention.

Tillage started on 30 September 1964, and Syrian soldiers indeed opened fire at an Israeli tractor working in a field in the southern sector of the Israeli-Syrian border. Such small scale clashes in the same sector were repeated on 7, 8, and 9 October 1964, but the ILAF—Squadron 109 included—was not scrambled to support.

MOUND DAN CLASH

The next point of friction along the Israeli-Syrian border was the border patrol track near Mound Dan, in the northern sector. This dispute was also cartographic and was not directly related to Water War issues; Israel claimed the ILDF border patrol track ran along the border line and Syria claimed the patrol's track was 50 meters (164 ft) to the east of the border line; the UNTSO seemed undecided about the exact location of the border line.

A clash seemed inevitable, especially after the ILDF tractors started to prepare the border patrol track for the coming winter. On 8 October 1964, Syria positioned a Panzer tank and an SU-100 tank destroyer opposite Mound Dan and the ILDF responded by positioning Centurion tanks.

ILDF Armored Corps Chief David Elazar was promoted to ILDF Command North Chief on 1 November 1964, so when the Syrian Panzer and SU-100 finally opened fire on 3 November 1964, it was only natural that the Centurion tanks were ordered to return fire. However, the ILDF tanks did not silence Syrian fire, and it was again UNTSO intervention that ended the clash.

Israeli troops and Syrian soldiers again exchanged fire on 4 and 12 November 1964, but these clashes were minor in scale and were both along the southern sector of the Israeli-Syrian border, nowhere near Mound Dan.

Mystère 11—landing at Ramat David—was one of the first four Squadron 109 QRA aircraft to be scrambled as LADDER 4 with Avi Oren in the cockpit. (PC)

LADDER first bombed the southern target, Mound Azazyat. (PC)

LADDER then attacked Mound Hamra. (PC)

ILAF readiness was stepped up during the weekend of 13 to 14 November 1964, but this stepped up readiness was not related to Command North activity at Mound Dan, but to Operation KINGFISHER—a special operation over Egypt—while the ILDF's evaluation was that tensions in the Mound Dan sector were fading away.

The ILAF's Operation KINGFISHER weekend readiness impact on Squadron 109 was minimal; Squadron 109 was to maintain regular daytime readiness on 13 November 1964 and normal nighttime readiness 13 to 14 November 1964, in line with the standing ILAF Readiness Order. While the ILAF Readiness Order stipulated Squadron 109 maintain four Mystères armed with two 250 kilogram (550 lb) bombs each, during daytime readiness, the ILAF's KINGFISHER weekend readiness required Squadron 109 maintain four Mystères armed with two napalm canisters each during daytime readiness on 14 November 1964.

While the ILAF geared for Operation KINGFISHER weekend readiness, Syrian soldiers opened fire at 13:25, aiming at an ILDF patrol along the border track near Mound Dan. The exchange of fire soon escalated to include tanks, and this time the ILDF's Sherman

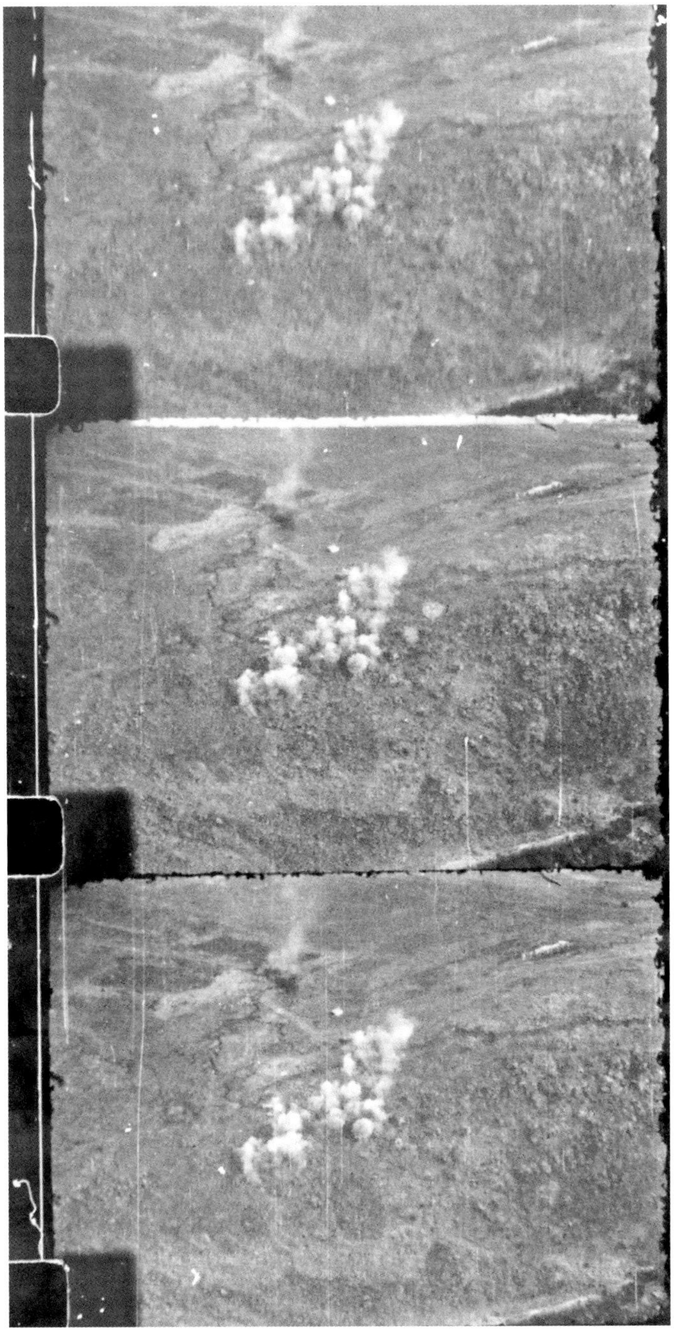

LADDER next strafed Mound Azazyat. (PC)

Another view—possibly from a Squadron 109 Mystère near Mound Hamra—during the ILAF strike on 13 November 1964. (PC)

and Centurion tankers claimed the destruction of two Syrian tanks. The Israeli tankers silenced the Syrian tanks, but by then, Syrian artillery was already in action, including the bombardment of kibbutz Dan and moshav Shar Yishuv; it was time to call for ILAF air support.

Circa 14:00, ILDF Chief of Staff Isaac Rabin asked Israeli Prime Minister and Minister of Defense Levy Eshkol for authorization to operate the ILAF against Syrian sources of fire. Authorization was duly granted, and at 14:12, the ILDF ordered the ILAF to attack the Syrian fortifications at Mound Azazyat and Mound Hamra, from where Syrian soldiers were showering fire aimed at Mount Dan.

At 14:17, the ILAF signaled bases and wings to prepare for attack against Syrian forces. Ramat David Wing Commander Ezekiel Somech was abroad, so Squadron 117 Commander David Ivry, as Ramat David Wing Acting Commander, ordered a shift to Readiness State C and preparations to strike. While Ramat David squadrons prepared to strike, ILAF Commander Ezer Weizman took over command and at 14:43 ordered the Ramat David Wing to scramble aircraft for a strike.

Squadron 109's four-ship formation LADDER—Ohad Shadmi in Mystère 14 and Irik Bester, Amihy Shmueli, and Avi Oren in Mystère 11—was the first ILAF strike formation to take-off at 14:47. In line with readiness for Operation KINGFISHER support, the first four readiness aircraft were loaded with two napalm canisters each. There was no comprehensive brief prior to the mission—after all it was a scramble—and LADDER was assigned with Mounds Hamra and Azazyat in the air while flying en route to the Mound Dan sector.

Squadron 109's LADDER formation was first to take-off and to attack; the four pilots flew to the border in combat formation, but rearranged in line astern for the attack, flying their attack passes while heading south-southeast and turning right at the end of the attack runs. LADDER first bombed the southern target (Mound Azazyat), with each Mystère dropping one napalm canister. Every pilot reported "in" and "out" during each of the attack passes. Upon completion of the first attack pass, they turned right and repeated the attack pattern against the northern target (Mound Hamra), with each Mystère dropping its second napalm canister. Repeating the right hand circuit pattern, LADDER returned to Mound Azazyat for a strafing pass and then back to Mound Hamra for a strafing pass, but by then Squadron 110 Vautours were preparing to bomb Mound Hamra, so LADDER gave way and returned to Ramat David, with LADDER 4 landing at 15:17.

Post strike, LADDER 3 Amihy Shmueli—identified as "CPT Ami," a Mystère pilot—shared his recollections with reporters:

> We were a formation of four Mystère aircraft. Our targets were Mound Azazyat and Mound Hamra. At first, we identified Mound Azazyat and attacked immediately. It is a hill stretching from north to south, with two bunkers at the south side and two bunkers at the north side. Two aircraft attacked the bunkers at the north side and two aircraft attacked the bunkers at the south side. We dived and dropped napalm bombs. From Mound Azazyat we flew to Mound Hamra; south of the mound we saw several fortified buildings and to the north were artillery and mortar emplacements. Again, we attacked with napalm. We then strafed. We were over the targets for twelve minutes and after our attack we could not see any movement of soldiers or vehicles; we only saw fire and smoke. During disengagement we saw the Vautours initiate their strike.

The second Squadron 109 formation was APARTMENT: Ami Gadish, Hanan Tamir, Uri Even-Nir, and Menahem Nehushtan. Their Mystères were armed with four 250 kilogram (550 lb) bombs each, as external fuel tanks were not needed for the short flight from Ramat David to Mound Dan and back.

APARTMENT departed Ramat David at 15:11; it was the fourth and final strike formation to depart Ramat David (or the fifth strike formation to take-off and the fourth to attack since Squadron 110's Vautours departed Ramat David in two formations, but regrouped in the air and attacked as one formation).

APARTMENT was unable to bomb Mound Hamra, since the Syrian fort was engulfed with smoke from preceding strikes. While trying to attack Mound Hamra, APARTMENT noted a position northwest of Mound Hamra from where kibbutz Dan was targeted. APARTMENT flew one dummy pass over this position, then bombed and strafed until the source of the fire seemed silent. It was then that APARTMENT noted another source of Syrian fire that was probably Mound Hamra. APARTMENT entered a strafing pass just as a pair of Squadron 105 SMB2s initiated a bombing pass against the same target; the melee ended without incident, as the Squadron 105 SMB2s continued strafing passes and the Squadron 109 Mystères disengaged. By then Syrian AAA fire was noted, Syrian MiGs were reported, and the UNTSO cease-fire deadline of 15:30 was approaching, so no more Squadron 109 formations were scrambled and the 13 November 1964 Mound Dan clash was practically over.

MOUND DAN CLASH IMPACT

Squadron 109 started the Mound Dan clash with nine serviceable Mystères, and by the end of the day fielded thirteen serviceable Mystères. SYAF did not intervene during the Mound Dan clash, but as a precautionary action against possible SYAF reprisal, the ILAF ordered EPs to report to squadrons, mobilized reserves, and stepped up readiness. Prime Minister and Minister of Defense Levy Eshkol and ILDF Chief of Staff Isaac Rabin visited Ramat David the morning of Saturday, 14 November 1964, to meet the pilots who were at the forefront of the Mound Dan clash.

The ILAF scrambled thirty-two attack aircraft in eleven formations from three air bases, but only nineteen aircraft in five formations from two air bases actually attacked prior to the UNTSO cease-fire at 15:30. Seventeen of the attacking aircraft, in four formations, were from Ramat David—the balance were two Squadron 105 SMB2s from Hatzor—and this number included eight Squadron 109 Mystères in two formations. Squadron 109 was the only ILAF squadron to attack with two formations. The Squadron 109 Mystères dropped eight napalm canisters and fifteen 250 kilogram (550 lb) bombs, since one bomb hung up.

From the ILAF's perspective, the Mound Dan clash was extremely successful and the ILAF viewed this action as a probable pattern for future operations, as explained in an ILAF post-Mound Dan official publication:

> Air action is a new type of reprisal operation. Instead of ILDF special forces invading Syrian fortifications at night that harassed Israeli settlements, aircraft were operated in daylight. Both actions involve an incursion into enemy territory, but in case of aircraft, the chances

Squadron 109 Commander Ohad Shadmi beside Mystère 06 on an air-to-ground QRA armed with two napalm canisters; Shadmi first flew 4506 on 18 November 1964. David Porat ferried 4506 from IAI at Lod to Ramat David on 14 November 1964 to bolster Squadron 109's strength due to Readiness State C; otherwise ferry flights were not flown on Saturdays. (PC)

Mystère 11—which Avi Oren flew as LADDER 4 on 13 November 1964—on air-to-ground QRA with two 250 kilogram (550 lb) bombs. (PC)

are higher to destroy the fortifications with minimum casualties to our forces.

Israel derived great pleasure from a subsequent UNTSO report that Syria initiated the clash—opening fire at 13:27 and starting artillery bombardment from 13:49—and that the ILAF's action concluded prior to the UNTSO agreed cease-fire at 15:30. The UNTSO report did not refer to the question whether the ILDF patrol was west or east of the border line, but it was reported that a UNTSO officer and surveyor stated that the ILDF patrol was indeed west of the border line.

ILAF action did not silence Syrian fire, but it signaled Syria that Israel would not tolerate artillery bombardment of settlements and that, due to Syria's numerical and topographic superiority over ILDF artillery, the Israeli reaction to Syrian artillery bombardment of Israeli settlements would be ILAF air strikes.

Readiness State C remained in force until 15 November 1964, and was relaxed to Readiness State B after another ILDF patrol along the border track in the Mound Dan sector completed its mission without event circa 13:00 on 15 November 1964. It went back to Readiness State A after another eventless ILDF patrol along the border track in the Mound Dan sector on 17 November 1964.

Small scale clashes involving a brief exchange of light arms fire erupted on 16 and 17 November 1964, and Syrian soldiers again opened fire at the ILDF patrol along the border track in the Mound Dan sector on 1 December 1964. Syria restrained from artillery bombardment of Israeli settlements and ILAF attack aircraft, including Squadron 109 Mystères, were not scrambled to support subsequent small scale clashes along the Israeli-Syrian border.

ILAF YEAR 1964 TERM 3

Four Flying School Class 44 graduates who attended Squadron Ouragan 113 OTU Course 24 during ILAF Year 1964 Term 2 were assigned to Squadron 109 at the start of ILAF Year 1964 Term 3: Michael Dvir, Giora Goren, Nadav Israeli, and Jacob Tal. Assigned from Squadron 109 at the same time were Deputy A Amihy Shmueli, Isaac Barzilai to Squadron 101 Shahak, and Daniel Ilan to Squadron 110 Vautour. Deputy B Uri Even-Nir was promoted to Deputy A and Ami Gadish took over as Deputy B.

Squadron 109 regular pilots during ILAF Year 1964 Term 3: standing (left to right): Tamir, Bester, Gadish, Shadmi, Even-Nir, Porat, and Nehushtan; and sitting (left to right): Friedman (Perry), Tal, Goren, Israeli, Dvir, and Lanis. (PC)

Mystère 07 departs Ramat David with flaps at zero deflection. Squadron 109 Commander Ohad Shadmi tested take off with deflected flaps on 29 November 1964 in 4505 and 4514 exactly a month before AIR2 issued a standard procedure for Mystère take off. (PC)

ATTACK AIRCRAFT EVALUATION REPORT

Air Department Chief Moti Hod signed a survey of potential attack aircraft on 11 December 1964, thus concluding the work of an ILAF delegation that evaluated British and French attack aircraft during October and November 1964.

Evaluated British attack aircraft were the Buccaneer, Canberra, Harrier, and Hunter. Evaluated French attack aircraft included the Mirage IIIE, Mirage IIIF2, Mirage IV, and Super Vautour. The medium attack aircraft types under consideration to replace the ten-ton Mystère were the then-seven-ton Harrier development aircraft—that would evolve into an operational eleven-ton combat aircraft by 1969—the eleven-ton Hunter and the fourteen-ton Mirage IIIE.

Even though the British Harrier and Hunter should have been ruled out on the spot—the Harrier was too new and the Hunter was too old—and the French Mirage IIIE would be the recommended medium attack aircraft by default, the actual recommendations concerning a new medium attack aircraft for the ILAF were ambiguous. The evaluation indeed discarded the Hunter as a potential future ILAF medium attack aircraft, but did not rate the Harrier and Mirage IIIE. Instead, it was recommended to continue to maintain interest in the Harrier and Mirage IIIE—even though the Harrier would only enter service in 1969, which was too late for the ILAF's requirement, while the Mirage IIIE was already operational, with deliveries to the FRAF starting in January 1964—while acquiring FRAF surplus SMB2 aircraft as a stopgap solution for the ILAF's medium attack aircraft requirement; a recommendation that impacted Squadron 109 within a short while.

TAKE OFF WITH FLAPS

The Mystère's take-off ambiguity was settled on 29 December 1964, when AIR2 issued a standard procedure for Mystère take-off.

The AIR2 standardization order was derived from a series of IAI test flights from 28 August until 2 October 1964 and a subsequent series of Squadron 109 flights aimed at validating the IAI recommendations with a broad base of aircraft and pilots.

The IAI measured Mystère take-off distances in four configurations:

- Empty fuel tanks and bomb racks
- Full fuel tanks and two napalm canisters
- Full fuel tanks and two 250 kilogram (550 lb) bombs
- Full fuel tanks and twelve T-10 rockets

The conclusion was the deflection of flaps shortened take-off distances and the greatest gain was accomplished at a flap setting of forty-five degrees. The improvement ranged from 300 meters (984 ft) measured at 13°C (55°F) to 450 meters (1,476 ft) expected

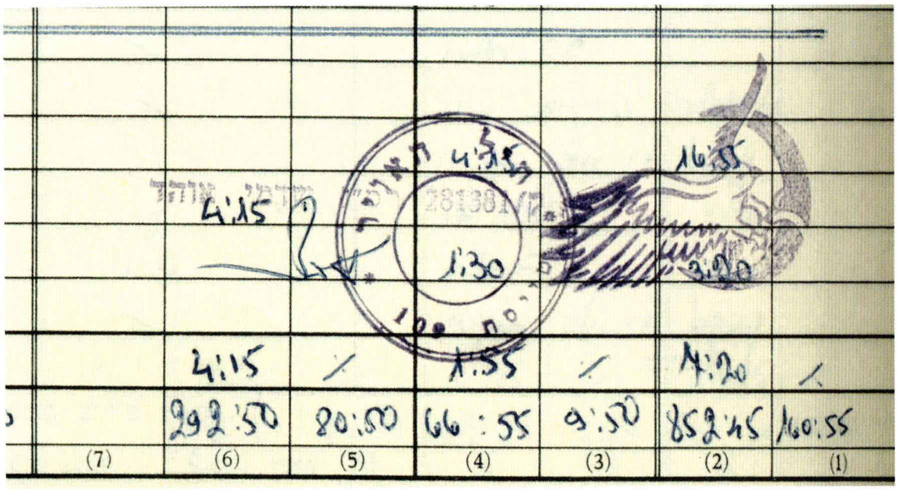

Squadron 109's Commander stamp (1956–1964) was composed of the round Squadron 109 stamp and the horizontal Squadron 109 Commander name stamp; only after Ohad Shadmi entered office as Squadron 109 Commander was the third stamp of the Squadron 109 badge added, as was custom in other squadrons, as illustrated in this extract from a Squadron 109 pilot's January 1965 logbook page. (PC)

at 30°C (86°F) in configuration with napalm down to 80 to 100 meters (262 to 328 ft) in configuration with rockets.

The new Mystère take-off drill was:

- The aircraft will stand at the start of the runway with deployed flaps, trimmed back and the green light off.
- The nose wheel will be in contact with the ground and the pilot will not apply pressure on the stick from brake release to lift off [compared with the previous procedure to lifting the nose wheel at 120 knots].
- Lift off speed is 115% of stall speed in the same configuration and the flaps are set so lift off speed with forty-five degrees flaps is:
  - 141 knots in configuration with full fuel tanks and two napalm canisters.
  - 140 knots in configuration with full fuel tanks and two 250 kilogram (550 lb) bombs.
  - 145 knots in configuration with full fuel tanks and twelve T-10 rockets.
- The pilot will pull the stick when the aircraft reaches lift off speed.
- The undercarriage will be retracted after the aircraft attains 160 knots.
- The flaps will be retracted after undercarriage retraction; it is recommended to retract the flaps in phases in order to avoid a rapid change in aircraft pitch.

SQUADRON 109 SMB2

ILAF Commander Ezer Weizman presented the 11 December 1964 survey during an ILDF General Staff meeting on 1 February 1965. The ILDF embraced the recommendation to acquire FRAF surplus SMB2s as a stopgap solution for the ILAF's medium attack requirement and a budget was allocated for procurement of sixteen SMB2s.

At the time, ILAF ORBAT included twenty-nine SMB2s equipping Squadron 105 at Hatzor and thirty-six Mystères assigned to Squadron 109 at Ramat David and Squadron 116 at Tel Nof. The acquisition of sixteen SMB2s was expected to enable transition of one squadron from the Mystère to the SMB2, as well as returning the remaining Mystère squadron to a full standard of twenty-four aircraft, plus ample reserve.

Squadron 109 was selected for transition from the Mystère to the SMB2, and the planned schedule was to introduce the SMB2 into Squadron 109 service during ILAF Year 1965 Term 2.

HOPE FOR SKYHAWK

The ILAF's fantasy for future heavy and medium attack aircraft were the F-4 Phantom and A-4 Skyhawk. American aircraft were considered superior to French aircraft, primarily in propulsion and weapon systems, with corresponding superiority in range, load, and hitting power.

The US was reluctant to supply combat aircraft to Israel, and the Israeli acquisition of combat aircraft from France perfectly suited US foreign policy considerations. However, from April 1964, the US negotiated sale of F-104 Starfighters to Jordan. The Jordanian alternative to the F-104's Starfighter acquisition was the purchase of MiG-21s from the USSR, since there was no suitable British Mach 2 combat aircraft to replace the JOAF's Hunters.

In order to ease Israeli objections to the sale of F-104 Starfighters to Jordan, President Lyndon Johnson dispatched Under Secretary of State for Political Affairs William Averell Harriman to Israel, from 24 February 1965 until 2 March 1965. During discussions, Israel demanded the US supply to Israel a heavy attack aircraft type—preferably the F-4 Phantom, but the B-66 Destroyer was mentioned as an acceptable alternative—to counterbalance the sale of F-104 Starfighters to Jordan.

The Israeli focus on the heavy attack aircraft type was probably due to the prior acceptance of the SMB2 as a stopgap medium attack aircraft type and the view that the requirement for a heavy attack aircraft type was more pressing, and the fact that in this class, the only readily available French alternative, the Mirage IV, was too expensive for Israel and too heavy for the ILAF.

The ILAF's dream duo of light and heavy attack aircraft were the American A-4 Skyhawk and F-4 Phantom—these contemporary paintings illustrated the heavy punch of the light attack aircraft and the brute power of the heavy attack aircraft—with light attack aircraft planned to reequip Squadron 109. (PC)

The product of this round of discussions was a Memorandum of Understanding signed on 10 March 1965. From Squadron 109's point of view and from the ILAF's medium attack aircraft requirement perspective, the most important clause in this Memorandum was the US undertaking the sale of combat aircraft to Israel if equivalent combat aircraft were not available from other suppliers; the exact, vague phrase in the 10 March 1965 Memorandum of Understanding was:

> The United States is further prepared to ensure an opportunity for Israel to purchase a certain number of combat aircraft—if not from Western sources, then from the United States.

The US interpretation of the 10 March 1965 Memorandum of Understanding was revealed the same day in a telegram from the Department of State to the US Embassy in Jordan:

> After extended negotiations ... reached agreement with Israelis that was prerequisite to our completing the Memorandum of Understanding with King Hussein. Package includes Israeli assurances against being first in the area to go nuclear, an Israeli agreement to acquiesce in US arms sales to Jordan, renewed US assurances of opposition to aggression in the area, and US agreement to sell Israel on favorable credit terms military equipment in quantities and kinds comparable to US sales to

> Jordan, plus "less than twenty-four" aircraft after 1966 if Israel is unable obtain them from Western European sources... On aircraft, you may assure the King that we have encouraged Israel to look to traditional sources of supply. In conformity with our position on the question of aircraft for Jordan, we would also tell Israel that if it is unable to meet its requirement in Europe, we would consider direct sale of a few aircraft (about the same number as Jordan is asking). As the King knows, we have not discussed possible sale of the F-104 series aircraft with Israel and do not plan to do so. Unless the Soviet bloc provides more and higher performance aircraft to Arabs sufficient to change the strategic situation, we will not change our position during the life of this agreement.

Israel's interpretation of the same 10 March 1965 Memorandum was quite different. From the Israeli point of view, the door for acquisition of US-made combat aircraft for the ILAF was not yet fully opened, but it was certainly no longer locked and sealed. In light of this development, Israel started to reevaluate the wisdom of the SMB2 acquisition for the ILAF versus presentation of proof to the US that no suitable French combat aircraft were available to fulfill the ILAF's medium attack aircraft requirement, in which case the US—in line with the 10 March 1965 Memorandum—would be obliged to sell medium attack aircraft to Israel.

MYSTÈRE RANGES

The ILAF's preoccupation with a plan for an air superiority campaign that would be launched at the start of a future war brought up the Mystère's range issues. The Mystère was designed as an interceptor and was adapted for attack missions after the ILAF introduced newer interceptors—the SMB2 from 1959 and the Shahak from 1962—but the ILAF never viewed the Mystère's attack capabilities as adequate, and for this reason the ILAF initiated efforts to replace the Mystère with a more suitable attack aircraft at an earlier point in the Mystère's lifetime.

Squadron 109 Commander Ohad Shadmi—here presenting a Mystère ordnance exhibition to visitors at Ramat David during winter of 1965—flew two SEAB mission range research flights on 1 February 1965 in 4532 and on 2 February 1965 in 4526. (PC)

On 14 March 1965, Squadron 109 Navigation and Performance Officer Hanan Tamir reported that the Mystère's manual range graphs did not cover all configurations, were not accurate enough and were, in most cases, very optimistic. As a result, the squadron conducted research to yield actual fuel consumption during typical SEAB mission profiles that included low altitude penetration with two 250 kilogram (550 lb) bombs and full fuel tanks, an attack time of eight minutes with one bombing run and three strafing passes, disengagement at low altitude, and RTB at medium altitude.

The average results were a fuel consumption of 300 kilograms (660 lbs) for taxi and take-off, 43 kilograms (95 lbs) per minute during low altitude penetration with bombs, 40 kilograms (88 lbs) per minute during low altitude disengagement without bombs, 280 kilograms (617 lbs) during a seven and a half minute climb to 25,000 feet that covered 93 kilometers (58 miles), 22.5 kilograms (49.6 lbs) per minute during RTB cruise at Mach 0.76 (350 knots) at 25,000 feet, and 50 kilograms (110 lbs) of fuel during descent from 25,000 feet to 2,000 feet, which covered 74 kilometers (46 miles). Average fuel consumption during the attack ranged from 350 to 450 kilograms (771 to 992 lbs), depending on attack profiles.

The results were the Mystère's actual radius of action in configuration for the SEAB profile mission was only 270 kilometers (168 miles) for the low-low-low mission profile or 335 kilometers (208 miles) for the low-low-high mission profile.

SILT READINESS

Operation SILT superseded Operation EAGLE as the ILAF's standing order for operations against Syria in the wake of an escalation during a border clash. Continued clashes along the Israeli-Syrian border were mostly small scale. Israel decided to use every border clash as cause for an attack on Syrian heavy engineering equipment involved in the Syrian water diversion project. However, Syria's heavy engineering equipment was mostly five to fifteen kilometers (three to nine miles) or more from the border, thus necessitating Israel to commit long range tank fire, artillery bombardment, and air strikes to the task.

The ILAF was on readiness to activate Operation SILT during a major border clash on 16 to 17 March 1965, but Syria restrained from bombarding Israeli settlements, thus giving Israel no cause for ILAF intervention.

EXERCISE MIGHT

The tactical training phase of ILAF Year 1964 Term 3 emphasized nighttime operations in preparation for end of term Exercise MIGHT, a large scale ILAF maneuver that ran from 29 to 31 March 1965.

Training for nighttime operations mostly involved regular and EP pilots, but not reserve pilots; from 1 to 28 March 1965, during the preparation period prior to Exercise MIGHT, regular pilot David Porat flew one nighttime training sortie as an illuminator, EP pilot Reuben Rosen flew four nighttime training sorties (one bombing and strafing, one navigation, and two napalm and strafing), and reserve pilot Asaf Ben-Nun did not fly any nighttime training sorties.

Regular and EP pilots initiated Exercise MIGHT missions on 29 March 1965: Ohad Shadmi flew his first MIGHT sortie in Mystère 15; David Porat flew one MIGHT SEAB practice mission (against Hatzor in Mystère 06); and Reuben Rosen flew one MIGHT SEAB training mission in Mystère 26.

Reserve pilots joined regular and EP pilots from 30 to 31 March 1965: Squadron 109 Commander Ohad Shadmi flew two MIGHT daytime sorties on 30 March 1965 (SEAB Hatzor in 4506 and attack Halutza in 4510) and two MIGHT sorties on 31 March 1965 (both attack Halutza, both in 4505, and both daytime); regular pilot David Porat flew two MIGHT missions on 30 March 1965 (one daytime SEAB and one nighttime support as an attacker) and two MIGHT missions on 31 March 1965 (both support); EP pilot Reuben Rosen flew three MIGHT missions on 30 March

Asaf Ben-Nun and Reuben Rosen flew Mystère 25 during Exercise MIGHT in July 1965. (PC)

1965 (one daytime SEAB, one daytime support, and one nighttime support as an illuminator) and one MIGHT mission on 31 March 1965 (daytime support); and reserve pilot Asaf Ben-Nun flew one MIGHT mission on 30 March 1965 and three MIGHT missions on 31 March 1965—all four sorties were daytime support.

MIGHT again exercised the ILAF's doctrine of an air superiority offensive followed by an air support campaign; the air superiority phase was flown during daylight as usual, while a night strike was added to the air support phase, but the ILAF was still oriented toward daytime operations and the number of nighttime sorties flown was only a fraction of the daytime sorties, yet the volume of ILAF night operations during MIGHT was an improvement over previous exercises and an indication of the future.

SMB2 CONVERSION COURSE

The plan to purchase sixteen SMB2s and convert Squadron 109 from the Mystère to the SMB2 during ILAF Year 1965 Term 2 was still in force. Thus, no Flying School Class 45 and Squadron 113 OTU Course 25 graduates were assigned to Squadron 109 at the start of ILAF Year 1965 Term 1, while in preparation for implementation of Squadron 109's transition from the Mystère to the SMB2, a group of six Squadron 109 regular pilots—Deputy A Uri Even-Nir, Deputy B Ami Gadish, Hanan Tamir, Irik Bester, Menahem Nehushtan, and David Porat—attended a Squadron 105 SMB2 conversion course at the start of ILAF Year 1965 Term 1.

The six Squadron 109 pilots attending the Squadron 105 SMB2 conversion course did not deploy to Hatzor for the duration of

Squadron 109 pilots attended Squadron 105's ILAF Year 1965 Term 1 SMB2 Conversion Course together with three Flying School Class 45 graduates slated for service with Squadron 105: standing (left to right): Tamir, Bester, Nehushtan, Gadish, SMB2 Conversion Course Commander Aki Arzi, Raviv, and Flum; and crouching (left to right): Porat, Even-Nir, and Sella. (PC)

conversion course, instead departing Ramat David every morning in Piper liaison aircraft and attending the SMB2 conversion course lessons and flights prior to their return to Ramat David in the Pipers at the end of the day.

The SMB2 conversion course solo day was on 16 April 1965; David Porat soloed in SMB2 08.

Also on 16 April 1965, Squadron 109 Commander Ohad Shadmi started to refresh his SMB2 skills; Shadmi was already an experienced SMB2 pilot and at the time was one of the most experienced ILAF SMB2 pilots after flying the SMB2 from conversion in France during 1958 until assignment as Squadron 109 Commander in 1964, Coincidentally, Shadmi's SMB2 refresher flight started on 16 April 1965 in SMB2 04, the same SMB2 he first flew in Israel back in February 1959.

Compared to the Mystère, the SMB2's innovations were its afterburner and the autocommand control system. These innovations, among other improvements, resulted in the SMB2's superior performance. The Mystère pilots were also impressed with the SMB2's roomy cockpit and better ergonomics.

The shortened Squadron 105 SMB2 conversion course for experienced Squadron 109 pilots covered Exercises 1 to 12; David Porat flew eleven sorties in six flying days from 16 to 22 April 1965 and accumulated 5:30 flight hours.

SMB2 SHORTFALL

The ILAF selected the SMB2 as a stopgap future medium attack aircraft and the ILDF allocated for the acquisition of sixteen SMB2s, but the FRAF was reluctant to release SMB2s to Israel, since the SMB2 was still viewed as a vital component of the FRAF's ORBAT. AIR3 Chief Jacob Nevo explained on 25 April 1965:

> Ferry flight planning [of SMB2s] has been delayed due to recent reports concerning the number and type of aircraft. Until the situation is cleared it is recommended:
>
> - To finish (SMB2) conversion of Squadron 109 pilots and maintainers.
>
> - To view Squadron 109 as continuing to operate as a Mystère squadron without any changes.
>
> - To press for the acceptance of operational [SMB2] aircraft and to raise reservations concerning the acceptance of seven test [SMB2] aircraft.
>
> - To evaluate the implications of modifying these seven [test] aircraft into operational [aircraft].

The AIR3 Chief's view was that even if the ILAF would accept the seven test SMB2s on offer and even if the ILAF would convert these test SMB2s to operational aircraft, then the number of available SMB2s would not be sufficient to maintain two SMB2 squadrons.

SKYHAWK SUPERSEDES SMB2

By June 1965, it was clear that France was unable to spare for export more than the seven nonstandard pre-series production airframes and development SMB2s. Not only was the number of available aircraft well below the ILAF requirement, but the actual operational value of these aircraft was questionable.

Furthermore, in line with the Memorandum of Understanding between Israel and the US, if Israel was not able to acquire French combat aircraft, then the US would be obliged to supply Israel with equivalent aircraft!

However, while France was unable to supply Israel with an adequate number of standard SMB2s, the US was not yet willing to accept that Israel had exhausted the European attack aircraft option, as explained in a 6 May 1965 memorandum to the US Secretary of Defense from the Joint Chiefs of Staff:

> The sale to Israel of US offensive weapons, such as tanks and aircraft, can be expected to generate Arab reactions which would be detrimental to US political, military, and economic interests in the Middle East... Although the Israelis have requested 75 combat aircraft—presumably bomber aircraft—the Memorandum of Understanding, as understood by the United States, provided for no more than 24 aircraft. The Joint Chiefs of

Squadron 109 Commander Ohad Shadmi flew Mystère 25 during Israel Independence Day 17's flyover on 6 May 1965. (PC)

Squadron 109 regular pilot David Porat flew Mystère 09 during Israel Independence Day 17's flyover on 6 May 1965. (PC)

Squadron 109 reserve pilot Asaf Ben-Nun flew Mystère 71 during Israel Independence Day 17's flyover on 6 May 1965. At some point during the early 1960s, the practice of covering aircraft numbers attending public displays was changed to slightly modifying the numbers of aircraft attending public displays with the addition of a third digit, which was sometimes a prefix and sometimes a suffix; Mystère 71's number was thus changed to 771. In many cases the modified, three-digits public display number was not changed to a normal ILAF two-digit number immediately afterward, so aircraft that were on public display continued to fly with three-digit numbers for a while. (PC)

Staff believe that the addition of even 24 jet light bombers to the Israeli inventory would provide a significant relative increase in Israeli military capability, and the addition of 75 bomber aircraft would create a drastic change in the present military balance which cannot be justified on military grounds... Israel's combat aircraft needs have been filled in the past from United Kingdom and French sources. The United States should avoid the sale of any US combat aircraft to Israel, particularly bomber aircraft. Every effort should be made to persuade Israel to continue to satisfy its combat aircraft requirements from Western European sources. The British Canberra Mk II or the French Vautour II B (especially if it were equipped with the Spey engine) would give Israel a satisfactory bombing capability. Both aircraft are expected to be available... If a political decision is made to sell US aircraft, bomber aircraft should not be offered, since this would increase the severity of the Arab reaction. If US aircraft must be provided, the F-5 is the best available compromise on the basis of performance, cost, political considerations, and impact on US military posture. Although its performance does not meet the stated Israeli requirement, it is probable that Israel would accept the F-5 in order to obtain a US aircraft.

The United States' view of the 10 March 1965 Memorandum of Understanding was emphasized in a 5 June 1965 telegram from the US Department of State to the US Embassy in Israel:

> The clear consensus is that it is contrary to US interests to sell military aircraft to Israel.
>
> We are committed to sell Israel aircraft only if Israel cannot obtain suitable aircraft from Western European sources. In any event, we would not sell supersonic aircraft, the number would not exceed 24, and delivery would not be until 1967. We are also most reluctant to sell a bomber, or even an attack aircraft, but to avoid charges of bad faith, we propose to stick for this round with the precise language of the Memorandum of Understanding [i.e., certain number of combat aircraft] and March 10 Agreed Minutes [i.e., certain number of mutually agreed type].
>
> We propose to tell the Israeli Embassy here we expect detailed evidence of a GOI effort to procure Western European aircraft.
>
> If, after intensive effort, the GOI is unable to find suitable aircraft, we intend to canvass Western European sources ourselves.
>
> Since we wish to steer Israel to Europe, rather than whet its appetite for US aircraft, we do not now intend to furnish the GOI information on availability, price, characteristics, or recommendations regarding potentially available US combat aircraft. Supplying such information before conclusion of the investigation of Western European possibilities could destroy credibility of the US insistence of thorough search for Western European aircraft. However, we will provide certain information on the costliness of selected US aircraft we do not intend to sell with a view to encouraging the Israelis to search for suitable foreign aircraft.

Though the content of this telegram was unknown to Israel at the time, it certainly expressed the ILAF's appetite for made in the

Squadron 109 Mystère 82 honors (left to right) ILAF Commander Ezer Weizman, Simon Peres, and Ramat David Wing Commander Ezekiel Somech during Peres' visit to Ramat David on 2 June 1965, a few days after Peres resigned from his position as Deputy Defense Minister on 25 May 1965. (PC)

USA combat aircraft and highlighted the fact that at the time, the ILAF was highly motivated to rule out potential European attack aircraft. The telegram also indicated the US Department of State rejected the US Chiefs of Staff recommendation to sell the F-5 to Israel, because the F-5 was supersonic, while the US Department of State preferred a non-supersonic aircraft, thus playing into the hands of the ILAF, which preferred the A-4 Skyhawk over the F-5 Freedom Fighter. The telegram also set a schedule for the potential sale of US combat aircraft to Israel, with deliveries not expected before 1967.

The profound ILAF preference for an American attack aircraft was indeed emphasized on 18 July 1965, in an ILAF Commander memo to the Deputy Minister of Defense that also elaborated on the background of the ILAF requirement:

> Enemy air forces and defenses became stronger in recent years. This development presents the ILAF with two challenges:
>
> - More targets in general and more long range targets in particular. The EGAF tends to base at the rear a considerable part of its ORBAT, especially bombers and SSMs.
> - Improvements in air defenses, including the introduction of the SA-2, force us to penetrate and attack at low level in order to preserve surprise and operate underneath the engagement envelope of the missiles.
>
> The solution to these two challenges is to increase ORBAT and load because:
>
> - Long range requires more fuel at the expense of bombs.
> - Low altitude increases fuel consumption, again at the expense of bombs.
>
> Therefore, we came to the conclusion that in light of present reality, it is no longer viable to emphasize versatility, but to tailor to a mission the most suitable aircraft... The ILAF therefore requires two types of attack aircraft:
>
> - Long range (heavy) attack aircraft...
> - Short range (light) attack aircraft...

The requirement for fifty heavy attack aircraft was promoted as first priority. The second priority requirement was for 100 to 120 light attack aircraft.

The three preferred types for light attack aircraft in order of preference were the eleven-ton A-4 Skyhawk, the sixteen-ton F-100 Super Sabre, and the nine-ton F-5 Freedom Fighter. The change from medium attack aircraft to light attack aircraft was presumably aimed to explain the inclusion of the A-4 Skyhawk and F-5 Freedom Fighter, while the memo also stated that there were no available European attack aircraft that suitably fulfilled the ILAF requirement, again ignoring the French thirteen- to fourteen-ton Mirage IIIE that was in FRAF service since 1964, was optimized for low level operations, was available to Israel, and could fulfill the ILAF's requirement.

Either way, by the summer of 1964, the prospects for Squadron 109's transition from the Mystère to the SMB2 seemed slim, the A-4 Skyhawk was the ILAF's frontrunner for a future light attack aircraft, and the Skyhawk superseded the SMB2 as the most likely future aircraft of Squadron 109.

ILAF YEAR 1965 TERM 2

Flying School Class 46 and Squadron 113 Ouragan OTU Course 26 graduates assigned to Squadron 109 at the start of ILAF Year 1965 Term 2 were Avi Gilad, David Lavi, Samuel Ringel, Aviem Sella, and Ran Zur. Solo day was on 30 July 1965; Aviem Sella soloed in Mystère 06. The assignment of junior pilots to Squadron 109 Mystère signaled that the plan to convert Squadron 109 from the Mystère to the SMB2 was no longer relevant.

Senior Squadron 109 pilots assigned to the Squadron 101 Shahak conversion course at the start of ILAF Year 1965 Term 2 were David Porat and Avi Oren; upon completion of the Squadron 101 Shahak conversion course, Porat and Oren were assigned to Squadron 117 Shahak, but continued to fly Squadron 109 Mystères from time to time in order to preserve their Mystère qualification until accomplishment of the Shahak combat qualification.

DEAD STICK LANDING AT NIGHT

The ILAF's effort to improve nighttime qualifications continued and Squadron 109's nighttime training sorties mostly involved navigation in singles and attacks in three-ship formations of one illuminator and two bombers. Reserve pilot Asaf Ben-Nun flew seventeen training sorties during ILAF Year 1965 Term 2 totaling 12:50 flight hours, including fourteen daytime sorties (totaling 9:55 flight hours) and three nighttime sorties (totaling 2:55 flight hours) that covered navigation (one sortie), attack (one sortie), and illumination (one sortie).

Pilots Asher Neeman and Giora Ben-Dov practiced navigation the evening of 16 September 1965. They were planned to fly the same route in singles at a time interval, with Neeman ahead of Ben-Dov. While flying south along the coastline at 20,000 feet in Mystère 11, Neeman experienced an engine cut, but managed a dead stick landing at Tel Nof; this was the only known nighttime engine-less emergency landing in Squadron 109 Mystère history.

PLAN SAMUEL A

The next round in the saga of American attack aircraft for the ILAF—and for that matter a new aircraft for Squadron 109—was ILAF Commander Ezer Weizman's presentation of the ILAF's Plan SAMUEL A in Washington during October 1965.

ILAF Commander Ezer Weizman presented Plan SAMUEL A on 12 October 1965. Plan SAMUEL A covered the acquisition of 210

Avi Gilad (covering his face with his hand) being "baptized" by HAS service persons after flying his Mystère solo flight on 30 July 1965. (PC)

The ILAF's fully French frontline fighter aircraft ORBAT on display in November 1965 (left to right): the Vautour, Shahak, SMB2, Mystère, Ouragan, and Fouga. At the time, the ILAF aspired to replace the Mystère, Ouragan, and SMB2—in that order—with the A-4 Skyhawk and to succeed the Vautour with the F-4 Phantom or A-6 Intruder; the Squadron 109 Mystère on display was 4515 with a prefix digit 7, while Mystère 71—also a Squadron 109 aircraft—was, at the time, undergoing Level D maintenance. (PC)

aircraft in two phases. Phase A included 120 light attack aircraft and thirty heavy attack aircraft. Phase B added forty-five light attack aircraft and fifteen heavy attack aircraft. Unequivocally, the ILAF's preferred light attack aircraft was the A-4 Skyhawk, while the F-4 Phantom was the preferred heavy attack aircraft; the A-6 Intruder was an acceptable alternative.

Israel asked the US to take over from France as its principle combat aircraft source and the negative US response was expressed during the follow up discussion on 13 October 1965. The US representatives rejected Israel's request and emphasized the US view of the 10 March 1965 Memorandum: up to twenty-four aircraft to be supplied only after Israel honestly rejected alternative European attack aircraft, such as the Super Vautour, Mirage IIIE, and Mirage IIIF2.

The US reaction to ILAF Plan SAMUEL A was summarized on 25 October 1965, in a memo to President Lyndon Johnson from Robert Komer of the National Security Council Staff:

> You'll recall that last March we promised that if Israel would lie low on Jordan arms, we'd sell some tanks and "up to 24 combat aircraft" if they couldn't get them anywhere else.
>
> Again predictably, the Israelis have made a blue sky opening bid—not for just twenty-four, but for 210 new fighter-bombers. Their air chief of staff was just here proposing in effect that we take over the modernization of the whole Israeli air force, on the grounds that neither France nor the UK—the only other suppliers—can provide the planes.
>
> State and DOD told him that he'd better go back to the French and British, and that selling 210 planes —even for dollars over several years—was out of the question. Nonetheless, it is true that we produce far better aircraft for the money, and that France and the UK probably can't meet Israel's total need (in fact, the Israelis are already back in, claiming that a new approach in Paris produced nothing).
>
> We'll keep stalling the Israelis along, making clear that we simply can't talk about becoming their chief suppliers, but not slamming the door on a small sale in 1966... Israel is happy enough about tanks and is asking enough other things from us ... that we can play hard to get on planes for a few months yet. But we'd recommend keeping the option open if you approve.

SAMUEL A PLAN B

The ILDF's General Staff discussed the implications of the US rejection of ILAF Plan SAMUEL A on 1 November 1965. ILAF Commander Ezer Weizman presented his vision of an ideal future ILAF ORBAT that would include 150 A-4 Skyhawks, fifty A-6 Intruders, and 100 Mirages. ILDF Chief of Staff Isaac Rabin also viewed 100 A-4 Skyhawks for the ILAF as an optimal plan, but doubted whether it was practical. The ILDF Chief of Staff thus concluded that the ILAF would wait three months for positive developments concerning A-4 Skyhawk acquisition and, if no breakthrough was accomplished, during the following three months the ILAF would revert to an optional plan to acquire the eighteen-ton Mirage 5 Raam—a heavier and simplified version of the fourteen-ton Mirage IIIE—which was specifically tailored to the ILAF's operational requirement and was within the ILAF's reach as a very capable alternative, and not a lot more expensive than the desired A-4 Skyhawk.

On 2 November 1965, AIR2 issued yet another survey of the potential future ILAF ORBAT entitled "ILAF ORBAT 1968 to 1970 - Discussion of Quality and Quantity." AIR2's view of an adequate ILAF ORBAT for the 1970s was 180 A-4 Skyhawks, sixty A-6 Intruders, and seventy Mirages.

The A-4 Skyhawk was still the ILAF's preference for a future light attack aircraft, but in line with US advice from 13 October 1965 and in line with the ILDF Chief of Staff's directive from 1 November 1965, the Israeli acquisition effort returned to the European market and the ILAF formulated an alternative requirement for the acquisition of 100 Mirage 5 Raam attack aircraft.

ILAF YEAR 1965 TERM 3

In order to match planned expansion of ORBAT, the ILAF started to gradually output more pilots from flying school classes, from an average output of nine graduates for Flying School Class 21 to 30, an average output of thirteen graduates for Flying School Class 31 to 40, and an average output of fifteen graduates for Flying School Class 41 to 50. However, there were two peaked outputs from the flying school classes: the March 1965 Flying School Class 46 with a record output (from 1956 to 1967) of twenty-seven graduates, and the July 1965 Flying School Class 47 with twenty-four graduates slated for piloting combat aircraft.

The sudden surge in the number of Flying School Class 47 graduates—and in the number of the preceding Flying School Class 46 graduates—strained the ILAF's progressional path from Flying School graduation to operational squadron.

Pilots' progress at the time included a Squadron 113 Ouragan OTU course during the term after graduation from Flying School and then assignment to either Squadron 107 Ouragan, Squadron 113 Ouragan, Squadron 109 Mystère, Squadron 116 Mystère, or Squadron 105 SMB2; Vautour and Shahak squadrons only accepted pilots with at least one term of experience in the Mystère or SMB2. Flying School Class 47 and Squadron 113 OTU Course 27 graduates posted to Squadron 109 at the start of ILAF Year 1965 Term 3 included Uri Keidar, Yuval Neeman, and Ami Rokeach, whose solo day was on 10 December 1965.

INTRUDER AND RAAM

The US rejected Israel's intention to base the complete ILAF reequipment plan on the acquisition of American attack aircraft as explained in a 21 January 1966 memorandum from US President Deputy Special Assistant for National Security Affairs to the US President Special Assistant for National Security Affairs in the wake of the former's discussion with an Israeli diplomat that same day:

> On planes, I told him Israel had made a grievous error in trying to take a whole arm when we extended a hand. When we grudgingly said last March that up to twenty-four planes might just be feasible as a bonus if none were available in Europe, the Israeli response was the Weizman approach, asking us in effect to take over supply of the whole Israeli airforce—with an initial commitment of 210 planes. This had led us to draw right back into our shells. If they wanted to increase the chance of a helpful response, I would advise them to inform us officially as soon as possible... that, while they still thought the Weizman proposal was the most sensible, they now recognized our reluctance to become the prime Israeli airforce supplier. Therefore, they would continue to seek primarily European sources. However, they did have a much smaller requirement for low level intruders which they hoped we would supply... I also said that, were I an Israeli, I would not ask for more than the twenty-four aircraft mentioned last March, and simply express hope that we might later make a further sale of like magnitude. I think he got the drift.

This discussion seemingly signaled Israel that the US would be willing to fulfil the ILAF's requirement for forty-five A-6 Intruders, but not the ILAF's requirement for 165 A-4 Skyhawks. Such willingness seemed likely, as it complied with the two terms of the 10 March 1965 Memorandum of Understanding: the US would supply a small quantity of aircraft of a type unavailable to Israel from European sources.

Therefore, in an ILDF General Staff discussion on 24 January 1966, ILDF Chief of Staff Isaac Rabin expressed his satisfaction with the acquisition of A-6 Intruders to fulfil the ILAF's requirement for a heavy attack aircraft, an acquisition that was in his opinion beyond Israel's realistic expectations. As for the ILAF requirement for a light attack aircraft, the ILDF decision to go ahead with acquisition of the Mirage 5 Raam from France was still in force; the Mirage 5 Raam was still Squadron 109 Mystère's replacement.

FROM INTRUDER TO SKYHAWK

US willingness to supply Israel with the A-6 Intruder was indeed —as phrased by ILDF Chief of Staff Isaac Rabin on 24 January 1965—"too good to be true." In another memorandum to the US president dated 8 February 1966, the US President Deputy Special Assistant for National Security Affairs still used the phrase "low level intruder," but this phrase no longer referred specifically to the A-6 Intruder:

> If we decide to sell Israel aircraft, we can only get what we want in return by providing a low level intruder. There's no point in offering an interceptor if Israel doesn't want one (and could buy from France if it did). It wants the fancy A–6 (at least $62 million for twenty-four stripped down versions), but we could probably get it to

Squadron 109 Commander Ohad Shadmi saved Mystère 15 on 20 February 1966 when—upon RTB from attack training (napalm and strafe) over range—the right wheel leg did not detract. Shadmi retracted the undercarriage and landed on the external fuel tanks. The landing was so successful that the aircraft stopped on the runway only a few feet beside the centerline and was flying again within days. (PC)

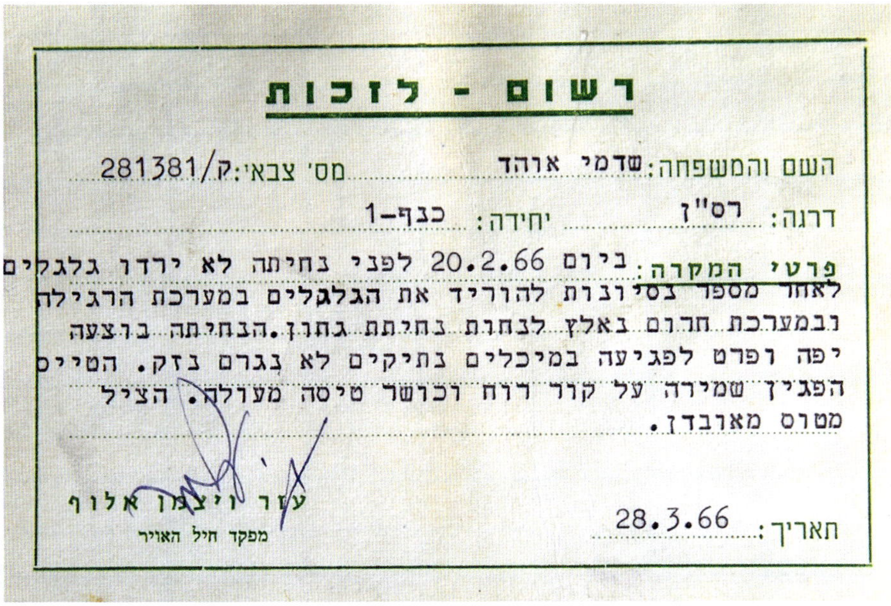

רשום - לזכות

השם והמשפחה: שדמי אוהד מס' צבאי: 281381/ק

דרגה: רס"ן יחידה: כנף-1

פרטי המקרה: ביום 20.2.66 לפני נחיתה לא ירדו גלגלים לאחר מספר נסיונות להוריד את הגלגלים במערכת הרגילה ובמערכת חרום באלץ לנחות נחיתת גחון. הנחיתה בוצעה יפה ופרט לפגיעה במיכלים בתיקים לא נגרם נזק. הטייס הפגין שמירה על קור רוח וכושר טיסה מעולה. הציל מטוס מאובדן.

עזר ויצמן אלוף
מפקד חיל האויר

תאריך: 28.3.66

ILAF Commander Ezer Weizman signed the Green Endorsement awarded to Squadron 109 Commander Ohad Shadmi for saving Mystère 15 on 28 March 1966; the Green Endorsement stated: "On 20 February 1966, before landing, the wheels did not detract [and] after several attempts to detract the wheels with the regular system and the emergency system was forced to land on its belly. The landing was performed well without any damage except to the external fuel tanks. The pilot displayed cool headedness and superb piloting skills and saved an aircraft."

> settle for the smaller, cheaper A–4E (around $24 million for the same number).
>
> VI. Recommendations. Offer Israel now ... up to twenty-four intruder type aircraft, with an option to purchase twenty-four more next year, provided that Israel will in return: (1) continue buying most of its aircraft in Europe so we don't become their prime supplier, thus outraging the Arabs; (2) actively, if quietly, support controlled US arms sales to Jordan as being in Israel's interest just as much as ours; (3) not use our aircraft as nuclear weapons carriers; and (4) maintain full secrecy till we decide when and how to publicize all such arms deals.

Apparently, both the US Defense Department and State Department were strongly against furnishing Israel with the A-6 Intruder, as indicated during a presidential meeting on Israel and Jordan matters on 11 February 1966:

> Plane Sales to Israel/Jordan. [US State] Secretary Rusk described the proposal being recommended, i.e., the sale of forty-eight aircraft to Israel. He saw dangers even in selling the A-4E, but much stronger political, as well as military arguments against selling the A-6, which the Israelis now wanted. There was also the nuclear angle. At the same time, it was proposed we offer Jordan thirty-six F-104s or F-5s.
>
> [USA Defense] Secretary McNamara felt we could not even consider the A-6. It was an extremely complicated aircraft and the bugs hadn't even been worked out yet. We had only one squadron. There were security problems with its electronics. Its price was four times as expensive as the A-4E. There was a shortage in our own supply for Vietnam. Selling the A-6 would also inflame the Middle East arms race, in particular scaring the Arabs about Israeli nuclear capabilities, since it was designed as a nuclear weapons carrier.
>
> The President asked Secretary McNamara to take on the job of dealing with the Israelis on this matter. He noted the pressure he was under from Congress on Israeli matters. He had already had to talk with twelve Congressmen, plus [Israel] Foreign Minister Eban. So McNamara should call Eban back here and tell him we couldn't possibly sell A-6s for the reasons McNamara had given. McNamara should find out if Israel was willing to have us sell to Jordan. He should tell the Israelis that we would sell them "X" aircraft and give them "X" dollars in aid if they would sew up everyone in Congress to keep quiet about our Jordan and Israeli sales. McNamara should say that our proposition was a final one; all the pressure in the world would not change it.

Accordingly, US Defense Secretary Robert McNamara conveyed the final offer in a meeting with Israel Foreign Minister Abba Eban on 12 February 1966:

> After the usual amenities, the Secretary opened the meeting by saying the US is operating in the Middle East "on very slender margins" and that there are accordingly several things we definitely cannot do: (1) we cannot be a major arms supplier to Israel or any Arab country; (2) we cannot sell to any country a sophisticated airplane like the A-6; and (3) we cannot sell supersonics of any kind to Jordan unless Israel concurs in the sale and effectively

> supports it among its friends in the United States, both in- and outside of Congress. He stressed the point that, in the absence of Israeli concurrence and support, the US would not sell aircraft to Jordan.
>
> The Secretary said that, if Israel can meet that basic condition and certain others, the US is prepared to sell Israel twenty-four A-4Es and to give it an option to buy an additional twenty-four, either now or later. The Secretary said the cost of such airplanes would be approximately $26 million for twenty-four and that credit terms would be the same as those that governed the [SAM] Hawk purchase (10% down, 3-1/2% interest, and a 10-year repayment). He said that four additional conditions would attach to our willingness to make this sale: (1) that Israel agree to continue to look to Europe for the bulk of its aircraft requirements and not regard the US as a major arms supplier; (2) that Israel reiterate its undertaking not to be the first power in the Middle East to manufacture nuclear weapons, and its acceptance of periodic inspection of Dimona; (3) that Israel agree not to use any US-supplied aircraft as a nuclear weapons carrier; and (4) that Israel agree to full secrecy on all matters until the USG decides when and how to publicize.

Israel and the ILDF and ILAF were deeply disappointed on the one hand and very satisfied on the other. US willingness to supply combat aircraft to Israel was a major breakthrough and a remarkable accomplishment for Israeli diplomacy. The proposed A-4 Skyhawk was the ILAF's preferred light attack aircraft, but a comparable French light attack aircraft was readily available to Israel, while there was no French equivalent to the A-6 Intruder. Since the US insisted Israel should continue buying aircraft from Europe and since the ILAF's requirement for light combat aircraft was much larger than the forty-eight A-4 Skyhawks offered, Israel decided to go ahead with the acquisition of two types of light combat aircraft. During an ILDF General Staff discussion on 21 February 1966, ILDF Chief of Staff Isaac Rabin expressed his disappointment about the US decision, summarizing the ILDF's preference to acquire ninety-six light attack aircraft for the ILAF: the forty-eight A-4 Skyhawks offered and forty-eight Mirage 5 Raams from France.

AHIT AND RAAM PRELIMINARY CONTRACTS

Israel wasted no time. A preliminary contract for thrity Mirage 5 Raams—plus an option that covered an additional eighteen—was signed on 14 March 1966. A preliminary contract for forty-eight A-4 Skyhawks was signed on 18 March 1966. The Israeli code for the still classified and not-yet-publicized Ahit contract was Program RUGBY.

ILAF modernization and expansion was finally starting to become a reality. Accordingly, on 30 March 1966, an AIR2 forum discussed the impact of the Ahit and Raam introduction. AIR2's recommendation was that Tel Nof-based Squadron 119 Shahak would reequip with the Raam as the first Mirage 5 squadron and that Ramat David-based Squadron 109 Mystère would reequip with the Ahit as the first A-4 Skyhawk squadron. Deliveries of the Ahit and Raam were expected to start during late 1967 or early 1968, thus setting a time frame for Squadron 109's transition from the Mystère to the Ahit.

SILT SCRAMBLE

Clashes continued along the Israeli-Syrian border, but Syrian artillery did not bombard Israeli settlements and the ILAF was not authorized to fly counterbattery missions.

Ahit and Raam acquisition were the final accomplishments of Ezer Weizman during his term as ILAF Commander from July 1958 until April 1966. Weizman visited Ramat David prior to the ILAF Commander handover in April 1966, where he bid farewell to Squadron 109 service persons. (PC)

Squadron 109 Mystères—including Aviem Sella in Mystère 34—and Squadron 110 Vautours were scrambled in line with SILT on 30 March 1966, during a major exchange of fire in the southern sector of the Israeli-Syrian border. The ILDF evaluated that Syrian artillery fired some 250 shells, but all were aimed at ILDF positions; none was aimed at Israeli settlements and not one strayed in the direction of Israeli settlements. The ILDF had no reason to authorize an ILAF SILT action and the Squadron 109 Mystères and Squadron 110 Vautours returned to Ramat David without attacking Syrian targets.

The Syrian internalization of Israel's red lines posed a problem for the ILDF, which could not mount effective counterbattery action against Syrian artillery without ILAF support and was unable to effectively engage Syrian heavy engineering equipment involved in the Syrian water diversion project works at ranges of more than 15 kilometers (nine miles) or so without ILAF support.

AHIT AND RAAM FULL CONTRACTS

Israel ordered fifty Raams in a contract signed on 7 April 1966. Negotiation for a full contract of Ahit was more complicated, since the US offered Israel a degraded A-4E designated the A-4H. The A-4H lacked an RWR system, bombing computer with gyro sight, and wiring for the AGM-45 Shrike ARM. The US rejected an Israeli request for advanced A-4H compatible ordnance, including AGM-12 Bullpup missiles, AIM-9 Sidewinder missiles, Rockeye cluster bombs, and napalm canisters. The US agreed to modify the A-4H with a braking chute, to assist with replacing the US standard 20 millimeter guns with ILAF standard 30 millimeter guns, and to include in the contract two "buddy" air-to-air refuel pods.

Amidst negotiation of the full contract, the US announced the sale to Israel of "tactical aircraft" on 20 May 1966. Also, Israel restrained from reprisal actions against Syria in the wake of terror attacks Israel related to the Syrian-sponsored PLO. The tough

Squadron 109 pilots participating in Israel Independence Day 18's flyover on 25 April 1966: standing (left to right): Arzi, Bina, Gadish, Even-Nir, Shadmi, Milo, Ben-Nun, and Gilad; kneeling (left to right): Rokeach, Tamir, Hochman, and Sella; and crouching (left to right): Yadid, Neeman, Goren, Yariv, and Neeman. (PC)

Squadron 109 aircraft—including Mystère 32—assemble prior to Israel Independence Day 18's flyover on 25 April 1966. Ohad Shadmi flew Mystère 83, Asaf Ben-Nun flew Mystère 26, and Aviem Sella flew Mystère 10. (PC)

On the ground and in the air, Squadron 109's seventeen-ship formation flown during Israel Independence Day 18's flyover on 25 April 1966 was one of the largest, most complicated, and most impressive ILAF Mystère flyover formations ever. (PC)

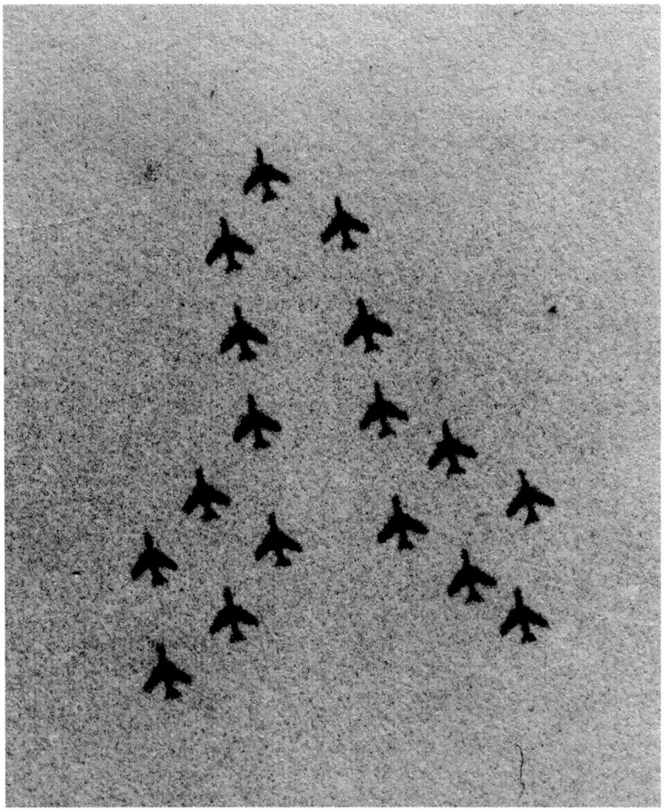

On the ground and in the air, Squadron 109's seventeen-ship formation flown during Israel Independence Day 18's flyover on 25 April 1966 was one of the largest, most complicated, and most impressive ILAF Mystère flyover formations ever. (PC)

negotiation ended in signature of the Ahit contract on 2 June 1966. The contract covered forty-eight A-4H Skyhawks—in US-specified standard and without Israel's requested ordnance —for delivery to Israel from September 1967. The contract's value was seventy million US dollars, including approximately twenty million US dollars for equipment and ordnance. Squadron 109 Mystère's successor was at last on order.

SHAFRIR 2 FOR SQUADRON 109?

As indicated, the ILAF's Shafrir 2 operational requirement rated the Mystère at the lowest priority for integration with Shafrir 2. This attitude was emphasized on 6 July 1966, when AIR2 issued a recommendation for a Shafrir 2 equipment plan. AIR2 recommended equipping all Shahak interceptors and then all Raam interdictors with the Shafrir 2, but only half of the Ahit, SMB2, and Vautour attack aircraft and none of the Ouragans and Mystères.

Thus, if Squadron 109 aircraft were to be equipped with the Shafrir 2, then this would not happen during the Mystère era, but sometime after the start of the Ahit age.

SMALL SILT

With the Ahit contract sealed and signed, Israel was no longer willing to restrain reprisal in the wake of Syrian and/or Syrian-sponsored PLO terror attacks; the next was on 13 July 1966, when an ILDF vehicle drove over a mine and two soldiers and a citizen were killed. The attack was within undisputed Israeli territory and ILDF trackers traced footprints from the scene to the Israeli-Syrian border. An Israeli reprisal action against Syria seemed inevitable.

The next morning, in order to be prepared for possible reprisal action, AIR3 distributed OPOR SMALL SILT. The objectives were to destroy Syrian engineering equipment and to attack surrounding AAA emplacements. Four Squadron 109 Mystères were to attack from 16:00 with four Squadron 110 Vautours following up, while five formations were to be in the air and on hold, flying racetracks west of the Israeli-Syrian border and waiting for orders to attack Syrian targets. Two Shahak four-ship formations were to fly CAP and two Shahaks and one Vautour were to be on alert for post combat BDA photography.

That same morning, the Israeli government approved an ILDF reprisal operation and authorized Prime Minister and Minister of Defense Levy Eshkol to decide—in coordination with the ILDF—the nature of the reprisal operation. The ILDF Chief of Staff recommended attacking Syrian heavy engineering equipment engaged in water resource diversion work from the air that same afternoon and the Prime Minister and Minister of Defense accepted this recommendation.

The ILAF switched to Readiness Level C from 11:15 and at 13:00 the ILDF issued OPOR WIND to cover ILAF action as well as ILDF readiness. This was the first aerial retribution operation against Syria since 1951, as all ILAF strike operations against Syria from 1951 to 1966 were air support missions.

Squadron 109's formation call sign TAILOR—Ohad Shadmi in Mystère 05, with Daniel Lanis, Haggai Ronen, and Jacob Yariv — departed Ramat David at 15:50. Each Mystère was armed with four 250 kilogram (550 lb) bombs. TAILOR attacked at 16:00 and the four Mystères flew east, crossed the east coast of the Sea of Galilee some three kilometers (two miles) north of En Gev, penetrated the Golan Heights some eight kilometers (five miles) deep, turned left (north), bombed, and turned left again for the flight back west.

Two Vautour formations followed and attacked, but the strike was then called off because Syrian interceptors were scrambled. The ILAF ordered the remaining attack formations to return to

Ramat David Wing 1 Maintenance Squadron Commander Josef Kvodi (standing fourth from the left) bid farewell to Squadron 109 on 25 June 1966 in the presence of Squadron 109 Commander Ohad Shadmi (standing fifth from the left) and Squadron 109 Technical Flight Commander Zohar Ben-Haim (standing sixth from the left). (PC)

A unique fifteen-ship formation flown during Flying School Class 50's graduation parade flyover on 7 July 1966 encompassed four Shahaks, three Vautours, two SMB2s, two Mystères, two Ouragans, and two Fougas; it is not yet known if the participating Mystères were from Squadron 109 or Squadron 116, or both. (PC)

base and the clash continued as an air-to-air action between ILAF Shahaks and SYAF MiG-21s.

From the integration of pilot debriefs and BDA photographs AIR4 concluded that the Squadron 109 Mystères and Squadron 110 Vautours hit six tractors, two motorized drills, one truck, and one AAA emplacement.

NO SHAFRIR 2 FOR SQUADRON 109

On 25 July 1965, AIR Department Chief Menahem Bar rejected AIR2's recommendation to equip ILAF interceptors and attack aircraft with Shafrir 2 in two phases and in two batches of 440 missiles. The lion's share of the ILAF's budget was committed to acquisition of the Ahit and Raam. The AIR Department Chief thus suggested approving the purchase of only sixty missiles for delivery from 1967 until 1969 to equip Shahak interceptors.

LANDING CRAFT CLASH

The Sea of Galilee was wholly within Israeli territory in line with 1949's Armistice Agreement between Israel and Syria, but the border line on the northeast side of the lake nearly overlapped the water line, thus giving Syria access to the Sea of Galilee. Israel was determined to exercise control over the whole Sea of Galilee through regular patrols of ILNF boats, including a small landing craft that was used because of its ability to get close to the shore. On many occasions, Syrian soldiers stationed along the northeast side of the Sea of Galilee opened fire at the landing craft as it came close to the water line, so ILDF orders limited the landing craft from getting closer than 250 meters (820 ft) from the northeast water line of the lake; none of these clashes triggered air action until 15 August 1966.

Tension along the Israeli-Syrian border in the wake of the 14 July 1966 clash motivated the ILDF to limit the landing craft to no closer than 500 meters (1,640 ft) from the northeast water line of the lake, but somehow, at 03:30 on 15 August 1966, the small landing craft ran aground opposite the disputed water line.

Syrian forces opened fire at the stranded landing craft from 04:54 and an hour later, a pair of Squadron 109 Mystères was scrambled for support. The two Mystère pilots—Ohad Shadmi in Mystère 07 and Aki Arzi—flew over Syrian fortifications for six minutes (circa 06:10), in order to deter Syrian soldiers from firing at the landing craft. The Mystères did not attack, but did not deter either, and Syrian fire ceased circa 07:00 for unknown reasons.

The clash restarted circa 09:00, when SYAF MiG-17s attacked the landing craft, and this second round—that included air combat and air strikes—lasted until a UNTSO imposed cease-fire at 10:30.

The high tension in the wake of the 14 July 1966 reprisal operation escalated into readiness for war in the wake of the 15 August 1966 landing craft clash; the small landing craft was still stranded when fire ceased on 15 August 1966 and recovery attempts continued until 26 August 1966, when the boat was finally recovered. Throughout this time, the ILAF was on readiness to support the recovery effort and to strike Syria if a renewed clash escalated into full scale war. None of this happened, since Syria did not renew fire.

Squadron 109 Commander Ohad Shadmi was scrambled in Mystère 07—in lead of a pair—on 15 August 1966 to support ILNF landing craft at the Sea of Galilee; the pair departed Ramat David at 06:10 and landed at 07:15. (PC)

SINAI STAR ANNIVERSARY 10

Israel, the ILDF, and the ILAF marked the Suez War's tenth anniversary in October 1966. In the wake of the October to November 1956 Suez War, the Israeli media referred to the Mystère interceptor as the "Sinai Star," allegedly one of the key military technology elements that secured Israeli victory in this conflict.

Ten years later, the Mystère was no longer a top tier interceptor, but an elderly attack aircraft fast approaching the end of its useful life. Only two regular officers and three reserve pilots in the October 1966 Squadron 109 roster were in ILAF service during the Suez War: Squadron 109 Commander Ohad Shadmi was a Squadron 101 Mystère pilot during the Suez War, Squadron 109 Technical Flight Commander Zohar Ben-Haim was a Squadron 105 Spitfire maintainer, Squadron 109 reserve pilot Asaf Ben-Nun was a Squadron 105 Mustang pilot, Squadron 109 reserve pilot Arie Dagan was a Squadron 105 Mustang pilot, and Squadron 109 reserve pilot Jacob Yariv was a Flying School Class 21 cadet.

The 1966 Squadron 109 Mystères were the same aircraft assigned to Squadrons 101 or 199 during the Suez War and were in almost exactly the same standard; the ILAF did not invest heavily in Mystère development—except for the addition of a braking chute and a few minor modifications—primarily because the Mystère was viewed as lacking growth potential for improvement and for a lengthy service career. As a matter of fact, the ILAF had been trying to replace the Mystère with a more capable attack aircraft since 1962, so there was really little point to invest in an aircraft that was slated for retirement, while by 1966, the Mystère's successor was already on order and the Mystère's replacement schedule was generally set for some time after 1968.

Squadron 109 Commander Ohad Shadmi summed up the Mystère's status for an October 1966 ILAF publication that marked the tenth anniversary of the Suez War:

> The Mystère is mainly flown by junior pilots who are training in it prior to progressing [to more advanced combat aircraft types]. We try to make their training

Squadron 109 EP pilot Aviem Sella flew OPOR 109/90—an interdiction training mission—on 14 October 1966 in Mystère 07; by then, the AIR3 OPOR designation system had changed from a prefix letter and suffix number to a unit/counter. (PC)

Ramat David Wing Squadron 109 Mystère, Squadron 110 Vautour, and Squadron 117 Shahak in the Suez War Day 10 flyover on 27 October 1966. Squadron 109 Commander Ohad Shadmi flew Mystère 44. (PC)

varied and cover all subjects relevant for fighter pilots. However, considering today the Mystère is limited in air-to-air capabilities, we are emphasizing air-to-ground operations.

The Mystère is an aircraft that aged early; it is more versatile than the comparable MiG-15 and its versatility enables it to successfully accomplish attack missions. It is maneuverable and pleasant to fly. After ten years in service, it is known as technically and operationally efficient; a fact that testifies to the ability and devotion of its maintainers.

The Mystère cannot equal modern attack aircraft such as the Skyhawk, which was developed as an attack aircraft. The Mystère's endurance and load performances are inferior to the Skyhawk, but within its endurance limits the Mystère can successfully accomplish its missions. For this reason, it will be worthy to operate this aircraft for a long time.

It is "fun" to fly in Mach 2 aircraft, but the ILAF must make the most of all its available assets. For an attack mission, the offensive ordnance of a Mystère is similar to that of a Shahak and it will accomplish similar results, so why not exploit its capabilities?

OPERATION GRINDER IMPACT

A terror attack that Israel ascribed to Syria and/or to the Syrian sponsored PLO occurred the night of 8 to 9 October 1966, when an Israeli Police Border Guard patrol drove over a mine in the southern sector of the Israeli-Syrian border; four Border Guard service persons were killed and two were injured. ILDF trackers traced footprints from the scene of the mining to the Israeli-Syrian border. Moreover, in a statement made in Damascus, Syria, on 9 October 1966, the PLO assumed responsibility for this mining attack, so the ILDF Chief of Staff proposed an immediate ILAF reprisal operation—with dozens of aircraft tasked to bomb targets in Syria—to the Israeli government. However, this time the government decided to demonstrate restraint.

Syria sponsored the PLO, but the PLO also operated against Israel from Jordan. During the night of 11 to 12 November 1966, an ILDF patrol vehicle patrolling along the Israeli Jordanian border track south of Hebron drove onto a mine; three ILDF soldiers were killed and six ILDF soldiers were wounded. The attack was within undisputed Israeli territory and ILDF trackers traced footprints from the scene of the mining to the Israeli Jordanian border. Regardless of Israeli restraint in the face of the similar terror attack in October 1966, and perhaps because of Israeli restraint in the face of the similar terror attack in October, an Israeli reprisal action against Jordan seemed inevitable.

West-affiliated Jordan was in between the hammer and the anvil: between Israel, whose policy was to launch a reprisal operation in the wake of a terror attack against the host nation of terrorists; and between extreme, East-affiliated Arab nations that sponsored the PLO.

The US was also in between the hammer and the anvil: between Israel, which indeed launched a massive reprisal operation (Operation GRINDER) on 13 November 1966; and between Jordan. On 18 November 1966, a Central Intelligence Agency memo summarized the aftermath of Operation GRINDER:

Four Squadron 107 Ouragan pilots attended an ILAF Year 1966 Term 3 Squadron 109 Mystère Conversion course: standing (left to right): Ben-Dov, Ronen, and Arzi; and sitting (left to right): Gilboa, Topaz, Schleider, and Bar-Ner. (PC)

A Squadron 107 Ouragan pilot who flew his Mystère solo in 4525 circa December 1966. (PC)

A Squadron 107 Ouragan pilot who flew his Mystère solo in 4544 circa December 1966. (PC)

The 13 November [1966] Israeli raid on the Hebron district of Jordan has shattered the *modus vivendi* which had lasted for several years along the Israeli Jordan border. During this period, King Hussein had made a sustained effort to avoid provocations against Israel. This has involved such steps as preventing Arab saboteurs from crossing from Jordan into Israel and keeping his armored forces east of the Jordan River. These measures have been politically unpopular at home and have subjected him to criticism from other Arab states.

Hence, Hussein is particularly bitter at the size of the attack and the damage it caused... the recent raid involved an infantry brigade supported by armor, aircraft, and artillery... Jordan's army was clearly humiliated in the process.

The Israeli attack badly damaged Hussein's position at home. It made him vulnerable to attack by disaffected elements of his population who argue that his policy of peaceful coexistence with Israel has been dictated by the US and has proven a failure...

Hussein is aware that such feelings exist and will probably try to propitiate both military and civilian elements by stationing significant army units, including armor, on the West Bank of the Jordan River... Hussein probably feels he cannot for the present use his security forces to prevent Syrian trained saboteurs from operating through Jordan into Israel. The result will probably be an increase in sabotage incidents, which in turn may result in further major Israeli retaliations...

Squadron 109 was not involved in Operation GRINDER's air action; the same ILAF consideration of geographical proximity that resulted in Ramat David squadrons spearheading the 13 November 1964 and 14 July 1966 clashes with Syria resulted in Hatzor and Tel Nof squadrons supporting Operation GRINDER.

However, Operation GRINDER could have had an impact on future plans for Squadron 109, since the US explored the possibility of suspending A-4 Skyhawk deliveries to Israel and accelerating F-104 Starfighter deliveries to Jordan in order to deter Israel from launching additional reprisal operations against Jordan on the one hand and to stabilize the situation in Jordan on the other, as suggested in a 20 November 1966 telegram from the US President Special Assistant to the President:

> The Israeli Jordan border situation remains explosive. Last Sunday's raid weakened King Hussein's ability to control terrorists operating into Israel from Jordan because he no longer has full cooperation of the army, which Israel badly mauled. Another Israeli strike in retaliation for new incidents that could happen would force Hussein to counterattack.
>
> Our first job, therefore, is to keep Israel from attacking again. [State] Secretary Rusk recommends a tough message to [Israel Prime Minister and Minister of Defense] Eshkol saying we would have to reassess last year's decision to supply military equipment if Israel attacks again...
>
> Sunday's attack badly damaged our ability to go on stabilizing Israel's Jordanian border... The Israelis have gravely damaged the unspoken truce we have helped them build with Hussein, including possibly the agreement in return for our plane and tank sale not to station Jordanian armor on the West Bank of the Jordan near Israel. They have upset your delicate and successful balancing act in selling jets to Jordan to keep the Soviets out. He is now reported to be receiving Soviet equipment offers and is making requests to us for substantial additional equipment. The Israelis must be made to realize that if they retaliate again in response to anything short of a major attack, our ability to stabilize the area may be crippled.

Eventually, the US decided to accelerate F-104 Starfighter deliveries to Jordan, but not to suspend A-4 Skyhawk deliveries to Israel as explained in a 22 November 1966 telegram from the US Department of State:

> The idea of suspending or slowing down arms deliveries to Israel has much appeal... After careful consideration, we have concluded for a number of reasons that such actions, whether publicly announced or privately conveyed to one or both parties, would not be wise at this juncture and might in fact be counterproductive. Regardless of the general indignation concerning the nature of the Israeli raid, public announcement of suspension of deliveries could be interpreted as a slap at Israel... We also have in mind most recent reports indicating the Israeli forces used were on much smaller scale than originally reported and that no significant, if any, US equipment was employed... In addition, publicly announced suspension of arms to Israel could lead to demand for the same to be applied to Jordan, and perhaps to the whole area. At the very least, this could reopen previous public questioning of US sales to Israel, Jordan, and Saudi Arabia that could do considerable damage to our policy interests, both in the short and longer run. Finally, suspension of deliveries would face us with the problem of developing a convincing rationale for their ultimate resumption. Even if the suspension were kept private, the fact of the suspension would probably surface, and if terrorism and present tensions continue it would be difficult to justify resumption unless the Israelis had renounced retaliation (which we judge as most unlikely)... If it could be demonstrated that Israel had violated agreements with us by using our equipment for aggression there would be no questioning our reaction to suspend shipments. In present circumstances, we believe measures short of suspension, such as the deliberate slowdown of shipments, would risk strong reactions that could undercut Israel's tacit agreement for recent US tank and aircraft sales to Jordan. In sum, in present circumstances we believe the disadvantages outweigh the advantages of suspension of arms deliveries to Israel...

Therefore, Operation GRINDER did not have an impact on Squadron 109's reequipment time line, but many believe that Operation GRINDER was the starting point for subsequent deterioration and escalation that would result in a Middle East war by June 1967 which, in turn, would have an impact upon the reequipment schedule of Squadron 109.

SKYHAWK SHIPMENT GESTURE AND REQUEST

In line with the post-GRINDER environment, on 21 December 1966, the US and Jordan agreed to the loan—or more accurately the deployment—of six USAF owned and operated F-104 Starfighters from January or February 1967 to bridge the gap until planned start of JOAF F-104 Starfighter deliveries from July 1967.

In order to appease Israel about the premature appearance of F-104 Starfighters in Jordan, the US suggested to increase the number of A-4 Skyhawks in the first shipment to Israel—scheduled for delivery during December 1967—from four to six. Israel, however, would request increasing the initial A-4 Skyhawk shipment from four to eight aircraft.

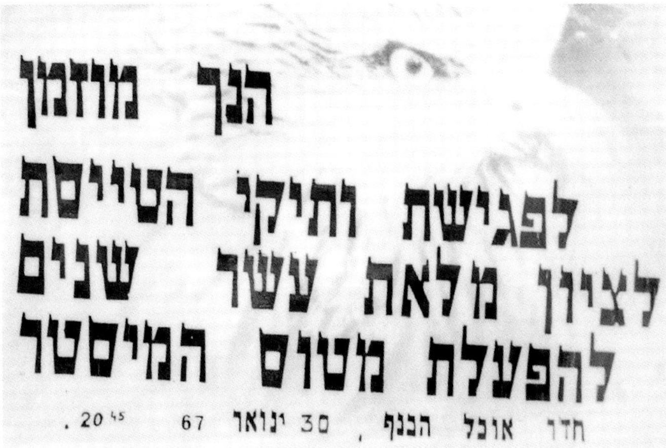

An invitation to Squadron 109 Mystère's tenth anniversary at Ramat David the evening of 30 January 1967. (PC)

MYSTÈRE 72

Squadron 109 practiced attack during the evening of 26 January 1967. After sunset on 26 January 1967, at 17:11, Aviem Sella flew Mystère 72 in 0:50 flight hour sorties and, upon return to Ramat David, the aircraft was subjected to turnaround for a follow up sortie that departed Ramat David around 21:00.

Aki Arzi flew Mystère 72 in the lead of a three-ship formation composed of an attacking pair—Arzi and Amos Zamir—and an illuminator flown by Uri Bina. The illuminator dropped flares while the attack pair flew bombing and strafing passes. It was during a strafing pass that Mystère 72 was suddenly engulfed in fire. When an aircraft was on fire, the standard drill was immediate ejection due to the danger of explosion, so Bina, Zamir, and the duty range officer Samuel Ringel all transmitted to Arzi to eject.

Arzi ejected and Mystère 72 crashed within the perimeter of the ILAF's new Hatzerim air base in the Negev Desert. The ejection was harsh; Arzi broke his left arm, but managed to walk and link up with the duty range team.

ILDF ARAB SOLIDARITY EVALUATION

In the wake of Mystère 72's accident, the ILAF's inventory was down to thirty-four Mystères—out of sixty-one delivered in 1956 and minus three returned to France and one nonstandard aircraft withdrawn from service for use as an instructional airframe—but this low number was no longer a cause for worry, since the ILAF expected to initiate introduction of forty-eight Ahits and fifty Raams within less than a year. Chief of Staff Isaac Rabin—in an ILDF General Staff meeting on 27 February 1967 in the presence of Prime Minister and Minister of Defense Levy Eshkol during which the ILDF's plan for Year 1967 was presented—referred to this point and to the general situation:

> ...we started this year with the opposite [enemy] side presenting us the following problems:
>
> (A) Arab solidarity...
> (B) Diversion [of water resources].
> (C) Clashes and sabotages along the borders.
>
> I think that during last year... the [Arab] solidarity... has been proven as not serious. I think... that Operation GRINDER surfaced this and proved it, and maybe even contributed to non-solidarity more than anything else. I do not think that this danger of Arab solidarity against Israel is the main issue that should draw our attention in the future.
>
> As for the diversion [of water resources]... I think that the 14 July [1966] air action completed prior action of armor and artillery to the point that diversion is no longer realistic...
>
> Concerning border clashes... There is no way to say that we came up with an appropriate answer...
>
> The problems that we face in the coming year... is not what the Arabs can do to us, but in what way can we exploit our power in the face of separatism in the Arab world...
>
> The problems the ILDF should be prepared for are:
>
> (A) Build up... In the air we will start to see the first of one hundred new aircraft...

However, it was indeed Arab solidarity—so dismissed in this 27 February 1967 discussion and evaluation—that within less than three months would initiate a dramatic deterioration that would challenge the ILDF Chief's dictum "what the Arabs can do to us" and would delay the ILAF's build up in general and Squadron 109's reequipment in particular.

ORDNANCE IMPROVEMENTS

Squadron 109 was slated for conversion to the Ahit. Preparations for transition to the Ahit were planned to start during ILAF Year 1967 Term 1, with setup team conversion in the US and to continue with the major milestone of initial deliveries towards the end of ILAF Year 1967 Term 2 or early in ILAF Year 1967 Term 3. All remaining Mystères were then planned to continue service with Squadron 116 at Tel Nof, since the second Ahit squadron was planned to be a new unit, rather than the conversion of an existing squadron, in order to accomplish both ILAF objectives: modernization and expansion.

Regardless, Squadron 109 did not stagnate with regard to developments and improvements. A lesson from the ILAF's November 1964, July 1966, and November 1966 involvement in border clashes was that for such short range missions, maximum offensive load was paramount. This lesson was implemented among the Mystère force from February 1967, when Squadron 116 was qualified to attack with the configuration of two 500 kilogram (1,100 lb) bombs on inner wing stations and two 250 kilogram (550 lb) bombs on outer wing stations, compared with maximum load thus far of four 250 kilogram (550 lb) bombs. Squadron 109 was also qualified for the same configuration around that

A visit to Ramat David on 19 March 1967 with Wing 1 Maintenance Squadron's Mystère Workshop in the background. (PC)

time, as Squadron 109 Commander Ohad Shadmi tested the new configuration in Mystère 44 on 23 January 1967.

Yet another Mystère ordnance innovation—an innovation that ripened after protracted development—was LBR and RPB, enabling the Mystère to lift four RPB units on two LBR units attached to outer wing stations. Squadron 116 was qualified with this combination during March 1967. Possibly, Squadron 116 was planned to be the only Mystère unit qualified with LBR and RPB due to plans to convert Squadron 109 from the Mystère to the Ahit within less than a year and, indeed, no Squadron 109 qualification flights of this combination have been unearthed thus far; yet, within months, Squadron 109 would fly missions with LBR and RPB.

NO NEW MYSTÈRE PILOTS FOR SQUADRON 109

Contrary to Mystère ordnance qualification policy, no new pilots were assigned to Squadron 109 for the Mystère conversion course; no Flying School Class 50 and Squadron 113 Ouragan OTU 30 graduates at the start of ILAF Year 1966 Term 3 and no Flying School Class 51 and Squadron 113 Ouragan OTU 31 graduates at the start of ILAF Year 1967 Term 1. Class 50 and 51 pilots slated to fly the Mystère were therefore assigned to Squadron 116 while Squadron 109 was preparing for the introduction of the Ahit.

Assigned to the squadron at the start of ILAF Year 1967 Term 1 as Squadron 109 Deputy B, Zvika Hess renewed his Mystère flights on 2 April 1967, after a break since 26 June 1964, when he last flew a Mystère as a Squadron 109 EP pilot due to assignment as a Squadron 119 Shahak regular pilot from 1964 until 1967.

COMBAT DAY ON FRIDAY THE SEVENTH

Friday, 7 April 1967, mirrored the action of Friday, 13 November 1964. A small scale clash escalated to the point that air strike readiness was authorized at 12:14 and attack aircraft were then scrambled. Squadron 109 launched four Mystères—Haggai Ronen, Nahum Merhavi, Zvika Hess, and Ilan Lior—that attacked with two 250 kilogram (550 lb) bombs per aircraft. The Squadron 109 Mystères operated over the southern sector of the Israeli-Syrian border and the attack was included in the first wave of ILAF strikes from 13:32 until close to 14:00.

A second Squadron 109 four-ship formation followed, but by the time it was in the air the ILAF was monitoring take-off of SYAF interceptors and all strike aircraft—including the second Squadron 109 formation—were called off and eventually ordered to return to base as ILAF Shahaks engaged SYAF MiG-21s in air combat over Syria.

The ILDF evaluated that the clash was over except for ongoing activity of ILAF and SYAF interceptors, but circa 14:45, Syrian artillery initiated a bombardment of Kibbutz Gadot, in the center sector of the Israeli-Syrian border. From 13 November 1964 until then, Syria mostly avoided artillery bombardment of Israeli settlements. Therefore, artillery bombardment of kibbutz Gadot triggered a second round of ILAF strikes this time against Syrian targets in the center sector from 13:25 until 16:16.

Squadron 109 again scrambled two four-ship formations, only this time both formations actually attacked.

The first second wave Squadron 109 formation—Ohad Shadmi in Mystère 11, David Lavi, Elisha Friedman (Perry) in Mystère 44, and Aviem Sella in Mystère 07—attacked artillery with

Aviem Sella flew Mystère 07 on 7 April 1967. (PC)

four Tadmor fused bombs per aircraft; the flight, from take-off to landing, lasted only fifteen minutes, thus demonstrating the close proximity of Ramat David to the Israeli-Syrian border.

The second, second-wave Squadron 109 formation was call sign ACID: Irik Bester, Giora Ben-Dov, Samuel Yadid, and Uri Keidar.

Again, SYAF interceptors appeared from 15:52, but this time ILAF strikes were not called off and the ILAF attacks continued until 16:16, while ILAF Shahaks engaged SYAF MiG-21s.

By the time action ended, the ILAF had launched 171 combat aircraft sorties versus thirty-four SYAF sorties. The ILAF attack sortie count was ninety-three, of which eighty-four actually attacked; seven were recalled without actually attacking. Squadron 109's share of the ILAF's total during the 7 April 1967 combat day was sixteen sorties (seventeen per cent), of which twelve sorties actually attacked and four sorties were recalled, returning to Ramat David without attacking.

FIGHTING WILL NOT BE RESUMED

Though 7 April 1967 was the largest scale Water War clash along the Israeli-Syrian border, Israel did not initially grasp the potential impacts of the clash, nor did the US, as explained in a 7 April 1967 State Department telegram:

> A major border clash centered in and around the Southern and Central Demilitarized Zones took place today. The trouble apparently began when an Israeli tractor plowing in the DZ near HaOn was fired upon by Syrians. The resulting battle lasted most of the day and involved mortar, artillery, and tank fire and several aerial dogfights.
>
> Israel claims to have downed seven Syrian MiG-21 aircraft without loss to its own air arm, and claims to have damaged several Syrian ground positions that had fired on Israeli cultivators and settlements.
>
> Syria also claims a victory, alleging that five Israeli aircraft were shot down and at least seventy Israelis killed in fighting that came about when Israel "insisted on aggression." Syria admits losing four MiGs and suffering five deaths.
>
> There are no reports yet from UN truce observers. We have no basis for assessing Israel's claim that the plowing that touched off the day's events was being done in a field that had been under regular cultivation by Israel for years. With both sides claiming victory, there is a fairly good chance that fighting will not be resumed tomorrow.

In line with his aforementioned 27 February 1967 analysis of the situation in the Middle East, ILDF Chief of Staff Isaac Rabin continued his line of thinking in an ILDF General Staff discussion of the situation on 26 April 1967:

> I evaluate that the Syrians were hit hard. I do not think this will collapse the Syrian regime... Essentially, our clash with the Syrian regime is, in my view, an all out clash... either this regime will change or be replaced... we have to be ready to change the [Syrian] regime policy or [to replace the Syrian] regime... As for [deployment to the Israeli-Syrian border of ILDF] forces... there are too many [ILDF] forces along the [border] line...

The ILDF Chief of Staff may have been out of line, since a decision to attempt to change or to replace another nation's regime was a matter of political policy and not a military issue, but the combination of the ILDF Chief of Staff's views and forecasts expressed on 27 February 1967 and 26 April 1967 were that due to shaky Arab solidarity, Syria's deployment was defensive and Israel would decide what would be the next phase in the conflict. This ILDF concept was proven absolutely unrealistic within less than a month.

SHAKY SOLIDARITY?

Tension along the Israeli-Syrian border remained high—an occasional exchange of fire along the Israeli-Syrian border continued, as well as PLO terror attacks along the Israeli Lebanese and Israeli Jordanian borders—but the ILDF did not view the situation as volatile. US analysis of the situation in the Middle East also seemed to rule out the potential for full scale war due to a weakness of Arab solidarity expressed in a 1 May 1967 memo from the US Under Secretary of State to the President:

> Israel has a safe margin of superiority over any combination of Arab forces likely to attack it and can be

> expected to maintain that position for at least the next five years. Arab numerical force superiority is more than matched by Israel's superiority in training, leadership, military doctrine, and maintenance of equipment. Moreover, the Arab states have made little progress in military coordination among themselves. Recent border clashes have demonstrated that short of general hostilities or Israeli occupation of Arab territory, the Arab states will not rush to one another's assistance. In practical terms, therefore, Israel's security must be measured by its ability to maintain military superiority over the UAR, the strongest single Arab state that can challenge Israel.

The Israeli concept and the US view seemed to have been confirmed on 2 May 1967, when Egyptian President Gamal Abed El Nasser admitted Egypt was willing to commit combat aircraft to assist in the defense of Syria, but this was not possible without basing Egyptian combat aircraft in Syria. According to contemporary reports, Syria rejected the Egyptian offer and this state of affairs again affirmed the ILDF concept that Arab solidarity was shaky and that Egypt would not stand by Syria in case another major clash erupted along the Israeli-Syrian border.

On 4 May 1967, while addressing the Israeli public prior to Israel Independence Day, ILDF General Staff Branch Chief Ezer Weizman revealed the ILAF would introduce the Ahit during the coming year and expressed the ILDF's evaluation that no major war between Israel and an Arab nation was expected during the following year, though more border clashes with Syria seemed a likely possibility.

A series of small scale terrorist attacks against Israeli infrastructure, traffic, and settlements started on 5 May 1967, and Israel held Syria responsible for these attacks. On 9 May 1967, Israeli Foreign Minister Abba Eben warned Syria that Israel would not tolerate terror attacks without reaction. An Israeli reprisal operation against Syria seemed inevitable. On 10 May 1967, Israel stressed to UNTSO that Israel viewed Syria as responsible for terror attacks in northern Israel's in a message that was addressed to Syria. The following day, Israeli Prime Minister and Minister of Defense Levy Eshkol stated that Israel may be forced to react against terrorists and against those who encourage terror attacks against Israel. Syria responded to the warning with a statement that Israel was planning an attack against Syria.

The war of words started to get out of control. On 13 May 1967, in an interview prior to Israel Independence Day, Israeli Prime Minister and Minister of Defense Levy Eshkol stated that Israel would react against terrorist attacks and against terrorists host nations, that Israel would thwart any plan to divert River Jordan water resources, and that Israel would defend its freedom of navigation in the Red Sea (the title of the interview in the Israeli newspaper *Davar* was "Eshkol Warns The Syrians"), so Syria again responded with claims that Israel was planning a large scale attack, that the Israeli warning was part of a collusion to overthrow the Syrian regime (as though Syria was aware of the ILDF Chief of Staff's opinion expressed on 26 April 1967), and that the Egyptian Syrian mutual defense treaty signed on 4 November 1966 would be implemented if Israel attacked Syria.

Possibly in an attempt to assess the status of Israeli preparedness for attack, a Syrian reconnaissance mission was flown over Israel along the Israeli-Syrian border on 14 May 1967.

Regardless of the evolving crisis, Israel was resolved to stage an Independence Day military march in Jerusalem on 15 May 1967. The Independence Day military march had been an Israeli show of force since 1949. The only drawback from the Israeli perspective was the inability to stage a full scale military show of force in Jerusalem, as the city had been divided between Israel and Jordan since 1948 and demilitarized since 1949. Ignoring Jordanian protests and UN condemnations, Israel staged Independence Day military marches in Jerusalem during 1950, 1951, 1958, and 1961.

Apparently, in response to the war of words and possibly as a result of the Syrian reconnaissance flight over Israel on 14 May 1967, the Egyptian army started to roll forward into Sinai, in the direction of the Egyptian-Israeli border. Was it merely coincidence that Israeli Prime Minister and Minister of Defense Levy Eshkol was notified that the Egyptian armed forces were marching across the Suez Canal into the Sinai Peninsula while he was standing on the guests of honor stage and reviewing the march of ILDF troops in Jerusalem on 15 May 1967?

NO REASON TO WORRY

The ILDF's concept that Arab solidarity was shaky was shattered during Israel Independence Day 19 on 15 May 1967. The ILDF's evaluation that war against an Arab nation was not expected during the time from Israel Independence Day 19 until Israel Independence Day 20 was being tested and would be proven wrong, yet at this early phase of the crisis, both Israel and the US evaluated—or hoped—that the situation would not get out of control and that there would be no deterioration towards war, as indicated on the evening of 15 May 1967 in a telegram from the US Embassy in Israel to the US Department of State:

> Bitan [from the Israeli Foreign Office] advises [US Assistant Secretary of State for Near Eastern and South Asian Affairs] Battle saw [Israeli Ambassador to the US] Harman this morning and expressed concern over reports of Egyptian troop concentration in the Canal area that blocked normal traffic and interpreted this development as an Egyptian demonstration of solidarity with the Syrians, who are apprehensive about possible Israeli intentions.
>
> Bitan said that following talks with [Israeli Prime Minister and Minister of Defense] Eshkol and [Israeli Foreign Minister] Eben, he authorized to give the following GOI reaction this representation:
>
> A. There is no Israeli troop concentration on the Syrian, Egyptian, or other frontier. (This corresponds with US Attaché's reconnaissance to this hour.)

B. GOI hopes infiltration and sabotage will stop.

C. If there is no further sabotage there is no reason for anyone to worry.

D. GOI interpretation of Egyptian demonstration of troop activities is that the Syrians are trying to involve Egypt in the Syrian Israeli issue, and if the Egyptian concentration is true then the Syrians could represent this as support.

GOI has no objection foregoing being transmitted to Cairo.

The situation with Syria is obviously precarious and, if additional serious sabotage incidents such as attacks on settlements, main roads, etc., continue it is impossible to predict GOI will sit idly by without reacting. However, I believe GOI is aware of risk escalation, disposed making minimum effective response, and exercises what to them would seem maximum patience. I doubt that they will be very impressed in any event with Nasser's foot shuffling one way or the other.

DEPARTURE FOR THE AHIT CONVERSION COURSE IN THE US

In line with initial Israeli evaluations that the evolving crisis was containable, previous plans for departure of ILAF pilots for the Ahit conversion course to the US were adhered to.

Squadron 109 Commander Ohad Shadmi and Squadron 109 Deputy A Haggai Ronen—along with former Squadron 110 Vautour commander Yossi Sarig and Squadron 105 SMB2 pilot Nissim Ashkenazi, who were assigned to command and deputize, respectively, a new Ahit squadron to be activated at Hatzor—departed Israel for the US A-4 Skyhawk conversion course one day after Israel Independence Day on 17 May 1967.

Squadron 109 Squadron Commander Ohad Shadmi was expected to stay in the US for several months, so Uri Even-Nir was assigned as Squadron 109 Acting Commander, but his assignment was short lived—very short lived.

RETURN FROM THE AHIT CONVERSION COURSE IN THE US

Israel viewed the public deployment of Egyptian forces in Sinai as a dramatic act aimed to deter Israel from attacking Syria. As already indicated, ILDF aspirations were indeed to change or replace the Syrian regime, but since the Israeli government had no immediate intentions to attack Syria, the crisis initially looked like an ostentatious Egyptian show of force primarily aimed at the Arab world in order to revive Arab solidarity, which the ILDF evaluated only weeks before as practically nonexistent and in the wake of Arab world criticism of Egypt, which did not stand by Jordan during Operation GRINDER in November 1966 and did not stand by Syria on 7 April 1967.

The next milestone in the crisis was on 17 May 1967, when it was made public that Egypt demanded the withdrawal of UNEF from observation posts in Sinai. The situation no longer looked like an empty act of Arab solidarity in a war of words between Israel and Syria, but a real danger, as UNEF started to withdraw from Sinai on 19 May 1967.

The Ahit conversion course team only visited the A-4 Skyhawk's manufacturing facility in California prior to recall to Israel; Squadron 109 Commander Ohad Shadmi is second from the left with Yossi Sarig fourth from the left. (PC)

Squadron 109 Commander Ohad Shadmi in dress uniform for deployment to the Ahit conversion course in the US with his ILAF wings, Suez War ribbon, and Squadron 109's symbol. Prior to departure to the US in May 1967, Shadmi last flew a Mystère (4507) on 11 April 1967 and last flew in Israel—from Ramat David to Dov Field and back—on 16 May 1967 in Piper 03 with Haggai Ronen. (PC)

Meanwhile, the ILAF suspended training from 18 May 1967; EP pilots reported to their squadrons and reserve pilots were then called for active duty, so by 19 May 1967, the ILAF was fully ready.

The Ahit conversion team pilots were recalled while visiting Douglas in California. They returned to Israel on 23 May 1967.

EGYPT WELCOMES WAR

In an attempt to cool down the region, Israeli Prime Minister and Minister of Defense Levy Eshkol stated on 22 May 1967:

> From this stand I would like to repeat and say to Arab nations, including Egypt and Syria, that we are not heading for attack. We have no interest in interfering with their security, territory, or legitimate rights. We will not interfere in their internal affairs, in their regimes, or in their regional and international relationships. We claim, in line with principle of mutuality, to apply the same principles towards us.
>
> During the first days of Egyptian armed forces deployment in Sinai, there were nations that viewed this deployment as a demonstrative action without military implications. Others can accept such interpretations, but since this deployment is close to our border, it is our opinion that we must take all precautionary steps against any possible development. Due to Egyptian deployment along the border and the withdrawal of UNEF, I ordered a limited mobilization of reserve forces that has already been completed.
>
> After completion of limited mobilization of reserves, I visited the ILDF. The magnificent quality of our armed forces that have been fostered and perfected over many years has reached a high standard. The ILDF can now face any test with the same devotion and talent that it has demonstrated in the past and even more.
>
> To end with, I call the regional nations to mutual respect of sovereignty, entirety, and international rights of every nation. Israel—fully confident in its power and spirit—is expressing its willingness to take part in an effort to bring quiet and peace to our region.

The Egyptian president's fiery response to the reasoned speech of Israeli Prime Minister and Minister of Defense came on 23 May 1967—the same day the Ahit conversion pilots returned to Israel—when Gamal Abed El Nasser announced the closure of the Strait of Tiran to Israeli shipping. The implications of this escalating act were explained in a US State Department telegram on 23 May 1967 to the US Embassy in the USSR:

> Within the past few hours, the situation in the Middle East has seriously worsened. Nasser has announced that the Gulf of Aqaba will be closed to Israeli flagships, and while we have Israel's commitment to consult with us before attempting to run the blockade, we cannot hope to restrain Israeli action much beyond the next twenty-four hours. Obviously, Nasser must be restrained from further hostile action if we are to avoid a serious flare up. We are concerned lest the Soviets may not be fully aware of Nasser's recent moves and the dangers they hold for peace in the area. Accordingly, we believe it would be useful for you to see [USSR Foreign Minister] Gromyko soonest to express our grave concern over the deterioration of the situation, cataloging for his information the following recent moves giving rise to this concern:
>
> 1. The Egyptians have mounted a massive military buildup in Sinai, despite the fact the Israelis at that time had taken no action on their side of the frontier that would justify this move.
>
> 2. This buildup has increased Egyptian military strength in the area from a normal level of 30,000 to 50,000.
>
> 3. The Egyptians have demanded withdrawal of UNEF and the Secretary General of the United Nations has complied.
>
> 4. The Egyptians have moved naval units south into the Red Sea toward the entrance to the Gulf of Aqaba.
>
> 5. Nasser has just announced the Gulf would be closed to Israeli flagships, adding that if "Israelis want war, we welcome it."

While the USSR's interpretation of the Middle East escalation from a war of words to preparations for war was different than that of the US, it seems the USSR was also against war in the Middle East, as expressed in a 23 May 1967 reply telegram from the US Embassy in the USSR to the US Department of State:

> I saw [USSR Foreign Minister] Gromyko... he said the Soviet Union considers war in this area is not needed by anyone. It would cause damage to the countries in that area and increase tensions in the world as a whole. This is not needed by the United States nor any other country. The Soviet Union's position was in accordance with its general political line, which was that peace should reign in that part of the world. All powers, and particularly the big ones, should prevent the development of a situation leading toward war. The Soviet Union has reached the conclusion that the reason for the current tensions was the policy of Israel, and certain circles or groups in Israel that had determined this policy... I said I thought it would be pointless at this time for us to argue the general question of Israeli Arab relations... I thought the important thing was to address ourselves to the immediate problem that was made particularly acute by the Egyptian action with respect to shipping in the Gulf of Aqaba. I pointed out that Nasser's actions had been taken after the statement of the Israeli government that it could not tolerate a blockade of the Gulf and a few hours after the statement of the US government that it considered these to be international waters.

Regardless of US best efforts to restore order in the Middle East, the USSR seemed indifferent, so it was a good time for the US to assess the military situation in the Middle East in a 23 May 1967 Central Intelligence Agency memo entitled "Overall Arab and Israeli Military Capabilities":

> The judgment of the intelligence community is that Israeli ground forces "can maintain internal security, defend successfully against simultaneous Arab attacks on all fronts, launch limited attacks simultaneously on all fronts, or hold on any three fronts while mounting successfully a major offensive on the fourth." In the air, the judgment is less clear: the Israelis "probably could defeat the Egyptian air force if Israel's air facilities were not damaged beyond repair."
>
> Those judgments rest essentially on the proposition that the quality of Israel's military leadership, its ability to organize operations and maintain its equipment in a high state of readiness, and the high morale and intelligence of the individual Israeli ground soldier will make up for Israel's quantitative inferiority in men and equipment. The Israelis have consistently stressed intensive training, with emphasis on armor, standardization of weapons, rapid and reliable communications, and a very strong tactical intelligence effort. Egyptian capabilities in these areas appear to be inferior.
>
> Moreover, in the air, the Israelis have been acutely conscious of the difficulty of defending their air facilities, and have made strenuous efforts to overcome the fact that their bases are a very short warning time from the Arab borders. They have "hardened" their fields with dispersed pens, for example. Israeli pilots and tactics are considered superior and, in terms of operationally assigned fighter aircraft rather than total inventory, Israel has a slight edge: 256 to 222.
>
> Israeli planning is based on a short war conducted by ground forces with air cover. If this assumption should prove wrong, Israel might well be in trouble, since the Arabs' quantitative superiority would come into play. At M+48 hours, for example, Israel would have 280,000 men vs. the Arabs' 117,000 deployed in the vicinity of the Israeli borders. But the total strength of the Arab armies is nearly 500,000, vs. the same 280,000 on the Israeli side.
>
> This is not to say that the rout of the Egyptians in 1956 will be repeated. The Egyptian forces have improved substantially in the past eleven years, and they have acquired considerable operational knowhow by rotating combat units in Yemen. Nevertheless, we consider that the Israeli forces have retained an overall superiority

The US assessment of the diplomatic and military situation in the Middle East was very realistic, but at this point in the crisis, it looked like the USSR was going to cooperate with the US in an effort to calm down the Middle East, while the principle provocative figure of escalation was Egypt President Gamal Abed El Nasser, who—when announcing the closure of the Strait of Tiran to Israeli shipping during a visit to an EGAF air base—claimed that he ordered the deployment of Egyptian forces to Sinai in light of information that Israel was amassing "thirteen brigades" along the Israeli-Syrian border, called former Israel Prime Minister David Ben-Gurion "a dog of imperialism," stated that the "[coming] war will be an opportunity for Israel to realize that whatever is written about [Israel] occupation of Sinai in 1956 was fabricated stories and nonsense" and, adding insult to injury, the Egyptian President—laughing and mocking with Egyptian fighter pilots—made an immortal statement: "they threaten war and we tell them 'Ahalan VaSahalan' (welcome)." The die had been cast.

CHAPTER 6

SIX DAY WAR

JUNE 1967

The ILAF suspended training on 17 May 1967 and was ready for war in line with Israel's defense doctrine as coined by former Prime Minister and Minister of Defense David Ben-Gurion, which emphasized:

- A brief conflict due to Israel's limited resources.
- Fighting on enemy soil due to Israel's lack of territorial depth.
- A decisive victory in order to deter enemies.

Israel's chosen course of action to accomplish this doctrine was an ILDF preemptive strike, with the ILAF spearheading the preemptive strike with an air superiority offensive.

PLAN FOCUS

The objective of the ILAF's AIR3 Plan FOCUS was to accomplish air superiority. FOCUS covered four scenarios: FOCUS A against Egypt; FOCUS B against Syria; FOCUS C against Egypt and Syria or Egypt, Syria, and Jordan; and FOCUS C, plus Iraq and Lebanon. The mission's definition was "neutralization of enemy air force through damage to runways and destruction of a maximum number of aircraft on the ground."

Navigational aids in ILAF combat aircraft were limited to a compass, map, and watch, so the professionalism and skills of formation leaders were crucial to securing the success of FOCUS. Surprise was critical; routes to targets were to be flown at extremely low altitude in order to escape enemy radar detection, but no altitudes were specified—the pilots were to fly the lowest they dared.

Returning formations were to disengage at low altitude. A climb to economical cruise altitude was recommended once safe separation from the enemy air defense threat was accomplished. Formations flying into SA-2 defended zones were to climb only

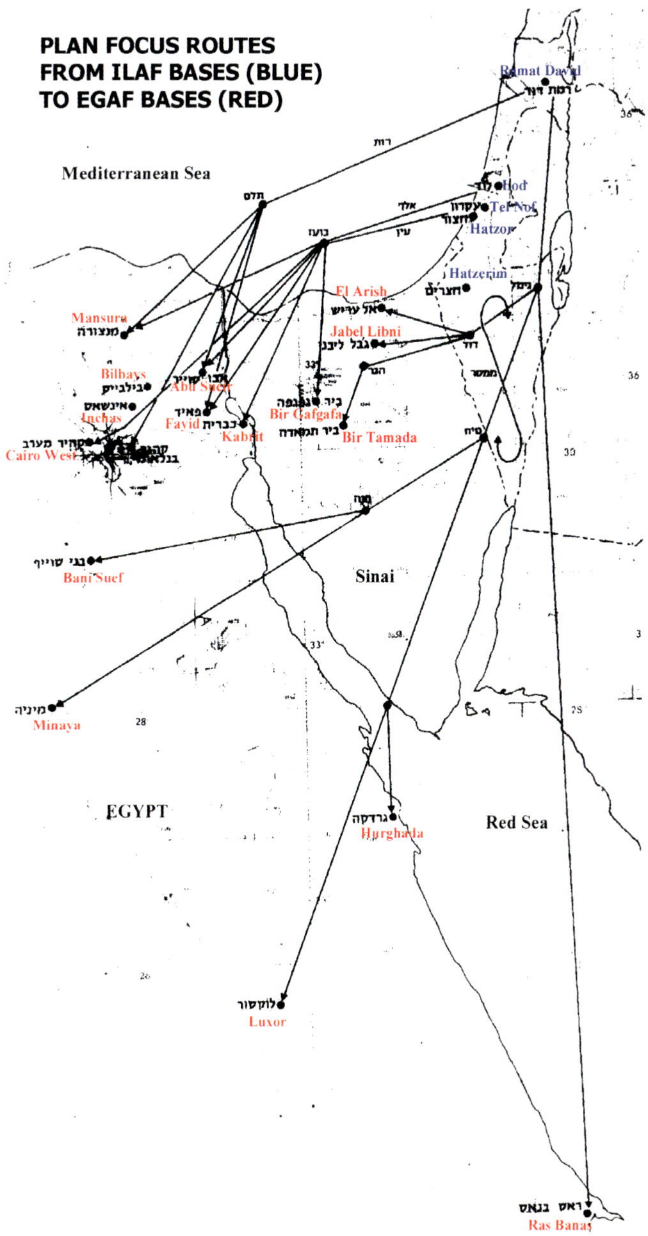

FOCUS first wave routes, including Squadron 109's routes from Ramat David to Bir Gafgafa, Bir Tamada, and Kabrit. (PC)

after flying out of the engagement envelope of the missiles. To aid planning, intelligence prepared a map of known SA-2 battery locations and an engagement envelope circle drawn around every battery. Substantial overlapping between SA-2 battery engagement circles resulted in the coverage of the entire Suez Canal Zone and Nile Delta, though obviously this was based on optimum high altitude, maximum range performance of the SA-2 batteries. Actual coverage was much more limited, especially against low flying aircraft.

A time of up to fifteen minutes per attack was assigned to each four-ship formation. During this period, the Mystères were to bomb and strafe. The bombing run was flown in line astern, with the second pair bombing immediately after the first pair. Since approach was at low altitude, the aircraft were to pull up to a minimum altitude that would guarantee a safe thirty-five degree dive bombing angle. For the strafing passes, the four-ship formation was to split into two pairs that would attack from a different direction each time. When a pair strafed, the air base was divided into two sectors, with the leader attacking targets in the left half of the air base and the wingman strafing targets in the right half of the air base. Strafing passes were also to be flown at low altitude; AIR3's recommendation was lower than 1,500 feet above ground level over targets defended by radar guided AAA. Formation leaders were to aspire to fly four strafing passes, depending on their real time evaluation of local AAA fire and their fuel state. The only preplanned constraint was that a formation would finish its attack within fifteen minutes before the next formation appeared over the target.

The Mystères were to bomb with 250 kilogram (550 lb) bombs or RPBs:

- The 250 kilogram (550 lb) bombs were equipped with two types of detonators: an impact fuse inside the bomb's nose cone and a "7-15" short delay fuse inside the bomb's tail. Long delay fused bombs—set to explode an hour or more after the bombing in order to disrupt enemy battle damage repair efforts—were also included. Detonators were also tailored for specific targets. A few enemy air bases had concrete runways, so formations assigned to attack these air bases were equipped with a 0.1 second delay fuse inside the bomb's nose cone. Runways prepared for heavy bomber operations were hardened, so aircraft planned to attack these air bases had their bombs equipped with a hardened penetration nose cone and only a "7-15" delay fuse in the bomb's tail section. The delivery profile for 250 kilogram (550 lb) bombs was a pop up and dive.
- The RPB was dropped in a high speed dash along the runway at low altitude. Immediately after release, a parachute was deployed in order to create separation between the RPB and the aircraft, and to point the RPB downward; when the RPB was pointed downward a rocket ignited to accelerate the RPB in the direction of the runway's surface to enhance penetration and ultimately create a deeper crater that would be more challenging for enemy battle damage repair teams.

Only the first wave of FOCUS was preplanned in detail; tentatively, the second wave plan was to mirror the first wave. Obviously, AIR3 was to utilize BDA data to plan the second wave, but if no new AIR3 orders were issued then a formation that returned from a first wave air base attack mission would fly a replay of the mission to the same target along the same route during the second wave.

FOCUS A

Egypt was Israel's principle enemy during the 1960s, and EGAF was the most powerful air arm facing Israel. The EGAF was numerically larger than the ILAF; in March 1967, AIR4 evaluated the EGAF fielded sixteen squadrons of frontline combat aircraft versus the ILAF's nine. Since the standard ILAF squadron included more aircraft than the standard EGAF squadron, and since ILAF serviceability was higher than the EGAF's, the actual gap between EGAF and ILAF fighter elements was smaller.

An Egyptian advantage was the sheer size of the Nile nation. The EGAF had many more air bases than the ILAF and some were beyond the low altitude mission profile scope of ILAF combat aircraft.

The first known FOCUS A task assignment program, prepared on 10 April 1967, included four Squadron 109 missions:

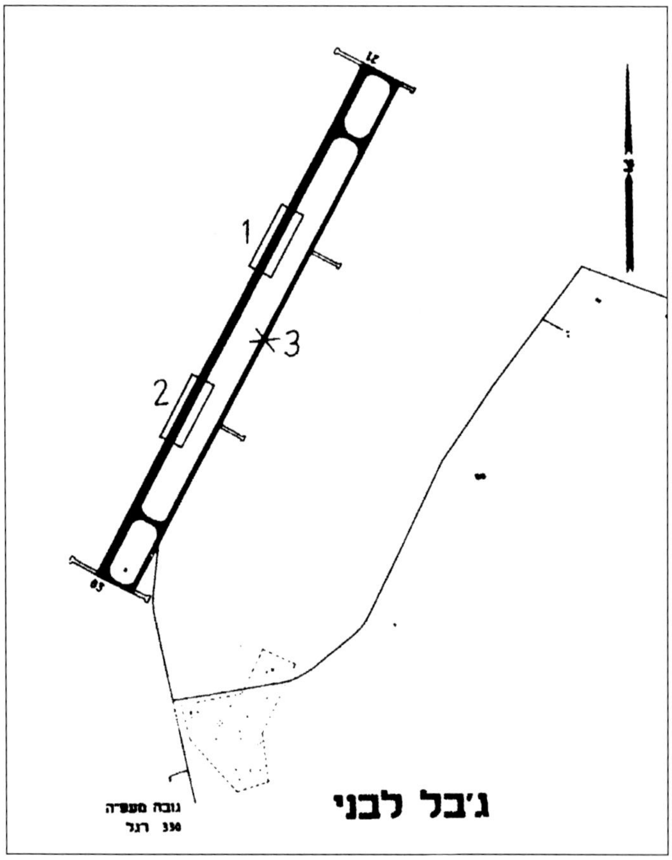

AIR3's OPOR FOCUS scheme of EGAF base Jabel Libni in Sinai, which was Squadron 109 FOCUS A's primary target; the primary aiming points were marked rectangularly, while secondary aiming points were marked with an X. (PC)

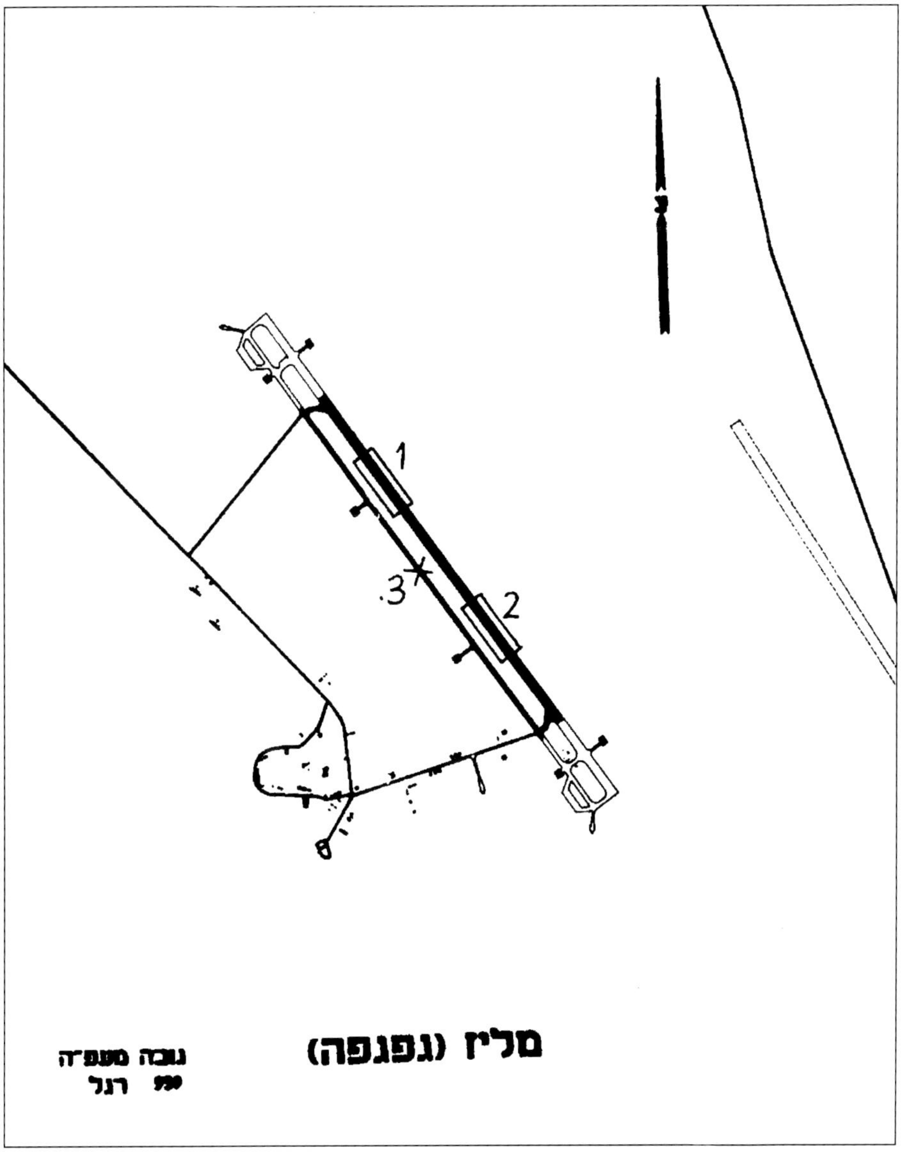

AIR3's OPOR FOCUS scheme of EGAF base Bir Gafgafa in Sinai, which was Squadron 109 FOCUS A's secondary target. (PC)

MIOR 109/1, tasked to bomb Jabel Libni air base aiming points 1 and 2 at H Hour with two 250 kilogram (550 lb) bombs per aircraft and then strafe resident aircraft.

MIOR 109/2, tasked to bomb Jabel Libni air base aiming points 1 and 2 at H+15 with six RPBs per aircraft and then strafe resident aircraft.

MIOR 109/3, tasked to bomb Bir Gafgafa air base aiming points 1 and 2 at H+15 with six RPBs per aircraft and then strafe resident aircraft.

MIOR 109/4, tasked to bomb Jabel Libni air base aiming points 1 and 2 at H+45 with two 250 kilogram (550 lb) bombs per aircraft and then strafe resident aircraft.

FOCUS B

Syria was Israel's most active and aggressive enemy during the first half of the 1960s. The SYAF was smaller than the ILAF and generally treated as no match. The March 1967 AIR4 evaluation referred to only four Syrian frontline squadrons against nine ILAF fighter squadrons.

In FOCUS A, the AIR3 planners had to spread the attack against thirteen Egyptian air bases, but in FOCUS B, the attack was concentrated against only five Syrian air bases. Because of this excess power issue, only FOCUS B included attacks against air defense targets and a massive air-to-air element including offensive combat air patrols over Syrian air bases. More formations were available per air base and a tighter schedule was set accordingly. If

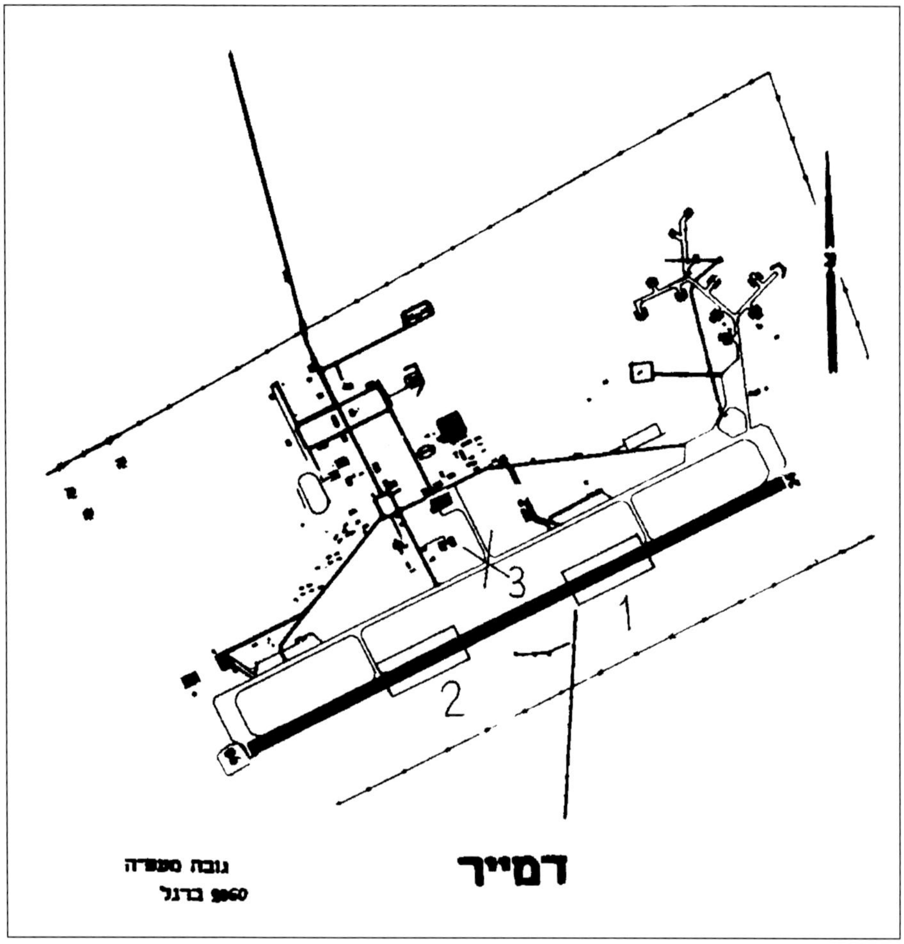

AIR3's OPOR FOCUS scheme of SYAF base Dumayr, northeast of Damascus, which was Squadron 109 FOCUS B's primary target. (PC)

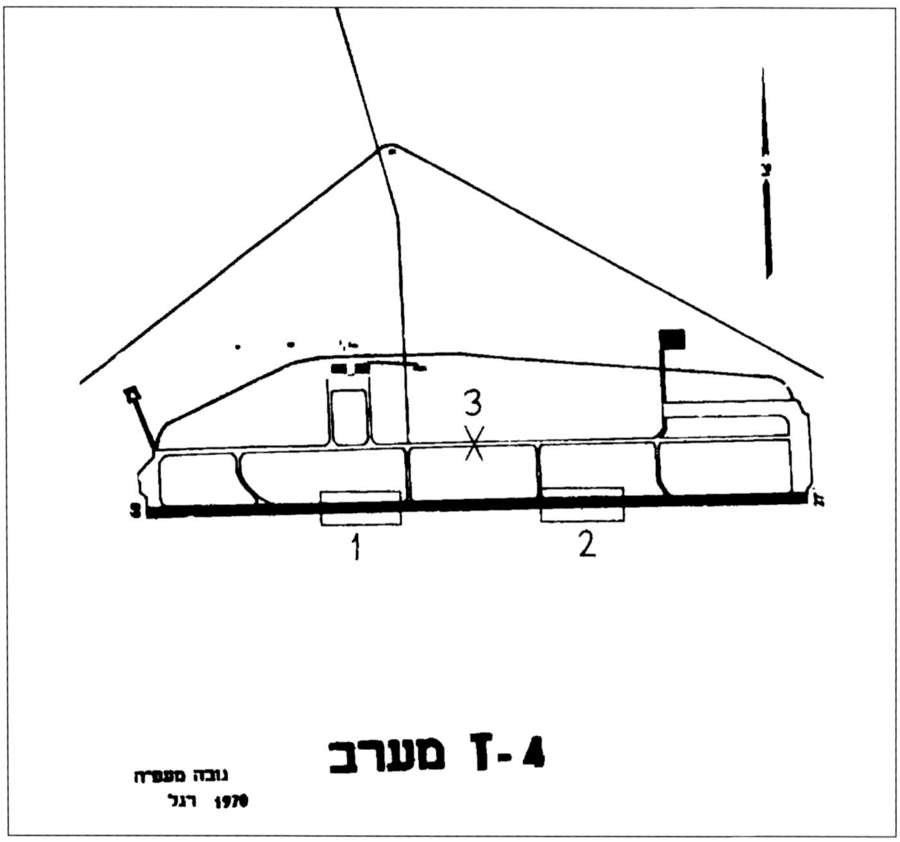

AIR3's OPOR FOCUS scheme of SYAF base T-4 east of Homs, which was Squadron 109 FOCUS B's secondary target. (PC)

four formations were planned to attack the EGAF's Cairo West air base during the first wave of FOCUS A, then no less than nine and up to eleven formations were planned to raid the SYAF's Mazzeh air base during the first wave of FOCUS B.

Squadron 109 was assigned with four FOCUS B attack missions:

MIOR 109/1, tasked to bomb Dumayr air base aiming points 1 and 2 at H+26 with six RPBs per aircraft and then strafe resident aircraft.
MIOR 109/2, tasked to bomb Dumayr air base aiming points 1 and 2 at H+36 with six RPBs per aircraft and then strafe resident aircraft.
MIOR 109/3, tasked to bomb T-4 air base aiming points 1 and 2 at H+16 with two 250 kilogram (550 lb) bombs per aircraft and then strafe resident aircraft.
MIOR 109/4, tasked to bomb T-4 air base aiming points 1 and 2 at H+26 with two 250 kilogram (550 lb) bombs per aircraft and then strafe resident aircraft.

FOCUS C

Israel's nightmare was war against an Arab coalition. Poor tiny Israel facing alone the mighty rich Arab world was an almost Armageddon scenario in the eyes of Israeli leadership of the 1950s and 1960s. When Israel's first Prime Minister and Minister of Defense David Ben-Gurion coined the Israeli defense strategy, he referred to a David versus Goliath scenario. The three simple elements of Ben-Gurion's brilliant defense concept were brief conflicts to be fought on enemy soil with swift operational decision.

The logic was that Israel's modest economy and small population could not sustain a lengthy war; Israeli territory had no "strategic depth" to withstand fighting on its own soil; and overwhelming and swift operational decisions were essential to deter Israel's enemies from pursuing another war in the future.

FOCUS C was AIR3's answer to a coalition that was to include the four nations sharing a border with Israel (Egypt, Jordan, Lebanon, and Syria), plus Iraq. From an air power perspective, Egypt was the main enemy. Jordanian and Lebanese air power was negligible, and Iraqi air power was relatively substantial but too far away to matter. Syrian air power was a quarter of the EGAF's strength and more tactically oriented than the EGAF, which fielded a substantial bomber force. AIR3 decided to ignore Lebanese and Iraqi air bases; FOCUS C targets were thirteen air bases in Egypt, three in Syria, and two in Jordan.

Squadron 109 missions in FOCUS C were a mix of FOCUS A and FOCUS B missions:

MIOR 109/1, tasked to bomb SYAF Dumayr air base aiming points 1 and 2 at H Hour with two 250 kilogram (550 lb) bombs per aircraft and then strafe resident aircraft.
MIOR 109/2, tasked to bomb SYAF Dumayr air base aiming points 1 and 2 at H+15 with two RPBs per aircraft and then strafe resident aircraft.
MIOR 109/3, tasked to bomb EGAF Bir Gafgafa air base aiming points 1 and 2 at H+15 with two 250 kilogram (550 lb) bombs per aircraft and then strafe resident aircraft.
MIOR 109/4, tasked to bomb SYAF Dumayr air base aiming points 1 and 2 at H+30 with two RPBs per aircraft and then strafe resident aircraft.

FOCUS UPDATE ON 23 MAY 1967

In light of the evolving crisis, the ILAF updated FOCUS A task assignments on 23 May 1967. The updated task assignment program covered a single wave over a time frame of eighty-five minutes from H Hour to H+85. The number of Egyptian air bases to be attacked was narrowed down to eight, with each repeatedly raided by four to seven formations, so the initial blow would be more focused and more concentrated: forty-two formations attacking eight air bases over eighty-five minutes compared to thirty-eight formations raiding twelve or thirteen air bases over ninety minutes.

The impact on Squadron 109 of the 23 May 1967 update of FOCUS A was minor; Squadron 109 was still tasked to launch four formations to raid two EGAF bases in Sinai, with the only change in the schedule of the attacks.

Jabel Libni was still Squadron 109's primary target, with MIOR 109/1 attacking from H Hour, MIOR 109/2 attacking from H+10, and MIOR 109/4 attacking from H+40; a total of four formations were tasked to raid Jabel Libni, including the three Squadron 109 formations and Squadron 113 Ouragan MIOR 113/6, which was tasked to attack Jabel Libni from H+25.

MIOR 109/3 was tasked to raid Bir Gafgafa from H+10 as the second formation out of five formations tasked to attack Bir Gafgafa during the first wave of FOCUS A.

CLEARLY NASSER HAS WON THE FIRST ROUND

The ILAF was thus ready to attack: aircraft were armed and pilots were briefed. The puzzling figure in the crisis was Egyptian President Gamal Abed El Nasser, who initiated the crisis on 14 to 15 May 1967, who escalated the crisis on 23 May 1967, and who was not willing to back off from the Israeli border and lift the Red Sea maritime blockade. A 26 May 1967 Central Intelligence Agency memo summed up the crisis until then:

> The first thing that calls for explanation in the present crisis is why Nasser chose at this moment to abandon his long standing reluctance to risk military confrontation with Israel.
>
> At the immediate moment, Nasser was probably prompted to initiate these maneuvers by Israeli threats against Syria. He probably felt he had to identify himself with Arab nationalist interests and that some action on his part would refurbish his image in the Arab world. These views, however, are probably insufficient to explain all the events that have occurred.
>
> He had probably decided (though he stated the contrary not long ago) that his armed forces were improved to the point where they could successfully stand off an Israeli offensive, even though they might be unable to defeat Israel decisively. Accordingly, he may

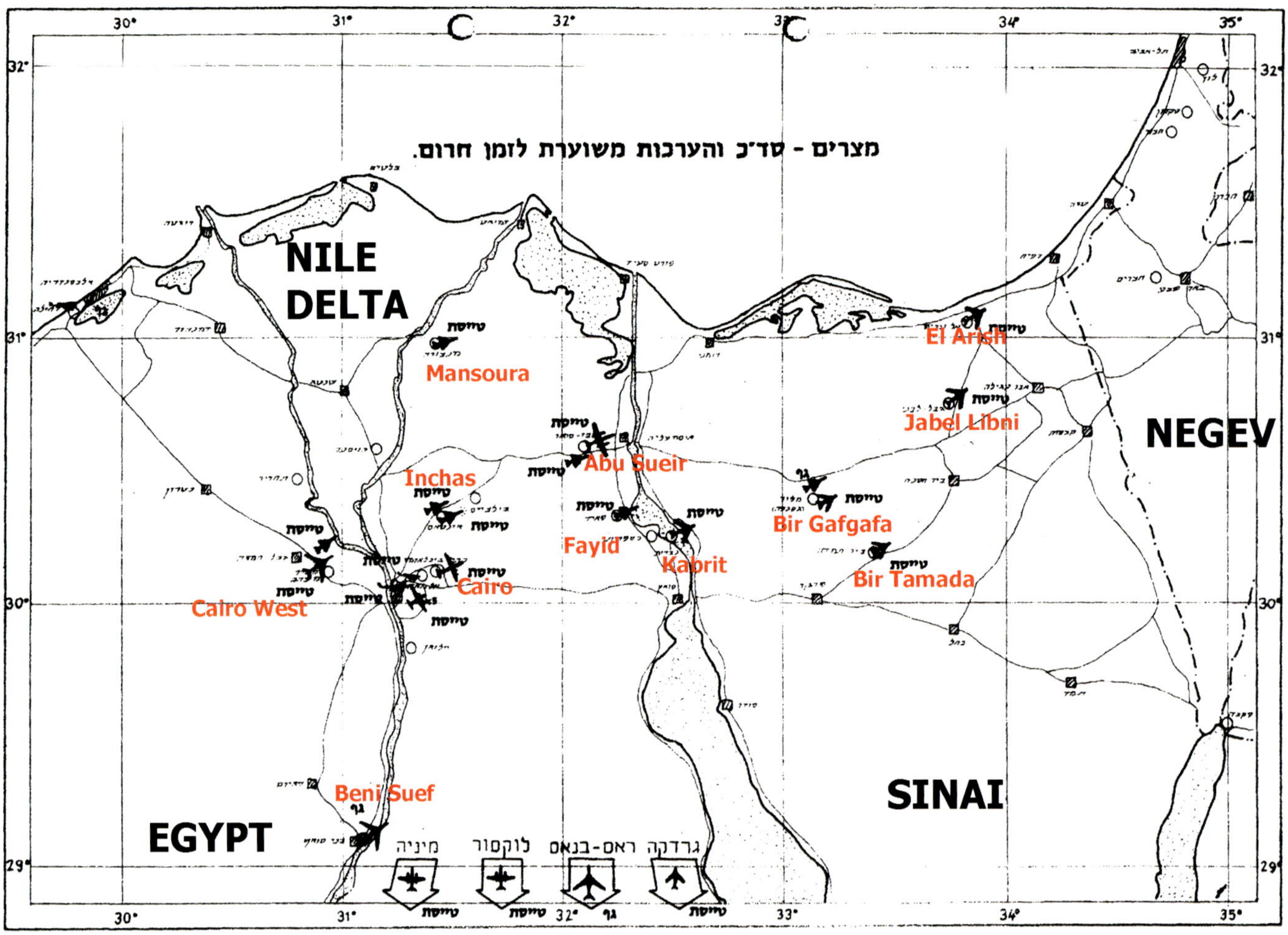

AIR3's OPOR FOCUS scheme of EGAF deployment; due to the Mystère's short range, Squadron 109 FOCUS targets were in Sinai, while the SMB2, Vautour, and Shahak were tasked to raid more distant targets in the Suez Canal Zone, River Nile Delta, and Upper Egypt. (PC)

have felt that if he could get his army properly deployed in the Sinai Peninsula and elsewhere, the chances of war would be acceptable.

It is possible the Soviets encouraged him in these views. We do not believe the whole operation is a Soviet plan, or even that the Soviets urged him to his present course of action, but their attitude must have been sufficiently permissive so that he knew he could count on political and logistic support from them in the course of the crisis. The interests of the Soviet Union itself would obviously be served by successes for Nasser at the expense of Israel and the US.

The US preoccupation with Vietnam and the bad blood occasioned thereby between the US and the USSR probably had some important influence on the nature of Nasser's decision, as well as its timing.

There may have been some element of desperation in Nasser's attitude arising from the parlous condition of the Egyptian economy, the worsening of relations with the US, a belief that some sort of US Israeli plot against him existed, and perhaps a fatalistic conclusion that a showdown with Israel must come sooner or later, and might best be provoked before Israel acquired nuclear weapons.

He may also have concluded, from a tactical point of view, that he could gamble on US influence and perhaps some Israeli indecisiveness to prevent an Israeli offensive at the early and most vulnerable stages of his deployments.

The movement of UAR troops seems to have gone smoothly and expertly. Yet there must have been in this, as in other crises, a large element of accident in the actual course of events. For example, Nasser probably did not

The Mystère's most common weapon was a 250 kilogram (550 lb) bomb, but Squadron 109's ordnance inventory also included napalm, rockets, rounds, and RPBs. (PC)

expect such a speedy departure of UN forces from Sharm El Sheikh, giving him opportunity for a quick seizure of the position and an announced closing of the Strait. He has thus far managed the crisis, from his point of view, with great skill and success.

Clearly Nasser has won the first round. It is possible that he may seek a military show down with Israel, designed to settle the whole problem once and for all. This seems to us highly unlikely. We still do not believe that Nasser considers his forces (together with those of other Arab states) capable of carrying such a campaign to a successful conclusion. And in our opinion they are not so capable. Moreover, we believe the Soviets would almost certainly advise Nasser against a military effort of this magnitude, perhaps with strong insistence.

The most likely course seems to be for Nasser to hold to his present winnings as long as he can, and in as full measure as he can. As of the moment he has vastly enhanced his own prestige in Egypt and throughout the Arab world, diminished the standing of Israel and, at least for the moment, administered a serious setback to the US. Moreover, by simply standing where he is he places the Israelis in an extremely difficult position. He keeps the crisis at high pitch, and as long as this continues the Israelis must remain mobilized. This they cannot do for long without adverse effects upon their economy.

The Israelis face dismaying choices. Surprised and shaken by Nasser's action, they failed to take the instant military counteraction which might have been most effective. If they attack now, they will face far more formidable opposition than in the rapid campaign of 1956. We believe they would still be able to drive the Egyptians away from the entrance to the Strait of Tiran, but it would certainly cost them heavy losses of men and materiel. We are not sure they have sufficient stockpiles of ammunition and equipment for a war lasting more than three or four weeks, and it is possible that they would not embark upon a major campaign without prior assurances from the US of adequate resupply. But the alternative for the Israelis is perilous. To acquiesce in the permanent closing of the Strait of Tiran would constitute an economic and political setback from which no early recovery would be foreseeable. The Israelis would expect—correctly we believe—that the Arabs over the long run would be encouraged to undertake new and still more dangerous harassments. We are inclined to believe that unless the US and other major powers take whatever steps are necessary to reopen the Strait, the Israelis will feel compelled to go to war.

In this event, they might choose to begin hostilities by attacking Syria and wait for the Egyptians to respond. If the Egyptians did not, Nasser would lose much of what he has gained. If they did, they would lose the advantage of their defensive positions.

The Soviets are unlikely to take vigorous steps to calm down the crisis so long as it continues to produce deleterious effects upon Israel (and the US) and advantages for Nasser. Nevertheless, they may be apprehensive about the future course of events. They may not have known in advance about the closing of the Strait. We do not believe they desire a Middle Eastern war or that they have planned with Nasser the destruction of Israel at this juncture. They will probably oppose by diplomatic and propagandistic means any efforts by the US and the Western Powers to open the Strait. But if we assume an attempt by the Western Powers to open the Strait by military force, we do not think the Soviets would use their own armed forces in opposition.

One almost certain objective of the Soviets is to see the US more firmly and publicly identified with Israel. This would have the obvious effect of making the entire Arab world—including in an ambivalent way even the more conservative states—convinced that the US is irrevocably committed to their common enemy. It would further weaken the US position in the area, threaten US oil interests, and strengthen the Soviet position as friend and protector of all Arabs against their imperialist foes. This Soviet aim has already been realized to a considerable degree. Moreover, the Soviets must be glad to see US attention diverted from Vietnam, but it does not seem likely that they think the Middle Eastern crisis will appreciably affect US military capabilities or intentions in Southeast Asia.

One important question is what the Soviets would do if the Israelis attacked the UAR and waged a successful campaign. Such an event would be a grave setback for Nasser and, by extension, for the USSR itself. Nevertheless, we do not believe the Soviets would intervene in the conflict with their own combat forces. They could, of course, use their bomber and missile forces against Israel, but they would be very unlikely to do so, though they might threaten it. They do not have the capability of introducing lesser kinds of forces (ground troops or volunteers) in this area with sufficient speed to be decisive, and we do not think they would try to do so. They would be cautious about the risk of armed confrontation with US forces. And they would probably count upon the political intervention of great powers, including themselves, to stop the fighting before Nasser had suffered too much damage.

The position of other Arab countries than the UAR is, at this stage of crisis, ancillary and comparatively unimportant. Conceivably, Syria might touch off larger hostilities by attacking Israel in force, but we believe both Nasser and the USSR would be opposed to such action. If war broke out Syrian forces would engage and other Arab states would send help, but it would not matter very much. The crisis in its present acute intensity is essentially one between Israel and the UAR, the US and the UAR, and (to a more moderate degree) between the US and the USSR. The course of events will depend upon the action and reactions of these powers.

ISRAEL WILL NOT DARE STEP OVER THE LINE

While the US was attempting to calm down the situation, the USSR seemed determined to heat up the situation. When the USSR Premier finally replied to the US President on 27 May 1967, the content did not refer to the two major issues—the Egyptian deployment of forces along the Egyptian-Israeli border and the Egyptian blockade of Red Sea shipping from and to Israel —but actually hinted the USSR would stand by Egypt and Syria in case of war:

> According to information being received by the Soviet government, the State of Israel is actively engaged in military preparations and evidently intends to carry out armed aggression against neighboring Arab states. Under conditions of extreme tension at the borders of Israel with the UAR and Syria, Israeli militant circles are attempting to impose upon their government, their country, and their people an "adventurist" action for the purpose of resolving all problems by military means. There is a danger that these circles may cause an armed conflict which would be fraught with important consequences for the cause of peace and international security.
>
> We understand that in the situation now taking shape much depends upon the United States and upon you personally, Mr. President, as to whether Israel will undertake such a reckless act. In this respect,

there cannot be any other view. If there will be no encouragement on the part of the US, then Israel will not dare step over the line.

In your letter of May 22, you called upon us to exercise our influence along with yours in the direction of restraint. We are for restraint. We are convinced that no matter how complex the situation in the area along the borders of Israel, Syria, and the United Arab Republic may be, measures must be found to prevent this conflict from becoming a military one. The situation is such that, in our opinion, this can be done. A new hotbed of war must not be permitted to develop in the world.

That's why we are in favor of a restraining influence, but, of course, not to the detriment of the lawful interests of the Arab states. Their actions are of a defensive nature. Moreover, it is precisely restraint that they are exercising and, as we know, they do not want a military conflict.

Of course, if the "adventurist" line should prevail and if arms should be used, this could be the beginning of far reaching events. Should Israel commit aggression and military operations begin, then we will render aid to those countries that are subjected to aggression.

Neither we, nor you, nor the Arab countries, nor the people of Israel are interested in a conflict. We appeal to you to take all necessary measures to prevent an armed conflict. We, for our part, will also undertake measures in that direction.

The USSR message was empty words, practically encouraging Egypt to pursue a hard line; perhaps a USSR intelligence evaluation concerning the Middle East military balance was different than US intelligence evaluation that clearly expected an Israeli victory.

ILAF READY FOR WAR

Possibly encouraged by USSR backup, the Egyptian president pursued hard line policy and tightened the ring around Israel on 30 May 1967, when Egypt and Jordan signed a mutual defense treaty. Jordanian armed forces were placed under Egyptian command and Egyptian commandos—presumably tasked to raid ILAF bases—deployed to Jordan; the Jordanian radar station at Aj'lun—which could potentially track every single aircraft taking off from ILAF bases—was linked to the Egyptian command and control system. Instead of calming down the situation, Egypt heated up the conflict that was no longer Israel against Egypt and Syria, but was escalated into Israel versus Egypt, Jordan, and Syria.

Throughout this tense time, the ILAF was on readiness to face an Arab offensive or to activate Plan FOCUS as the first phase of an Israeli preemptive strike. ILAF deployment was as follows:

Base	Wing	Squadron	Type
Ramat David	1	109	Mystère
Ramat David	1	110	Vautour
Ramat David	1	117	Shahak
Hatzor	4	101	Shahak
Hatzor	4	105	SMB2
Hatzor	4	113	Ouragan
Hatzerim	6	123	light helicopters
Hatzerim	6	147	Fouga
Tel Nof	-	103	medium transport
Tel Nof	-	116	Mystère
Tel Nof	-	119	Shahak
Tel Nof	-	124	medium helicopters
Dov Field	-	100	light transport
Lod	-	107	Ouragan
Lod	-	120	heavy transport

Only a minimum number of training flights were flown in order to preserve pilot combat qualifications, train ILAF AAA battalions defending ILAF bases, and maintain aircraft serviceability, while at the same time minimizing impact on the ILAF's readiness. Squadron 109 EP pilot Aviem Sella flew only four training sorties from 18 to 31 May 1967: three daytime SEAB practice missions against Ramat David, St Jean, and Megiddo, and one nighttime SEAB practice mission against Ramat David. Squadron 109 reserve pilot Asaf Ben-Nun flew six training sorties from 19 to 31 May 1967: four daytime SEAB practice missions against Ramat David, St Jean, and Megiddo, one nighttime SEAB practice mission against Ramat David, and one daytime live bombing practice.

HOW LONG A WAR WOULD LAST

A stalemate played into Arab hands because of the negative impact of the ILDF's mobilization of reserves on the Israeli economy. A new Israeli government entered office on 1 June 1967, with Moshe Dayan taking over from Prime Minister Levy Eshkol as Defense Minister. The new harder line government was a signal to the world that Israel would not tolerate the situation for much longer.

Also on 1 June 1967, the ILDF Intelligence Chief met the US Secretary of Defense. The ILDF Intelligence Chief described the military situation in the Middle East and the impact of the ILDF's mobilization on the Israeli economy, and summed up with his personal opinion that Israel should take action because there was no other way out. The US Secretary of Defense then asked only two questions: how long would a war last and how many casualties would Israel sustain?

The ILDF Intelligence Chief's answers—"seven days" and "less than in 1948"—probably satisfied his hosts to the point that the US Central Intelligence Agency Deputy Director summarized his notes with the following sentence:

Squadron 109 Commander Ohad Shadmi flew only one flight in a Mystère from 15 to 31 May 1967: SEAB practice in 4571 on 28 May 1967. (PC)

Arab solidarity, overconfidence, and arrogance as illustrated in a caricature published in a Lebanese newspaper on 31 May 1967: Egyptian, Iraqi, Jordanian, and Syrian armor are pointing guns at terrified, hapless, tiny Israel. (PC)

> I urged him to get a night's sleep and go back to Israel as soon as possible because he would be needed more there than here.

ISRAELI DECISION TO ATTACK

The US Central Intelligence Agency described the deadlock on 3 June 1967:

> Reporting during the past few days has focused on two primary aspects of the Near East crisis. One is the rapidly growing belief in Israel that time is running out, and that if Israel is not to suffer an ultimately fatal defeat it must very soon either strike or obtain absolutely ironclad security assurances from the West. The second aspect is the rise of a euphoric, bandwagon spirit among the Arab states, leading even moderate Arabs to believe that the time may in fact have come when the Arabs can close in on Israel with some hope of success.

That same day, Israel concluded from the US President's letter to the Israeli Prime Minister that diplomatic efforts—to force Egypt to withdraw its forces from the Egyptian-Israeli border and to lift the Red Sea blockade—had practically failed. Of special significance was the following paragraph:

> On the matter of liaison and communication, I believe our relations can be improved. We have completely and fully exchanged views with [ILDF Intelligence Chief] General Amit.

Arab solidarity's—a coalition of eight nations (Algeria, Egypt, Iraq, Jordan, Lebanon, Saudi Arabia, Sudan, and Syria) in this caricature that was published in a Lebanese newspaper on 31 May 1967—alleged ambition was to eliminate Israel, an alleged ambition that Israel had to treat seriously. (PC)

This paragraph could have been interpreted as US agreement with Israel's analysis of the situation and, in a way, as a hidden green light to an Israeli preemptive strike; the following day, the Israeli government decided to attack Egypt; D Day was 5 June 1967 and Operation FOCUS H Hour was 07:45.

SQUADRON 109 ON THE EVE OF THE SIX DAY WAR

Due to initiate conversion to the Ahit during ILAF Year 1967 Term 3, Squadron 109 had been operating the Mystère since December 1956, so service persons—in the air and on the ground —depended upon cumulative experience and traditions that had accumulated over more than a decade. The Mystère—with limited endurance, moderate performance, and a light load—was certainly an aging combat aircraft due for replacement, but it was still a valuable element in the ILAF's ORBAT.

On the eve of war, Squadron 109's inventory included sixteen Mystères, and all were planned to take part in FOCUS A's first wave, so expected serviceability was one hundred per cent.

Squadron 109's cadre of pilots included Commander Ohad Shadmi, Deputy A Haggai Ronen, Deputy B Zvika Hess, three regular pilots, ten EP pilots, seven reserve pilots, and one pilot on temporary assignment from Squadron 110 Vautour for a total of twenty-four ready for action. Additionally, Aki Arzi, who was grounded due to injuries sustained during his ejection from a Mystère in January 1967, was among the small group of senior pilots—"squadron executives" in ILAF slang—who rotated the task of duty officer in charge, or "fighting executive" in ILAF slang.

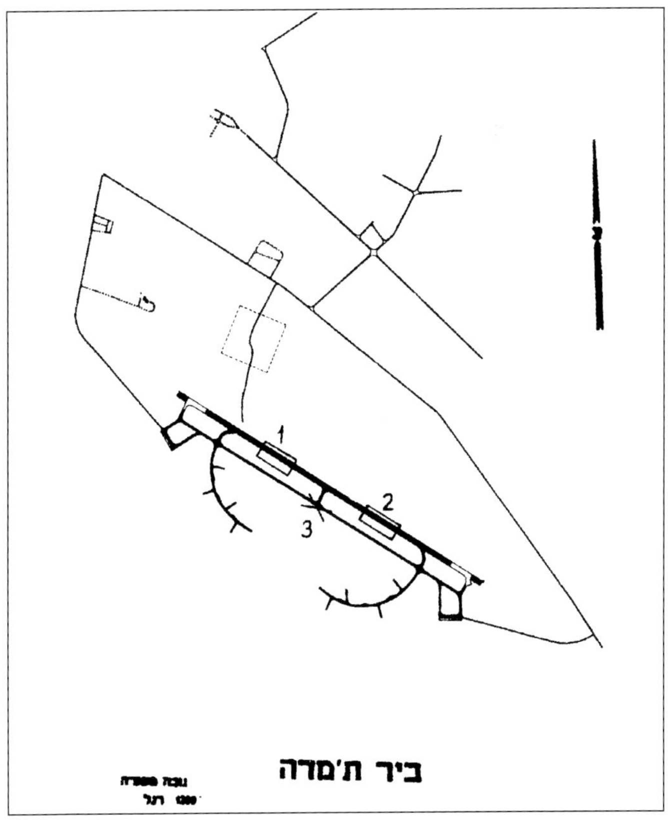

AIR3's OPOR FOCUS scheme of EGAF base Bir Tamada in Sinai; as with Bir Gafgafa and Jabel Libni, the aiming points at Bir Tamada were: principle aiming points 1 and 2 along the runway, plus secondary aiming point 3 midway along the parallel taxiway. (PC)

NO JABEL LIBNI FOR SQUADRON 109

Squadron 109's FOCUS A primary target was Jabel Libni, an EGAF forward base in Sinai, as three out of four Squadron 109 formations were tasked to raid Jabel Libni. However, in the final prewar FOCUS task assignment program prepared on 4 June 1967, Jabel Libni was deleted from the list of targets and the three

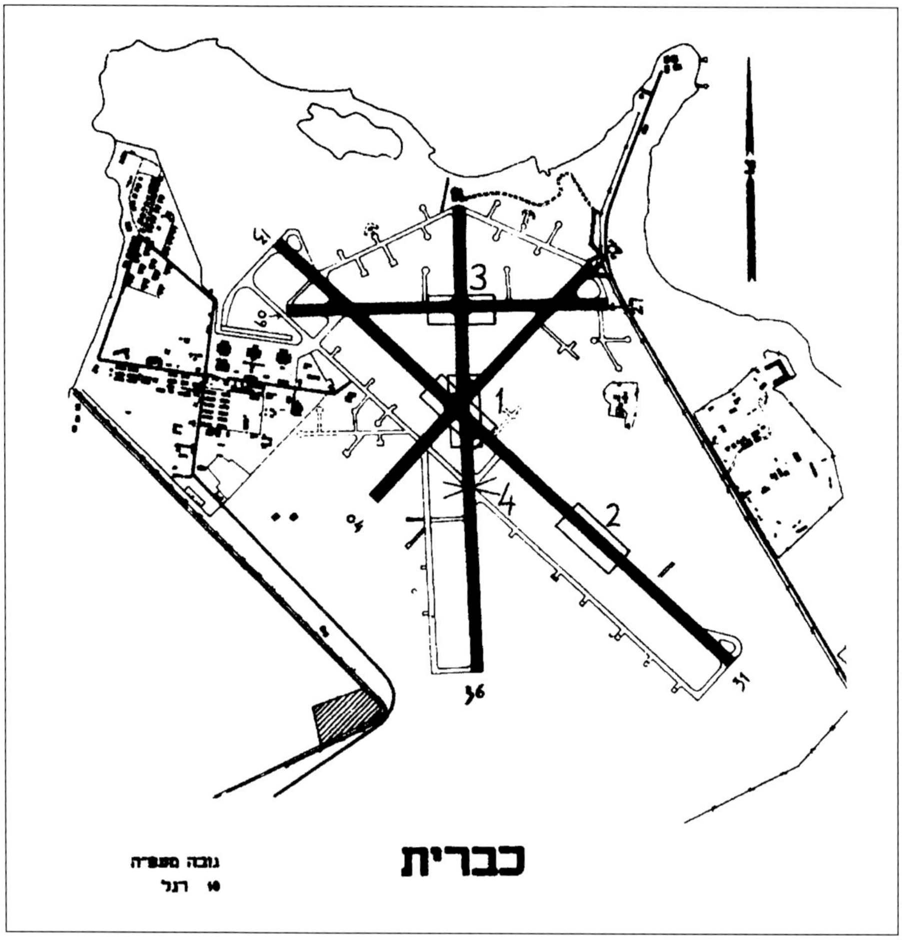

AIR3's OPOR FOCUS scheme of EGAF base Kabrit in the Suez Canal Zone; four runways were supposedly an insurance against an enemy attack, but Kabrit's runways were more suited to face changing wind conditions than to safeguard the air base's survival in the event of an attack. Three of the runways (04/22, 13/31, and 18/36) intersected with each other at a single point that obviously became aiming point 1; the intersection of runways 09/27 and 18/36 was aiming point 3, while aiming point 2 was halfway along runway 13/31 between aiming point 1 and the runway's southern threshold; and the sole secondary aiming point was at the intersection of runway 18/36 and the taxiway parallel to runway 13/31. A peculiar Kabrit feature was concrete runways. The ILAF aircraft tasked to attack Kabrit had nose section impact detonators replaced by a 0.1 second fused detonator. (PC)

Squadron 109 formations previously tasked to attack Jabel Libni were retasked:

> MIOR 109/1 to attack Kabrit from 08:25
> MIOR 109/2 to raid Kabrit from 08:40
> MIOR 109/4 to strike Bir Tamada from 08:00

While MIOR 109/3 was tasked to attack Bir Gafgafa from 08:10.

The final prewar ILAF FOCUS briefing took place inside the ILAF Commander's office the evening of 4 June 1967; in attendance were base commanders, wing commanders, and squadron commanders. ILAF Commander Moti Hod opened with a typically short, sharp sentence, "tomorrow we will wage war!"

AIR4 presented EGAF deployment and AIR3 detailed the final FOCUS task assignment program—that was not typed but handwritten to narrow down the circle of those informed.

Several issues were briefly emphasized, the foremost being surprise; radio silence, the complicated radio silence take-off drill, and low flying were also mentioned. AIR3 Chief Rafi Harlev recalled:

> Present commanders asked "how shall we brief crews under our command to react in the face of a technical malfunction during flight to the target?" and the answer was that a pilot facing malfunction should do whatever necessary—eject, turn back, or anything else—but under two conditions: do not climb and do not report. Radio silence and low altitude flying were paramount to accomplish surprise. Everything was plain and simple, everything was crystal clear.'

DAY 1 MIOR 109/4
SEAB BIR TAMADA TOT 08:00

COTTON 1 Shadmi in Mystère 06, take-off at 07:23, landing at 08:30
COTTON 2 Milo in Mystère 07, take-off at 07:23, landing at 08:30
COTTON 3 Bester in Mystère 14, take-off at 07:23, landing at 08:34
COTTON 4 Yariv in Mystère 82, take-off at 07:23, landing at 08:34

Bir Tamada was the southernmost of the three EGAF first line bases in Sinai, along with El Arish in the north and Jabel Libni to the south of El Arish. Behind this first line was Bir Gafgafa, the principle EGAF foothold in Sinai. Though geographically the southernmost of the four EGAF bases in Sinai, Bir Tamada was actually in central Sinai, to the southeast of Bir Gafgafa and west of a point roughly midway along the Egyptian-Israeli border.

Bir Tamada's layout was generally similar to Bir Gafgafa and Jabel Libni, with a single runway and a parallel taxiway. The air

Bir Tamada under ILAF attack during FOCUS wave 1 with one Il-14 already burning and one Il-14 not yet on fire. (PC)

Squadron 109 COTTON reported that all aircraft at Bir Tamada had been destroyed by the end of COTTON's attack, including these two Il-14 airlifters and one Mi-6 helicopter. (PC)

base installations at Bir Tamada were much more extensive than at Jabel Libni and somewhat less comprehensive than at Bir Gafgafa. The surrounding AAA was not as strong as at El Arish or Bir Gafgafa, but still had to be treated seriously, with three batteries dispersed along a line roughly parallel to the runway to the northwest. These included—from northeast to southwest —a battery of four 57 millimeter cannon, a battery of six 14.5 millimeter guns, and again a battery of four 57 millimeter cannon. Analysis of EGAF documents that Israel captured in Sinai revealed that EGAF Air Brigade 2 Squadron 25 MiG-17s were the aircraft deployed to Air Base 260 Bir Tamada during May 1967.

Five formations were tasked to raid Bir Tamada during FOCUS A's first wave the morning of 5 June 1967: a Squadron 101 Shahak formation from 07:45, a Squadron 107 Ouragan formation from 07:50, Squadron 109 MIOR 109/4, a Squadron 113 Ouragan formation from 08:10, and a Squadron 107 Ouragan formation from 08:25.

MIOR 109/4 was tasked to bomb aiming points 1 and 2 with two 250 kilogram (550 lb) bombs per Mystère. AAA was already active when COTTON bombed. While bombing, the COTTON pilots counted circa ten burning aircraft and noted that only two Il-14s, a MiG-17, and a helicopter were still intact; all of these four seemingly intact aircraft were claimed destroyed during subsequent COTTON strafing passes, so by the time COTTON finished the attack, all EGAF aircraft at Bir Tamada were reported destroyed.

DAY 1 MIOR 109/3
SEAB BIR GAFGAFA TOT 08:10

CONCRETE 1 Ronen in Mystère 10
CONCRETE 2 Sella in Mystère 11
CONCRETE 3 Gadish in Mystère 26
CONCRETE 4 Hochman in Mystère 09

EGAF Air Base 244 (Bir Gafgafa) was a classic "second line" base located at the rear of "first line" bases Bir Tamada, El Arish, and Jabel Libni. While the three "first line" air bases were the stepping stones of the MiG-17 attack force, a MiG-21 air-to-air unit was stationed at Bir Gafgafa to defend Sinai and the MiG-17s.

Roughly 100 kilometers (sixty-two miles) from the Suez Canal to the west and some 200 kilometers (124 miles) from the Egyptian-Israeli border to the east, Air Base 244 was ideally

CONCRETE strafing Mi-6 helicopters at Bir Gafgafa. (PC)

The ILAF's BDA team—left to right AIR2 Weapon Systems Section Chief Josef Afik, MAT5 Armament Section Chief Joe Ertz, MAT3 Attack Section Chief Yossi Sarig, and AIR3 Defense Section Chief Michael Haber—examine RPB impact at Bir Gafgafa. Squadron 109 CONCRETE was the only first wave formation to attack Bir Gafgafa with RPB. (PC)

placed to support EGAF operations in Sinai. Bir Gafgafa's layout was generally similar to Bir Tamada and Jabel Libni, with a single runway and a parallel taxiway, though air base installations at Air Base 244 were more extensive. In March 1967, AIR4 evaluated that massive AAA defended Bir Gafgafa: sixteen 14.5 millimeter machine guns northwest, twenty-four 37 millimeter cannon in four groups of six to the west, and twenty-one 57 millimeter cannon in four locations around the air base. The final prewar AIR4 report of EGAF deployment listed fourteen MiG-21s based at Bir Gafgafa.

Five formations were tasked to raid Bir Gafgafa during FOCUS A's first wave the morning of 5 June 1967: a Squadron 113 Ouragan formation from 07:45, a Squadron 113 Ouragan formation from 07:55, Squadron 109 MIOR 109/3, a Squadron 113 Ouragan formation from 08:25, and a Squadron 113 Ouragan formation from 08:40.

CONCRETE departed Ramat David at 07:34 and was tasked to bomb aiming points 1 and 2 with RPBs. The RPB pattern was more vulnerable to AAA and AAA fire damaged CONCRETE 2 and CONCRETE 3, but both pilots pressed ahead with the attack.

CONCRETE 4's RPBs hung up—a not uncommon occurrence at the time when the weapon was still new—but a few bombs more or less hardly mattered, since FOCUS was planned with wide margins of redundancy.

CONCRETE then flew two strafing passes. Ronen claimed two Mi-6s destroyed in a single pass. Sella targeted four MiG-21s seemingly on QRA, one of which was already burning.

On the way back to Ramat David, Ronen ordered CONCRETE 2 and 4 to jettison all external loads so that CONCRETE 4 could get rid of the hung up RPBs and CONCRETE 2 would be able to make it to Ramat David. The two wingmen landed first and then Ronen escorted Gadish to land Mystère 26 without a functioning airspeed indicator due to damage to the pitot tube; all four landed by 08:40.

Mystère 26's pitot tube was torn away and the air intake, leading edge of the right wing, and the elevator were all damaged, but the Mystère was flying again the night of 5 to 6 June 1967.

Mystère 11 returned with two large holes in the left wing that had to be replaced so it was grounded until 8 June 1967.

DAY 1 MIOR 109/1
SEAB KABRIT TOT 08:25

SULPHUR 1 Hess in Mystère 83
SULPHUR 2 Keidar in Mystère 32
SULPHUR 3 Dagan in Mystère 34
SULPHUR 4 Bina in Mystère 71

EGAF Air Base 228 (Kabrit), on the eastern coast of Lake Bitter, was the southernmost of the three Suez Canal Zone air bases attacked during the first wave of FOCUS. According to Egyptian fighter pilot Tahir Zaki—who claimed to have served as Kabrit Air Base Commander from early 1967 until April 1967 —two MiG-17 squadrons were based at Kabrit, while sixteen highly realistic MiG-17 dummies were dispersed along runway 13/31 and the parallel taxiway; an inventory that corresponds well with AIR4's evaluation that twenty-two MiG-17s and twenty-nine MiG-15s were present at Kabrit the morning of 5 June 1967.

A MiG-17 in between buildings at Kabrit during Squadron 109's attack on 5 June 1967 with Lake Bitter in the background. (PC)

Five formations were tasked to raid Kabrit during FOCUS A's first wave: three Squadron 105 SMB2 formations from 07:45 and two Squadron 109 Mystère formations from 08:25.

Squadron 109 was unable to fly a low altitude mission from Ramat David to Kabrit, so eight Mystères were deployed to Tel Nof on 4 June 1967. They flew in singles at low altitude in an attempt to conceal the telltale deployment from lurking Arab radar stations. All five formations were planned to fly along route AYN from Hatzor and Tel Nof to point BOAZ over the Mediterranean Sea, to the north of Bardavil, from where a straight line course to Kabrit was flown.

MIOR 109/1 was tasked to bomb aiming points 1 and 2 along runway 13/31. SULPHUR—which departed Tel Nof at 07:54—was the final first wave formation to bomb Kabrit at points 1 and 2. To complicate the enemy's battle damage repair effort and to bridge the gap until resumption of the attack during the expected second wave, the Mystères utilized delay fused bombs. Zvika Hess recalled:

> Two four-ship formations—half of our squadron—deployed from Ramat David to Tel Nof. We sneaked in singles to Tel Nof the previous afternoon and mingled with our Mystère sister squadron at Tel Nof. They took care of our aircraft and I attended the evening air base level briefing, where I was informed we were going to war.
>
> Number 2 experienced a radio malfunction, but it did not matter, as we did not say anything except for Number 3's call, "look, missiles!" As we approached Bardavil we saw what we figured—from our limited field of view at such a low altitude—were missiles. These were actually the tips of the sails of the local fishing boats.
>
> Smoke from preceding attacks made things difficult for us, but we bombed and flew three strafing passes, attacking MiG-17s in pens, buildings, and hangars. A huge tanker was in the Suez Canal east of Kabrit, so we had to fly over the masts of the tanker each time we disengaged. After the third strafing pass we looked for the SA-2 battery that was reportedly based east of Lake Bitter, but we were unable to find it. We flew low until we out-ranged the SA-2 engagement zone and we then climbed. Only then did we see that Number 2 had one bomb still hanging from his Mystère; obviously, he could not report because his radio did not function.
>
> While we were flying off Gaza's coast Number 4 reported high temperature, so I ordered him to land at Tel Nof and the three of us returned to Ramat David.

The ILAF—most likely erroneously—reported that all four Mystères landed at 09:00. The ILAF also reported Mystère 05 as flying Mission 109/1 (SULPHUR 4 Uri Bina) from 07:54 until 09:00 and Mission 109/3 (POTASH 3 Giora Ben-Dov) from 08:08 until 09:10. Obviously, only one pilot flew Mystère 05 during this

Three MiG-17s are visible in this view of Kabrit; the nearest is certainly a dummy; the destroyed aircraft outside the pen is a real MiG-17; and the furthest is probably a dummy. (PC)

time frame (POTASH 3 Giora Ben-Dov), while SULPHUR 4 Uri Bina flew Mystère 71. Bina, who aborted Mission 109/1 shortly after take-off and returned to Tel Nof, was also flying two missions at the same time according to ILAF reports.

DAY 1 MIOR 109/2
SEAB KABRIT TOT 08:40

POTASH 1 Ben-Nun in Mystère 44
POTASH 2 Friedman (Perry) in Mystère 25
POTASH 3 Ben-Dov in Mystère 05
POTASH 4 Yadid in Mystère 15

Dangerous delay fused bombs were already scattered around aiming points 1 and 2, so the second Squadron 109 Mystère

Mystère 44 on 30 June 1967, still without a kill marking. (PC)

Mystère 44 on 8 February 1968, already adorned with a kill marking. (PC)

formation to attack Kabrit targeted aiming points 3 and 4 with six RPBs per Mystère, but only three Mystères actually departed Tel Nof at 08:08, as Mystère 15 was unserviceable.

At the end of the low altitude RPB delivery pattern, POTASH 2 reported a MiG-17 was trailing the Mystères. Assaf Ben-Nun recalled:

> A MiG-17 threatened us, but our orders were to destroy as many aircraft as possible on the ground regardless of risk, so at first we ignored the MiG. After the first strafing pass I engaged the MiG-17 while ordering the other pilots to press on with the strafing passes. The MiG-17 had an afterburner and was absolutely superior to the Mystère. Moreover, our external fuel tanks were in short supply, so we were instructed to avoid dumping these tanks and I was foolish enough to fight that MiG-17 without jettisoning them.
>
> I could not disengage. The MiG zoomed skywards again and again. Each time he zoomed, I theoretically could disengage, but the risk was that he might dive right after the other Mystères and maybe even shoot down one. The final act of combat was when the MiG-17 zoomed upwards. I followed, but obviously I could not keep pace with the MiG-17. I had to let go and dive, but at exactly the same moment I noticed the MiG-17—though high above me—was also beginning to dive. I maneuvered my Mystère accordingly to create a situation with a slight chance—maybe 1 to 100—that the MiG-17's dive would place the Egyptian fighter right in front of me. I figured if he would drop right over me, or right behind me, then he would open fire, so I waited until I actually sensed his shadow. I still did not see him, but I sensed he was there and I squeezed the trigger. A moment later the MiG-17 dived right into my burst of gun fire.

The MiG-17 was definitely hit. POTASH then disengaged and due to a low fuel state returned to Tel Nof rather than to Ramat David, landing at 09:10.

Since the MiG-17 was not seen to crash, no air-to-air kill was credited to Asaf Ben-Nun in the initial postwar list of air-to-air kills that was issued on 5 July 1967. Only at a later date did AIR4 somehow conclude the MiG-17 crashed and Asaf Ben-Nun was credited with the first of his eventual total of five kills.

FROM FOCUS WAVE 1 TO FOCUS WAVE 2

The ILAF tasked forty-five formations to raid nine EGAF bases during FOCUS A wave 1. The ILAF's BDA was that 189 EGAF aircraft were destroyed during FOCUS A wave 1. Whether this BDA was absolutely accurate or not was pointless. What was not pointless was the fact that the EGAF was no longer able to strike Israel and was barely able to defend Egypt. The ILAF had accomplished air superiority.

Squadron 109's contribution was four formations (fifteen Mystères) that attacked three air bases. It is difficult to isolate the exact number of EGAF aircraft that Squadron 109 destroyed, but it was the overall impact that mattered.

DAY 1 09:35 TAKE OFF TO SEAB BIR GAFGAFA

CONCRETE 1 Ronen in 4507
CONCRETE 2 Bar in 4582
CONCRETE 3 Yariv in 4506
CONCRETE 4 Milo in 4509

The first second wave departure from Ramat David was accomplished at 09:35, when Squadron 109 CONCRETE took off to revisit Bir Gafgafa. The average turnaround was sixty-two minutes for aircraft and sixty minutes for the three pilots who flew first wave missions; CONCRETE 2 was flying his first FOCUS mission.

CONCRETE flew to Bir Gafgafa at medium altitude, since surprise did not matter anymore and because SA-2 batteries did not defend Bir Gafgafa.

CONCRETE bombed the runway and flew three strafing passes, but Bir Gafgafa was certainly defeated. Not a single intact aircraft remained, so the Mystère pilots strafed air base facilities and AAA emplacements.

CONCRETE 1, 3, and 4 landed at 10:35; CONCRETE 2 landed at 10:37.

DAY 1 09:55 MIOR 109/6 TAKE OFF TO SEAB KABRIT

COTTON 1 Shadmi in 4532
COTTON 2 Peled in 4583
COTTON 3 Gadish in 4510
COTTON 4 Hochman in 4514

Squadron 109 Commander Ohad Shadmi returned from his first Six Day War mission to Bir Tamada at 08:30 and took off on his second sortie at 09:55 to lead his COTTON section on a SEAB mission to Kabrit.

COTTON flew to the Suez Canal Zone at medium altitude, but upon getting closer to the Suez Canal Zone, the Mystères descended to low altitude to sneak below the engagement envelope of the defending SA-2 batteries.

During their bombing run, the Squadron 109 pilots saw two MiG-17s head on, on final approach to land at Kabrit. The first MiG-17 landed and was last seen taxiing in between hangars. The second MiG-17 aborted its landing and COTTON 1 and 3 intermittently engaged this MiG-17 while COTTON 2 and 4 strafed Kabrit.

Ami Gadish later reported he first attacked the MiG-17 immediately after the bombing run. The Mystère was climbing below the MiG-17, which was flying more or less straight and level when Gadish opened fire. Smoke and fire erupted from the underside of the MiG-17 aft of the wings. Gadish added two more bursts and the MiG-17 entered a spin, at which point the Israeli pilot was sure the Egyptian fighter was doomed, but the MiG-17 recovered from the spin at around 1,000 feet over Kabrit, burning and smoking.

COTTON 2 and 4 landed at 11:10; COTTON 1 and 3 landed at 11:12.

Mystère 10 on 12 June 1967, still without a kill marking. (PC)

Mystère 10 on 5 April 1968, already adorned with a kill marking. (PC)

The MiG-17 was not seen to crash, but AIR4 reported the MiG-17 was shot down, so Ami Gadish was credited with an air-to-air kill. This procedure was known to ILAF pilots as an "AIR4 kill," an air-to-air kill credit that was not confirmed visually—through reports of crash and/or ejection—but an air-to-air kill that was confirmed through intelligence channels.

In due time, Egyptian fighter pilot Mustafa Hafiz recalled an engagement that almost exactly matched in detail the report of Ami Gadish, but contrary to the AIR4 report, Mustafa Hafiz landed the damaged MiG-17.

DAY 1 11:26 TAKE OFF TO SEAB BIR TAMADA

POTASH 1 Ben-Nun in 4544
POTASH 2 Friedman (Perry) in 4525
POTASH 3 Bina in 4571
POTASH 4 Ben-Dov in 4505

The southernmost of the three EGAF first line attack bases in Sinai was defeated during the first wave, but a single formation attacked Bir Tamada during the second wave.

POTASH actually flew a "shuttle" mission: take-off from Tel Nof, attack Bir Tamada—bombing the parallel taxiway and then strafing AAA emplacements, as well as Egyptian military installations in the vicinity of the base—and back home to Ramat David, where they landed at 12:20.

DAY 1 11:27 TAKE OFF TO SEAB KABRIT

1 Bester in 4534
2 Lior in 4506
3 Neeman in 4507
4 Lanis in 4509

Mystère pilots reported that all aircraft targeted at Kabrit were evidently damaged by the time a close examination was possible; all except for one MiG-17 that was parked/hidden in between hangars and that Asher Neeman claimed as destroyed. The four Mystères returned to Ramat David at 12:32.

FROM FOCUS WAVE 2 TO FOCUS WAVE 3

The ILAF claimed destruction of 107 EGAF aircraft during FOCUS wave 2, so waves 1 and 2 destroyed 296 EGAF aircraft. Even if this claim was somewhat inflated, the exact number of destroyed EGAF aircraft was less important than the fact that most of the EGAF bases were neutralized, most of the EGAF's combat aircraft were destroyed, the EGAF lost the ability to conduct large scale offensive operations against Israel, and the ILAF won air superiority.

If Israel hoped a swift defeat of the EGAF would deter Jordan and Syria from joining the hostilities, then these hopes were shattered sometime after 11:00, when the SYAF scrambled formations to strike Israel; and at around 11:40, when Jordanian artillery started to bombard Ramat David. As a result, during FOCUS wave 3 the might of the ILAF—no longer fearing EGAF intervention—was directed against the JOAF and SYAF.

DAY 1 12:16 TAKE OFF FROM TEL NOF TO RAMAT DAVID

Mystère 15 missed FOCUS waves 1 and 2 due to a serviceability issue that was apparently solved by 12:16, when Samuel Yadid departed Tel Nof for a short ferry flight, arriving at Ramat David at 12:30.

DAY 1 12:49 MIOR 109/8 TAKE OFF TO SEAB MAZZEH

SULPHUR 1 Hess in 4514
SULPHUR 2 Lavi in 4510
SULPHUR 3 Dagan in 4582
SULPHUR 4 Merhavi in 4583

SULPHUR leader and sub leader returned from the FOCUS wave 1 SEAB Kabrit mission at 09:00 and were initially briefed to revisit Kabrit. The SULPHUR pilots were already in their cockpits when they saw two Hunters flying over Ramat David. Apparently, Jordan had joined the hostilities and SULPHUR's mission was changed to SEAB Amman, Jordan. This time, the SULPHUR Mystères got as far as the take-off point when a messenger arrived with an order to change the mission to SEAB Mazzeh, Syria.

Interestingly, Squadron 109 was not originally tasked to raid Mazzeh during FOCUS B or FOCUS C. Nevertheless, SULPHUR was tasked to initiate an attack against Mazzeh. Arie Dagan recalled:

> We crossed the border and flew over Lebanon at low altitude; local farmers waved their arms, unable to tell which side these metal birds were on and not knowing to where we headed. Number 2 reported a fuel system

malfunction and was ordered "RTB," so we pressed ahead as a three-ship formation.

Mount Hermon ridge was on our right and Lebanon Mountain ridge was on our left, but instead of viewing the scene I reconstructed our mission in my mind. Across the mountains we saw Damascus, changed heading, and surfed to the Damascus Basin. We then accelerated and pulled up with our view widening at a stroke. Damascus looked like a huge green oasis surrounded by an endless yellow desert.

I followed my leader, acquired the target, and aimed. The hits seemed to be accurate and dense smoke covered the intersection point of the runways. Urban areas were close by and AAA sprayed the sky. I looked at my wingman and ordered "turn back" to return for a strafing pass, as I clearly saw aircraft near the hangars and along the runway. Once again, I checked that my wingman was where he was supposed to be and then I aimed at a pair of MiG-17s. Just as we cleared the target my wingman reported he was hit and his cockpit was full of smoke. While pulling a tight turn to the left I noted his smoking aircraft climbing away, heading west.

We aborted the strike and regrouped with our friend in distress. He reported that even jettisoning the canopy did not improve his situation and he ejected over Lebanon. Our calls over the radio were not answered and only later did we learn that he was a POW in Lebanon.

We departed as a four-ship formation and returned two aircraft. Just as we crossed the Israeli Lebanese border back home, RCU warned us of hostile aircraft. We broke hard left and then back to our heading south as two friendly Mirages overtook us, waving their wings.

Merhavi ejected from Mystère 83 while Hess and Dagan returned to Ramat David at 13:23 and 13:26, respectively. The ILAF attributed the loss of Mystère 83 to AAA fire, while AMUC,

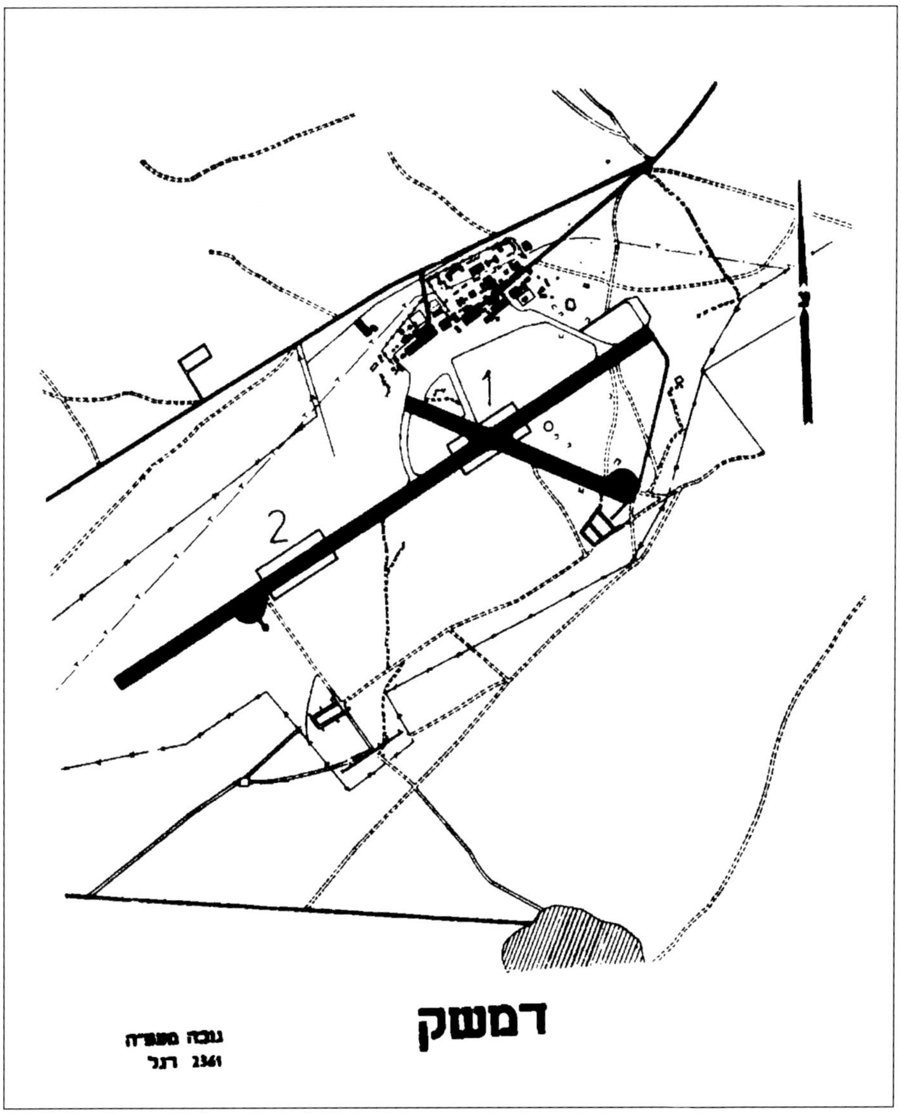

AIR3's OPOR FOCUS scheme of SYAF base Mazzeh, at the outskirts of Damascus, that SULPHUR attacked during FOCUS wave 3. (PC)

AMV1, and AMV3 linked Mystère 83's loss with a claim that SYAF MiG-17 pilot Zohair El Baowab shot down a Mystère. Due to the absence of hard evidence—such as Baowab's exact time of take-off and his full combat report—it is impossible at this point to confirm or rule out a link between the loss of Mystère 83 and Baowab's claim.

DAY 1 13:19 TAKE OFF TO SEAB BALY

CONCRETE 1 Ronen in 4532
CONCRETE 2 Zamir in 4505
CONCRETE 3 Gadish in 4507
CONCRETE 4 Keidar in 4544

The third formation to SEAB SYAF base Baly—at the time known to the ILAF as Marj' Real—was CONCRETE. The average turnaround per aircraft was seventy-three minutes and 183 minutes per three pilots—Ronen, Gadish, and Keidar—while Zamir was flying his first Six Day War sortie. Turnaround times, especially per pilot, increased along the timeline of the war.

The Mystères raided Baly unchallenged, claiming the destruction of two MiG-17s and a helicopter. The cumulative claim of the three formations that raided Baly was thirteen aircraft on the ground, so on the way back to Ramat David, CONCRETE reported that all visible aircraft at Baly had been destroyed. The next formation tasked to raid Baly was therefore retasked to attack another target while CONCRETE landed at 13:53.

DAY 1 13:49 MIOR 109/11 TAKE OFF TO SEAB BALY RETASKED TO SEAB DUMAYR

COTTON 1 Shadmi in 4509
COTTON 2 Bar in 4515
COTTON 3 Yadid in 4534

COTTON was tasked to attack Baly, but en route to Baly, CONCRETE reported that all targets at Baly had been destroyed so COTTON was diverted to SEAB Dumayr.

COTTON was the fourth formation tasked to raid Dumayr, but the third formation (Squadron 105 MENTHOL) reported that Dumayr was "neutralized," so COTTON was ordered to bomb AAA emplacements rather than the runway.

Upon arrival, the Mystère pilots noted a MiG-21 taking off from a parallel taxiway so Shadmi changed plans and ordered to bomb taxiway. A second MiG-21 taking off ran right into mushrooms of smoke from the explosions of COTTON 1's bombs and was seen to emerge intact.

COTTON claimed the destruction on the ground of five to eight aircraft. On their way back home to Ramat David, COTTON strafed and set fire two fuel storage tanks at Khan Ayash. The COTTON Mystères returned to Ramat David at 14:40.

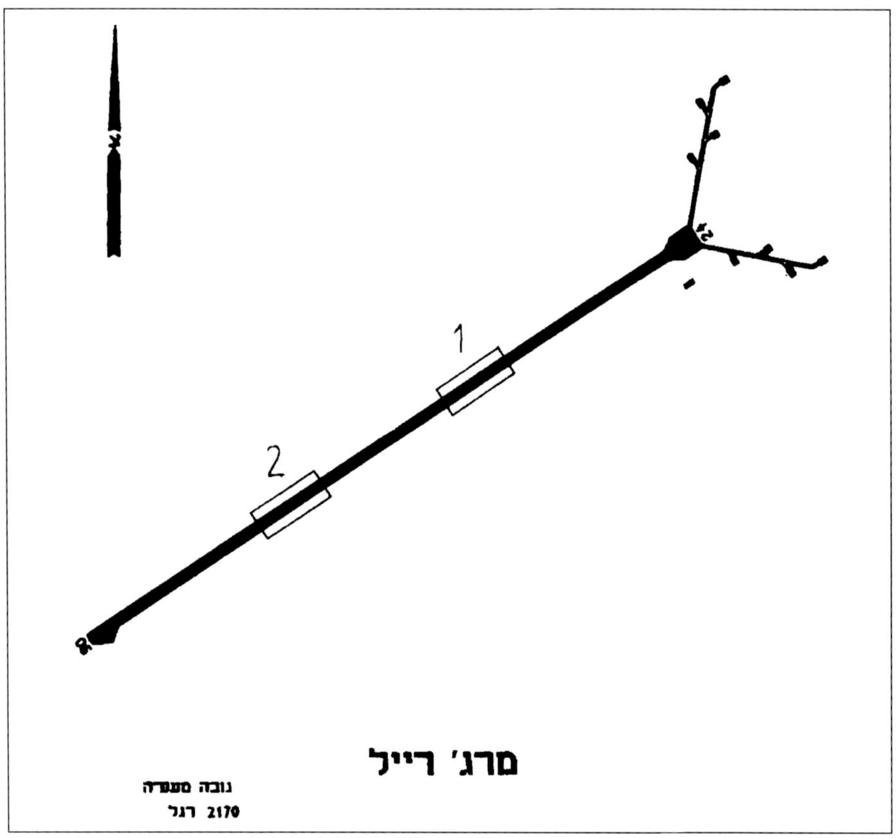

AIR3's OPOR FOCUS scheme of SYAF base Baly, south of Damascus—at the time known to the ILAF as Marj Real (Valley Real)—which CONCRETE attacked during FOCUS wave 3. (PC)

FROM FOCUS WAVE 3 TO 4

The ILAF destroyed the JOAF and neutralized the SYAF during FOCUS wave 3, so that by 14:00—after only six hours of fighting—the ILAF had established air superiority over all battlefields; prewar US assessments and ILDF evaluations were proven in combat and Israel was winning the war.

From 07:23 until 13:49, Squadron 109 generated eleven missions (forty-two sorties) that raided four EGAF bases and three SYAF bases. This high tempo of operations equated to circa 100 daylight sorties, or an average of four daylight sorties per pilot per day. The inevitable slowdown surfaced during FOCUS wave 4.

DAY 1 TAKE OFF 14:35 TO SEAB DUMAYR

MERCURY 1 Yariv in 4582
MERCURY 2 Hochman in 4506
MERCURY 3 Lanis in 4507

The sole Squadron 109 mission during FOCUS wave 4 was SEAB Dumayr. MERCURY pilots were actually briefed to attack Baly, but were retasked to raid Dumayr, since the ILAF had evaluated Baly as knocked out while Dumayr was still active.

MERCURY was the fifth formation to SEAB Dumayr, which was indeed very much alive. Yariv and Hochman bombed the runway while Lanis bombed the parallel taxiway. In the course of three strafing passes, MERCURY claimed the destruction of at least six MiG-21s.

AAA fire damaged MERCURY 1 during the third strafing pass, but all three Mystères returned safely to Ramat Davit, where they landed at 15:20.

FROM FOCUS WAVE 4 TO 5

The SEAB tempo slowed down around noon. This was not due to an Israeli siesta, but because the ILAF's objective of air superiority was accomplished. More and more air assets were diverted to patrol and support sooner than could have been expected prewar. Only ten FOCUS wave 4 SEAB missions departed ILAF bases from 14:15 until 15:40, and these included a single Squadron 109 SEAB mission.

FOCUS wave 5 was flown from 16:36 and again targeted EGAF bases. The last formation until then to take-off on a SEAB mission to Egypt departed Hatzor at 12:25. During this four hours and eleven minutes, all SEAB missions attacked Iraq, Jordan, and Syria. The time was right for the ILAF to return to SEAB Egypt in an effort to disrupt nighttime battle damage repair work.

DAY 1 TAKE OFF 16:37 TO SEAB FAYID

1 Bester in 4510
2 Sella in 4544
3 Ben-Nun in 4571
4 Neeman in 4532

Not one Squadron 109 Mystère departed Ramat David from 14:35 until 16:37; another positive indication that Israel was indeed winning the war. The four-ship formation that flew to Fayid was armed with bombs with hour delay detonators to disrupt battle damage repair activity, but they were tasked to bomb a recently spotted emergency runway near Fayid. The Mystère pilots noted that while bombing the "black line along the sand dunes," each bomb raised a large dust cloud of yellow sand. The alleged emergency runway was probably an Egyptian dummy.

There were no normal airfield facilities adjacent to the dummy runway so, at the end of bombing, the four Mystère pilots flew to strafe nearby Fayid. AAA fire welcomed the Squadron 109 pilots over Fayid. There were no visibly intact aircraft, so the Mystères strafed airfield facilities and then returned to Ramat David, landing at 17:50.

DAY 1 MIOR 109/15 TAKE OFF 17:28 TO SEAB KABRIT

SULPHUR 1 Hess in 4515
SULPHUR 2 Lior in 4505
SULPHUR 3 Dagan in 4506
SULPHUR 4 Ben-Dov in 4534

After a break of more than six hours, the ILAF again took off to SEAB Kabrit. SULPHUR was tasked to bomb runways and then strafe an SA-2 battery northeast of Kabrit. Zvika Hess recalled:

> We flew over land, cruising economically at 27,000 feet. As we descended to 6,000 feet over Bir Tamada, AAA fire targeted us. A minute or so after flying over the Sinai mountains towards the Suez Canal we saw two SA-2 missiles homing onto us. The SA-2 missiles were launched from a battery east of Shalufa. By then we were still descending, flying at 1,000 to 500 feet. The first missile crashed near the battery and the second missile flew farther away, but also crashed harmlessly.
>
> Our mission was to bomb the intersection of runways 31 and 36 and the intersection of the parallel taxiway with runway 36 [aiming points 1 and 4, respectively]. Our bombs were equipped with 7-15 and one hour delay fuses. We flew the bombing run from southeast to northwest, and as we finished bombing we turned right over the lake. AAA damaged Number 4 aircraft during the bombing run and the servo system hydraulic pressure dropped to zero.
>
> We then strafed an SA-2 battery north of Kabrit, east of Lake Bitter. The first pair attacked the battery's facilities: the sub leader hit the battery's radar and his wingman strafed generators. Our flight back home was uneventful until we split into pairs before landing. Number 3 escorted Number 4, who could not lower flaps or his undercarriage, so he performed a perfect landing on the two external fuel tanks.

SULPHUR 3 and 4 landed at 18:43; SULPHUR 1 and 2 landed at 18:48. Mystère 34 would fly again the following morning.

SULPHUR 4 landed on Mystère 34's external fuel tanks at the end of FOCUS wave 5 MIOR 109/15, but the Mystère was flying again the following day; Mystère 34 was photographed after RTB from a Six Day War mission. (PC)

FROM DAY 1 TO DAY 2

18:35 to 19:08 Ronen in 10 and Lavi in 09
19:40 to 20:35 Gadish in 05
20:10 to 20:50 Hochman in 71
20:34 to 21:05 Yadid in 10
02:54 to 03:41 Ronen in 32, Bina in 26 and Friedman (Perry) in 05
03:14 to 04:00 Yariv in 14, Neeman in 10 and Milo in 25

From five minutes before sunset at 18:40 on Day 1 until sunrise at 05:38 on Day 2, Squadron 109 generated eleven sorties.

CONCRETE—in a standard daytime two-ship support formation—flew interdiction along the Jordan Valley and attacked the Jericho sector with eight napalm canisters.

Gadish, Hochman, and Yadid were scrambled in singles. Gadish was tasked to silence Syrian artillery, but was unable to pinpoint the source of fire, so he was retasked to silence Jordanian artillery; the source of fire was again not pinpointed, so Gadish returned to bomb a Syrian target, as did Hochman and Yadid.

CONCRETE and MERCURY—in a standard nighttime three-ship support formation with one illuminator and two bombers—flew interdiction against Jordanian forces east of Jerusalem. A Squadron 110 Vautour assisted MERCURY with illumination.

DAY 2 05:00 TAKE OFF TO INTERDICTION AT DAWN

1 Bester in 44
2 Bar in 15
3 Lanis in 71
4 Lavi in 14

MIOR 109/1 COTTON 1 Shadmi in 07
MIOR 109/1 COTTON 2 Peled in 09
MIOR 109/1 COTTON 3 Gadish in 32
MIOR 109/1 COTTON 4 Zamir in 05

The two four-ship formations that departed Ramat David at 05:00 and 05:03 were tasked to interdict Jordanian forces along roads between Jericho and Jerusalem.

The first formation bombed a Jordanian camp east of Jerusalem, strafed vehicles, and returned to Ramat David by 05:38.

COTTON flew rocketry and strafing against military transport and returned to Ramat David by 05:52.

DAY 2 05:55 MIOR 109/3 TAKE OFF TO STRIKE SYRIA

SULPHUR 1 Hess in 10
SULPHUR 2 Keidar in 25

Interdiction along the road between Custom House and Quneitra.

DAY 2 07:02 MIOR 109/4 TAKE OFF TO ATTACK EGYPT

POTASH 1 Ben-Nun in 71
POTASH 2 Yadid in 09

The first (thus far) unearthed Squadron 109 Six Day War rocketry attack was flown by COTTON from 05:03 until 05:52 the morning of 6 June 1967. (PC)

POTASH 3 Ben-Dov in 07
POTASH 4 Lior in 82

ILAF air superiority resulted in heavy losses to Egyptian forces in Sinai. Flying a support mission—during support the formation was in contact with ALO or FAC, while during interdiction the formation was in contact with RCU—against Egyptian forces in the Bir Lahfan sector, POTASH reported hitting ten tanks, six armored vehicles, and ten other vehicles before RTB by 08:04.

DAY 2 07:41 TAKE OFF TO ATTACK EGYPT

1 Dagan in 26
2 Zamir in 10
3 Hochman in 05
4 Peled in 32

Attacked Egyptian forces in north Sinai and RTB by 08:50; while the Mystères were landing, an Iraqi Tu-16 bomber exchanged gun fire with Ramat David.

DAY 2 08:57 MIOR 109/6 TAKE OFF TO RAID JORDAN

COTTON 1 Shadmi in 15
COTTON 2 Bar in 25
COTTON 3 Bester in 34

Tasked to support an ILDF brigade engaging Jordanian forces in the Jenin sector, COTTON bombed and strafed before RTB by 09:35.

DAY 2 09:50 MIOR 109/7 TAKE OFF TO ATTACK EGYPT

SULPHUR 1 Hess in 14
SULPHUR 2 Lavi in 06
SULPHUR 3 Ben-Nun in 07
SULPHUR 4 Lanis in 82

Tasked to interdict along the road between Jabel Libni and Bir Gafgafa, SULPHUR claimed hitting some fifteen vehicles before RCU ordered to disengage due to enemy aircraft approaching to within less than 20 kilometers (twelve miles). Shahak pairs were vectored to intercept and were credited with two MiG-21 kills while SULPHUR RTB by 10:55.

DAY 2 10:10 TAKE OFF TO STRIKE SYRIA

1 Dagan in 05
2 Ben-Dov in 10
3 Lior in 71

Attacked Syrian fortifications at Golan and RTB by 10:42.

DAY 2 10:45 TAKE OFF TO STRIKE SYRIA

1 Yadid in 09
2 Keidar in 32
3 Keshet in 92

Squadron 116's Mystère 92 suffered battle damage during a Day 1 FOCUS wave 3 SEAB Mafraq mission and was forced to land at Ramat David. The Mystère was repaired and Squadron 116 tasked Uri Keshet to RTB 92. Instead of flying Mystère 92 straight from Ramat David to Tel Nof, Keshet integrated the ferry flight with a Squadron 109 attack mission against Syrian fortifications at Golan. The two Squadron 109 Mystères RTB by 11:33, while Keshet flew Mystère 92 to Tel Nof.

DAY 2 12:15 MIOR 109/10 TAKE OFF TO STRIKE SYRIA

MERCURY 1 Yariv in 05
MERCURY 2 Sella in 14
MERCURY 3 Neeman in 71
MERCURY 4 Milo in 06

Rocketry and strafing northeast of the Sea of Galilee; RTB by 13:07.

DAY 2 12:57 TAKE OFF TO RAID JORDAN

CONCRETE 1 Ronen in 25
CONCRETE 2 Bina in 26
CONCRETE 3 Hochman in 09
CONCRETE 4 Friedman (Perry) in 82

Interdiction of Jordanian forces in the Jericho sector; RTB by 13:47.

DAY 2 13:56 TAKE OFF TO STRIKE SYRIA

1 Gadish in 07
2 Zamir in 71
3 Yadid in 32
4 Peled in 10

Tasked to attack a Syrian frontline fort, but # 3 and # 4 had to RTB due to malfunction, so the pair was retasked to attack Syrian armor east of Gadot; RTB by 14:42.

DAY 2 16:05 TAKE OFF TO ATTACK EGYPT

1 Neeman in 25
2 Friedman (Perry) in 34

Tasked to support the ILDF in the Kuntila sector, but was retasked en route to interdict along the road between Bir Tamada and Bir Gafgafa. Observed armor near Bir Tamada and prepared to bomb when # 2 spotted two interceptors; # 1 decided to delay jettisoning bombs and tanks as the pair turned towards the interceptors until these were identified as friendly Shahaks. The pair then bombed and strafed armor near Bir Tamada. RTB by 17:16.

DAY 2 16:06 TAKE OFF TO ATTACK EGYPT

MERCURY 1 Yariv in 05
MERCURY 2 Sella in 07

Bombed barracks near Bir Gafgafa and then strafed along the road between Bir Gafgafa and Jabel Libni; RTB by 17:17.

DAY 2 16:27 TAKE OFF TO ATTACK EGYPT

CONCRETE 1 Ronen in 44
CONCRETE 2 Keidar in 26
CONCRETE 3 Bina in 06
CONCRETE 4 Lavi in 14

Tasked to interdict in the Bir Gafgafa sector; RTB by 17:42.

DAY 2 17:07 TAKE OFF TO ATTACK EGYPT

1 Bester in 32
2 Milo in 82
3 Bar in 09

Squadron 109 sight film frame from strafing; the terrain type indicates this was during a mission over Sinai. (PC)

Squadron 109 Commander Ohad Shadmi flew his seventh Six Day War mission the night of 6 to 7 June 1967 in Mystère 06. (PC)

Tasked to interdict in the Bir Tamada sector; RCU reported an SA-2 launch even though Bir Tamada was outside the Egyptian SA-2 engagement envelope. Nevertheless, the Mystères descended to low altitude until RCU reported that the danger was over. The Mystère pilots then resumed the mission and reported hitting some ten vehicles; RTB by 18:20.

DAY 2 18:14 MIOR 109/17 TAKE OFF TO RAID JORDAN

COTTON 1 Shadmi in 10
COTTON 2 Lior in 25

Briefed to attack Egypt, COTTON was retasked prior to take-off to support an ILDF brigade in the Jenin sector. ALO directed COTTON to seek Jordanian tanks and the Mystères attacked—first with napalm and then strafing—together with Ouragans. By the time a Squadron 116 pair arrived to relieve COTTON Shadmi was out of ammunition, but Lior was not, so he joined Squadron 116 NIXON to continue strafing a while longer. COTTON 1 RTB at 18:48 and COTTON 2 followed at 18:53.

FROM DAY 2 TO DAY 3

SULPHUR 1 Hess in 14
SULPHUR 2 Lanis in 34
SULPHUR 3 Ben-Nun in 44

POTASH 1 Ben-Nun in 09
POTASH 2 Shadmi in 06
POTASH 3 Lanis in 25

1 Bester in 34
2 Ben-Dov in 71
3 Keidar in 05

From dawn at 04:38 to dusk at 18:41 on Day 2, Squadron 109 generated seventeen attack missions (fifty-six sorties—including one by a Squadron 116 pilot in a Squadron 116 aircraft —in nine four-ship formations, four three-ship formations, and four pairs): seven attack missions (twenty-three sorties) against Egypt; five attack missions (seventeen sorties) against Jordan; and five attack missions (sixteen sorties) against Syria.

Operations slowed down during the night. SULPHUR flew MIOR 109/18 (support in the Jerusalem sector) from 18:33 until 19:15. POTASH flew MIOR 109/20 (interdiction between Jericho and Jerusalem) from 00:27 until 01:26, actually attacking vehicles in the Jericho sector with the leader illuminating and his wingmen bombing. The third three-ship formation also flew interdiction along the roads between Jericho and Jerusalem from 00:46 until 01:46.

Squadron 109 sight film frame; the terrain type hints this was during a mission over the West Bank. (PC)

DAY 3 04:30 MIOR 109/1 TAKE OFF TO RAID JORDAN

COTTON 1 Shadmi in 05
COTTON 2 Keidar in 09

Tasked to support the ILDF in the Qabatiya sector. Jordanian forces were already ordered to retreat from the West Bank at 15:30 on 6 June 1967, so COTTON did not pinpoint any Jordanian tanks in the Qabatiya sector and was diverted to interdict Jordanian forces in the Jericho sector. COTTON recced roads from Jerusalem to Hebron and Jericho, then attacked in the Jericho sector: first with rocketry against tanks, then strafing vehicles; RTB by 05:34.

DAY 3 05:52 TAKE OFF TO RAID JORDAN

CONCRETE 1 Ronen in 34
CONCRETE 2 Zamir in 44

Tasked to support the ILDF in the Qabatiya sector, CONCRETE attacked tents and tanks with rockets and guns and reported hitting tents and up to six tanks; RTB by 06:42.

DAY 3 06:11 TAKE OFF TO RAID JORDAN

1 Milo in 32
2 Sella in 07

Also tasked to support the ILDF in the Qabatiya sector, the Mystère pilots reported hitting five tanks and eight vehicles before RTB by 07:03.

DAY 3 06:42 TAKE OFF TO STRIKE SYRIA

MERCURY 1 Yariv in 10
MERCURY 2 Lior in 25
MERCURY 3 Neeman in 82
MERCURY 4 Bina in 15

Tasked to bomb two camps in the southern sector of Golan, MERCURY then strafed vehicles in the vicinity of the camps and RTB by 07:37.

DAY 3 07:17 TAKE OFF TO ATTACK EGYPT

1 Dagan in 05
2 Bar in 09
3 Gadish in 14

Attacked in the Bir Tamada sector; reported hitting five tanks, three armored vehicles, and several trucks, RTB by 08:20.

DAY 3 08:04 TAKE OFF TO RAID JORDAN

1 Yadid in 06
2 Friedman (Perry) in 26

Flew interdiction along the road from Jericho to Amman, rocketing and strafing until AAA fire damaged Mystère 06. Friedman (Perry) landed first and Yadid followed at 09:04, landing on the external fuel tanks.

DAY 3 08:19 MIOR 109/6 TAKE OFF TO STRIKE SYRIA

SULPHUR 1 Hess in 44
SULPHUR 2 Peled in 71

Bombed artillery in the northern sector of Golan, flew interdiction along the road from Quneitra to Damascus, and RTB by 09:00.

DAY 3 09:36 MIOR 109/8 TAKE OFF TO STRIKE SYRIA

CONCRETE 1 Ronen in 34
CONCRETE 2 Zamir in 14
CONCRETE 3 Ben-Nun in 25
CONCRETE 4 Hochman in 82

Bombed AAA emplacements outside Quneitra, strafed vehicles along the road from Quneitra to Damascus, and RTB by 10:20.

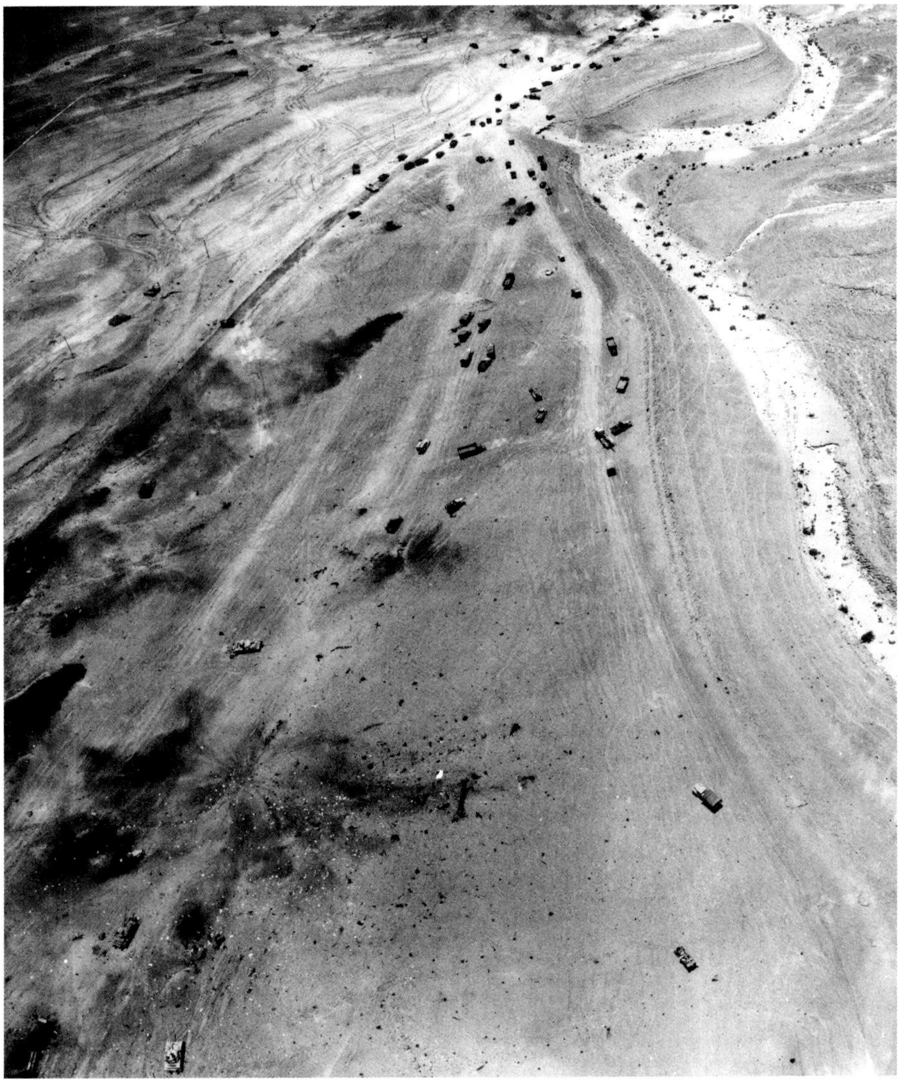

Air superiority impact on the Sinai Peninsula; destroyed or abandoned Egyptian vehicles. (PC)

DAY 3 10:10 TAKE OFF TO STRIKE SYRIA

1 Milo in 09
2 Lanis in 05

Attacked a Syrian post and AAA emplacement in the northern sector of Golan, strafed vehicles in the vicinity, and reported hitting some fifteen vehicles; RTB by 11:03.

DAY 3 10:32 TAKE OFF TO STRIKE SYRIA

1 Dagan in 10
2 Lior in 44
3 Neeman in 71
4 Bina in 15

Attacked mortars in the northern sector of Golan, east of Gadot; RTB by 11:32.

DAY 3 11:50 TAKE OFF TO RAID JORDAN

1 Gadish in 25
2 Friedman (Perry) in 82

Tasked to bomb a AAA emplacement south of Jericho, but this was not pinpointed, so the pair bombed and strafed vehicles in the Damia Bridge sector, some 50 kilometers (thirty-one miles) north of Jericho; they reported hitting three cannon and some twenty-four vehicles before RTB by 12:40.

DAY 3 12:02 TAKE OFF TO RAID JORDAN

MERCURY 1 Yariv in 14
MERCURY 2 Bar in 34

Tasked to interdict along the road east of the River Jordan and south of the Damia Bridge, but MERCURY 2 had to abort the

Squadron 109 sight film frame of enemy vehicles; the terrain indicates this is during a mission over the West Bank. (PC)

mission and RTB due to a malfunction, so MERCURY 1 pressed ahead alone and attacked the same targets as the previous pair prior to RTB by 13:05.

DAY 3 13:18 MIOR 109/13 TAKE OFF TO RAID JORDAN

SULPHUR 1 Hess in 09
SULPHUR 2) Hochman in 71
SULPHUR 3) Yadid in 05

By noon, the battered Jordanian forces had practically finished their retreat from the West Bank. Jordanian Brigade 40—one of the two Jordanian armor brigades—completed retreat from the northern sector of the West Bank with only eight tanks out of an initial deployment of nearly 100; the Jordanians attributed the lion's share of their losses in tanks and vehicles to Israeli air superiority and to the ILAF's air strikes. Accordingly, SULPHUR was the final Squadron 109 formation to attack Jordanian forces in the West Bank; the Mystère pilots targeted vehicles in the Jericho sector prior to RTB by 14:08.

DAY 3 15:54 TAKE OFF TO STRIKE SYRIA

1 Bester in 10
2 Lavi in 82
3 Ben-Dov in 25
4 Lanis in 14

While the ILDF was completing occupation of the West Bank from Jordan and while the ILDF was pushing back Egyptian forces in Sinai, the Israeli Syrian front was still mostly static, with mostly Syrian artillery bombardments and ILAF air strikes. With victory imminent in Sinai and the West Bank, Squadron 109 would now focus on softening Syrian forces in Golan. The four Mystères attacked mortars in the southern sector of Golan prior to RTB by 16:14.

DAY 3 15:57 MIOR 109/15 TAKE OFF TO STRIKE SYRIA

COTTON 1 Shadmi in 44
COTTON 2 Keidar in 26
COTTON 3 Ben-Nun in 07
COTTON 4 Sella in 34

Attacked a Syrian frontline fortification and a nearby AAA emplacement opposite Chorazin; RTB by 16:19.

DAY 3 16:00 TAKE OFF TO STRIKE SYRIA

CONCRETE 1 Ronen in 09
CONCRETE 2 Zamir in 05

Attacked the same targets as COTTON; RTB by 16:22.

DAY 3 17:19 TAKE OFF TO STRIKE SYRIA

1 Bester in 10
2 Lavi in 25
3 Ben-Dov in 07
4 Friedman (Perry) in 71

Bombed a Syrian fortification in the northern sector of Golan; RTB by 17:55.

DAY 3 17:20 MIOR 109/18 TAKE OFF TO STRIKE SYRIA

1 Dagan in 26
2 Peled in 34
3 Shadmi in 09
4 Bina in 05

Tasked to attack a Syrian fortification on top of Mound Faher, in the northern sector of Golan. Upon mission completion, RCU asked if it was possible to strafe the Syrian radar station near Daraa. They arrived over the Daraa sector but faced cloudy weather and could not find the radar station. The lead pair RTB at 18:24, while the trailing pair descended below the clouds, trying to find the radar station, but it was not pinpointed, so the trailing pair strafed vehicles in the Sheikh Maskin sector and RTB at 18:30.

DAY 3 17:50 TAKE OFF TO STRIKE SYRIA

POTASH 1 Ben-Nun in 14
POTASH 2 Lior in 82
POTASH 3 Neeman in 44
POTASH 4 Milo in 15

Tasked to attack Syrian tanks with napalm in the center sector of Golan. Tanks were not pinpointed, so they attacked trucks in

Squadron 109 Commander Ohad Shadmi and Squadron 109 Deputy A Haggai Ronen flew Mystère 09 from 17:20 until 18:30 and from 16:00 until 16:22, respectively, during Six Day War Day 3 on 7 June 1967. (PC)

A typical Syrian fortification at the Golan Heights; Squadron 109 attacked Syrian targets from Day 3 afternoon until Day 6 cease-fire. (PC)

trenches. By then Israel was winning the war and Egypt and Jordan were in full retreat from Sinai and the West Bank, respectively, so preservation of force started to matter and the pilots were briefed to avoid strafing over Golan to minimize exposure to AAA. Due to difficulty pinpointing targets not all the pilots dropped their napalm canisters, so POTASH 1 flew lead in another napalm delivery pass, strafing while at it. Mystère 14 was hit during this pass, so Ben-Nun pulled up and turned west, at which point the engine cut, the aircraft was on fire, and the cockpit was full of smoke. Ben-Nun delayed ejection because the regular afternoon wind blows from west to east, but was forced to eject when control was lost and the aircraft started to dive and roll.

The ILAF reported that Elisha Friedman (Perry) flew Mystère 10 from 12:44 until 13:43 during Day 4's strike Syria mission—the target was AAA emplacements in the Golan Heights—and that Ohad Shadmi flew Mystère 10 from 13:41 until 14:18 during Day 4's strike Syria mission that targeted a radar station in the southern sector of the Golan Heights with four bombs and strafing; obviously, two pilots could not fly the same aircraft at the same time, so either a reported aircraft number was erroneous or the mission times were in error; in this case Friedman (Perry) flew Mystère 10 and Shadmi flew Mystère 09. (PC)

Ben-Nun ejected west of the border, but the wind indeed drifted him east. Luckily landing on the right side of the border, Ben-Nun was fired at throughout his descent. Ben-Nun then ran west and took cover in a ditch until the arrival of ILDF troops, who evacuated him to Gadot, from where he was transported back to Ramat David, arriving in time to tell his story during the end of day squadron debrief.

FROM DAY 3 TO DAY 4

From dawn at 04:38 until dusk at 18:41 on Day 3, Squadron 109 generated nineteen attack missions (fifty-six sorties in eight four-ship formations, two three-ship formations, and nine pairs): one attack mission (three sorties) against Egypt; seven attack missions (fifteen sorties) against Jordan; and eleven attack missions (thirty-eight sorties) against Syria.

Day 3's division of missions and sorties mirrored wartime reality, as attack operations against Egypt and Jordan wound down and attack operations against Syria, especially from Ramat David, were stepped up.

Not a single Squadron 109 Mystère departed Ramat David from 17:50 on 7 June 1967 until 07:50 on 8 June 1967—a fourteen hour break that also indicated Israeli victory.

DAY 4 STRIKE SYRIA

07:50 to 08:33 Gadish in 24 and Yadid in 34
07:53 to 08:40 Hess in 09 and Sella in 10
08:14 to 09:04 Yariv in 82 and Lanis in 44
09:07 to 09:37 Dagan in 07 and Ben-Dov in 26
09:17 to 09:56 and 10:02 Neeman in 15 and Keidar in 71
09:37 to 10:02 Bester in 05 and Zamir in (35)
09:59 to 10:24 Bina in 25 and Lavi in 09
10:11 to 10:39 Noy in 32 (refreshment)
12:33 to 13:15 Ronen in 26 and Noy in 71
12:44 to 13:43 Milo in 15 and Friedman (Perry) in 10
13:41 to 14:18 Shadmi in 09 and Peled in 32
13:55 to 14:27 Gadish in 82 and Hochman in 07
14:02 to 14:28 Hess in 44 and Bar in 32
14:28 to 15:09 Yariv in 05 and Lior in 25
15:50 to 16:13 Neeman in 71 and Sella in 10
16:20 to 16:44 Bester in 15 and Noy in 34
16:42 to 17:06 Bina in 26 and Lanis in 07
16:45 to 17:20 Ronen in 32 and Keidar in 05
17:03 to 17:26 Yadid in 25 and Ben-Dov in 44
17:19 to 17:39 Hochman in 09 and Bar in 82
17:28 to 17:54 Shadmi in 34 and Lior in 10
17:38 to 18:07 Hess in 15 and Lavi in 71
17:48 to 18:17 Bester in 11 (test)
18:02 to 18:25 Neeman in 26 and Friedman (Perry) in 32
18:05 to 18:32 Bina in 05 and Peled in 07
18:15 to 18:42 Dagan in 44 and Zamir in 25
18:26 to 18:54 Ronen in 09 and Sella in 82

While the ILDF was completing its occupation of Sinai and the West Bank, exchange of fire along the Israeli-Syrian border continued and Squadron 109 generated twenty-five missions (fifty sorties) that attacked Syrian targets: AAA, artillery, fortifications, mortars, and radar.

Most missions (seventeen) lasted up to thirty minutes and most missions involved attacking with four bombs. Additionally, Squadron 109 generated one pilot refreshment flight and one aircraft test flight; the former to refresh EP pilot Dani Noy, who returned to Israel from Uganda; and the latter to test Mystère 11.

FROM DAY 4 TO DAY 5

MERCURY 1 Yariv in 10
MERCURY 2 Dagan in 34
MERCURY 3 Milo in 11

Squadron 109 generated a single mission from sunset at 18:42 on Day 4 until sunrise at 04:38 on Day 5; MERCURY departed Ramat David at 20:15 to silence Syrian artillery and RTB by 20:51.

DAY 5 STRIKE SYRIA

09:25 to 09:57 Gadish in 09 and Zamir in 11
09:43 to 10:17 Hochman in 32 and Friedman (Perry) in 71
10:30 to 10:53 Shadmi in 10 and Ben-Dov in 26
10:44 to 11:28 Hess in 44 and Keidar in 82
11:44 to 12:15 Bester in 05 and Lanis in 34
12:00 to 12:25 Yadid in 25 and Peled in 09
12:11 to 12:45 Ronen in 15 and Noy in 11
12:28 to 13:00 Milo in 32 and Sella in 10
12:34 to 13:07 Dagan in 82 and Bar in 71
13:05 to 13:42 Neeman in 44 and Lior in (05)
13:44 to 14:20 Ben-Nun in 34 and Milo in 25
14:14 to 14:45 Yariv in 09 and Zamir in 11
14:30 to 15:15 Gadish in 15 and Friedman (Perry) in 82
15:36 to 16:02 Hochman in 71 and Ben-Dov in 05
16:53 to 17:30 Shadmi in 25 and Lanis in 34
17:45 to 18:20 Hess in 07 and Peled in 11
18:18 to 18:47 Ronen in 26 and Noy in 15
18:30 to 19:09 Bester in 10 and Yadid in 44

The ILDF offensive against Syria—with objective of taking over the Golan Heights—started during Day 5, with Squadron 109 continuing to strike Syria during eighteen missions (thirty-six sorties) targeting AAA, armor, artillery, camps, fortifications, mortars, and vehicles with bombs, napalm, rockets, and guns.

FROM DAY 5 TO DAY 6

COTTON 1 Shadmi in 09
COTTON 2 Yadid in 26
COTTON 3 Gadish in 71
1 Bester in 05
2 Hochman in 82
3 Neeman in 34

Squadron 109 generated two missions from sunset at 18:42 on Day 5 until sunrise at 04:38 on Day 6; both were tasked to silence Syrian artillery, flying from 23:15 until 23:50 and from 00:15 until 00:59.

DAY 6 STRIKE SYRIA IN PAIRS

04:38 to 04:57 Ronen in 09 and Ben-Dov in 26
04:51 to 05:17 Hess in 07 and Zamir in 32
05:03 to 05:38 Dagan in 34 and Sella in 82
05:12 to 05:45 Yariv in 10 and Bar in 44
05:35 to 06:10 Ben-Nun in 05 and Friedman (Perry) in 71
05:48 to 06:05 Ben-Dov in 25 (test)
06:37 to 06:48 Bina in 15 and Keidar in 09
06:56 to 07:25 Ronen in 32 and Lanis in 44
07:12 to 07:38 Hess in 11 and Zamir in 71
07:34 to 08:30 Dagan in 07 and Noy in 05
08:01 to 08:38 Milo in 25 and Lavi in 09
08:19 to 08:52 Yariv in 06 and Lior in 32
08:44 to 09:03 Ben-Nun in 71 and Gadish in 44
08:49 to 09:20 Bester in 11 and Friedman (Perry) in 07
09:30 to 09:52 Shadmi in 15 and Sella in 05
09:54 to 10:26 Hochman in 25 and Bar in 09
10:13 to 10:50 Yadid in 71 and Keidar 32
10:45 to 11:15 Neeman in 06 and Noy in 44
11:14 to 11:39 Bina in 11 and Lanis in 07
11:21 to 11:58 Ronen in 10 and Lior in 05

While the ILDF was pushing Syrian forces east of the Golan Heights, Squadron 109 continued to strike Syrian targets with nineteen pairs (thirty-eight sorties) that departed Ramat David from 04:38 until 11:21. Most missions were not issued with MIOR, but were scrambled to a holding pattern; while holding in a racetrack pattern, RCU radioed a target and authorized a pair to attack armor, artillery, camps, fortifications, headquarters, and vehicles, mostly with bombs and guns.

DAY 6 12:02 TAKE OFF TO STRIKE SYRIA

MERCURY 1 Yariv in 09
MERCURY 2 Lavi in 26
MERCURY 3 Milo in 15
MERCURY 4 Friedman (Perry) in 25

The small stretch of land known as the Golan Heights—some sixty kilometers (thirty-seven miles) long and circa 30 kilometers (nineteen miles) wide—could not sustain more than a few attack formations at a time. In order to ease control and increase punch, a switch from pairs to four-ship formations was accomplished around midday. MERCURY was tasked to bomb and strafe in the Butmiya sector, southwest of Rafeed in the southern sector of Golan, prior to RTB by 12:40.

Air superiority impact on the Golan Heights; destroyed or abandoned Syrian Panzer tanks. (PC)

DAY 6 12:47 TAKE OFF TO STRIKE SYRIA

COTTON 1 Shadmi in 06
COTTON 2 Neeman in 71
COTTON 3 Ben-Nun in 32
COTTON 4 Hochman in 11

Tasked to bomb a Syrian fort near Taufik, in the southern sector of Golan; RTB by 13:11.

DAY 6 13:08 TAKE OFF TO STRIKE SYRIA

SULPHUR 1 Hess in 82
SULPHUR 2 Yadid in 34
SULPHUR 3 Bina in 44
SULPHUR 4 Ben-Dov in 07

Tasked to attack a fortification and mortars near Skopiya, in the southern sector of Golan; RTB by 13:30.

DAY 6 14:55 TAKE OFF TO STRIKE SYRIA

CONCRETE 1 Ronen in 05
CONCRETE 2 Noy in 10
CONCRETE 3 Dagan in 15
CONCRETE 4 Lanis in 32

Tasked to attack along the road between Quneitra and Damascus; RTB by 15:23.

DAY 6 15:41 TAKE OFF TO STRIKE SYRIA

1 Gadish in 05
2 Zamir in 82
3 Bar in 11

Scrambled to support the ILDF at Golan; ALO/FAC asked them to patrol along roads and to look for enemy activity; they did not observe enemy activity and did not attack, RTB by 16:35.

THE END OF WAR

Israel initiated the Six Day War with a preemptive strike on 5 June 1967. The UN ended the Six Day War with a cease-fire from 10 June 1967. Within six days, Israel defeated Arab armed forces and occupied the Sinai Peninsula from Egypt, the West Bank from Jordan, and the Golan Heights from Syria.

Squadron 109 flew 337 combat sorties (including one flown by a Squadron 116 pilot in a Squadron 116 aircraft; excluding five ferry, refreshment, and test sorties): fourteen SEAB missions (fifty-three sorties) during Day 1 and twenty-nine nighttime support sorties and 103 daytime support missions (255 sorties) from Day 2 to 6. The division of Squadron 109 daytime support missions was eight (twenty-six sorties) against Egypt, twelve (thirty-two sorties) against Jordan, and eighty-three (197 sorties) against Syria.

Squadron 109 generated more missions/sorties than Squadron 116, primarily because its main theatre of operations was Golan, so the duration of most Squadron 109 missions/sorties was up to thirty minutes. The Mystère proved to be an efficient and robust attack aircraft; expended ordnance included bombs, napalm, rockets, rounds, and RPBs, while many Mystères returned with battle damage. Squadron 109's cumulative claim amounted to dozens of aircraft and hundreds of vehicles; it is impossible to correlate between Squadron 109's claims and actual destruction, but there can be little doubt that FOCUS devastated the Arab air forces and that subsequent Israeli air superiority exposed Arab armed forces to ILAF strikes. A relevant example is Jordanian Brigade 40, which entered combat in the northern sector of the West Bank with nearly 100 modern Patton tanks, engaged ancient ILDF Sherman tanks in combat, and retreated from the West Bank with only eight tanks, attributing the lion's share of losses to ILAF air strikes.

Squadron 109 started the war with sixteen Mystères and ended the war with fourteen; one Mystère was lost during a SEAB mission and one Mystère was lost during a support mission. The ILAF's Mystère ORBAT dropped from thirty-three at the start of the war to only twenty-six by the end. Mystère replacement was more urgent than ever.

A Squadron 109 end of Six Day War photo: standing (left to right): Squadron 109 Commander Ohad Shadmi, Ilan Lior, Aki Arzi, Deputy B Zvika Hess, Deputy A Haggai Ronen, Asher Neeman, David Peled, Ami Gadish, Uri Keidar, Shlomo Milo, Daniel Lanis, and Dani Noy; sitting on the wing (left to right): Aviem Sella, Amos Zamir, David Lavi, Jacob Yariv, Arie Dagan, Elisha Friedman (Perry), Irik Bester, and Uzi Hochman; and standing on the wing (left to right): Giora Ben-Dov, Amos Bar, Samuel Yadid, Uri Bina, and Asaf Ben-Nun. (PC)

CHAPTER 7

FROM MYSTÈRE TO SKYHAWK

1967-1968

Squadron 109 was planned to start transitioning from the Mystère to the Ahit during ILAF Year 1967 Term 3 (December 1967 until March 1968). The Ahit's introduction was more urgent than ever due to ILAF losses during the Six Day War. Though Squadron 109's losses were relatively light—only two out of sixteen while overall ILAF losses were more than forty out of some 200—were significant, and the number of remaining Mystères was twenty-six, which was only two more than the ILAF's standard per squadron. The ILAF was anxious to introduce the Ahit and Raam not only in line with prewar plans for modernization and expansion, but also in order to replace Six Day War combat losses. Yet, it was at this crucial point that France placed an embargo and the US announced a suspension.

MORE MUSCLE

Israel hoped the French embargo and US suspension were temporary diplomatic measures that would soon be lifted, especially in light of USSR shipments of arms to Egypt and Syria. Therefore, immediately after the Six Day War cease-fire, ILAF Commander Moti Hod emphasized an urgent requirement to replace Six Day War combat losses on top of Ahit and Raam orders:

> In the recent war, the ILAF lost some forty attack aircraft. There is an urgent requirement to replace losses and to expand the force with the additional acquisition of attack aircraft in line with the ILAF's five year plan... Some twelve Ahits and twelve Raams are due for delivery during ILAF Year 1967,

Squadron 109 Mystères 44 and 71 attended the Ramat David Wing Commander handover parade on 30 June 1967. (PC)

with deliveries of forty-eight Ahits and fifty Raams due for completion by ILAF Year 1968... It is therefore recommended:

- To explore the possibility of purchasing at least forty Shahak, Vautour, and SMB2 aircraft from the FRAF to replace our losses.
- To continue acquisition of the Raam to field 100 Raams, while increasing production from three to five per month.
- To order fifty J79 powered Mirage F1s—plus fifty as an option—for deliveries starting in three years.

Apparently, ILAF Commander Moti Hod emphasized—in a departure from previous ILAF Commander Ezer Weizman's point of view—attack aircraft "with the ability to defeat enemy aircraft," and for this reason recommended the acquisition of 150 Mach 2 Mirages and no more subsonic Ahits, so the ILAF's ORBAT would include 330 combat aircraft by ILAF Year 1969, with the introduction of the J79 powered Mirage F1 from ILAF Year 1970.

SCALE DOWN

US suspension was still an abstract issue for the ILAF, since Ahit deliveries—scheduled to start during autumn of 1967—were not impacted yet and since Ahit conversion courses continued.

Squadron 109 Commander Ohad Shadmi and Squadron 109 Deputy A Haggai Ronen departed to the US again on 29 June 1967 to resume the Ahit conversion course that the Six Day War interrupted. Uri Even-Nir was again assigned as Squadron 109 Commander (Acting).

Since Squadron 109 was planned to transition from the Mystère to the Ahit and since the end of war division was fourteen Mystères assigned to Squadron 109 and only twelve assigned to Squadron 116, four Mystères (09, 10, 11, and 26) were reassigned from Squadron 109 to Squadron 116, so that by early July 1967, the respective Mystère inventories were ten and sixteen. Reassignment of Mystères from Squadron 109 to Squadron 116 also indicated that Squadron 109 initiated a scale down and reassignment of Mystère human and material assets in preparation for conversion to the Ahit, since it was hoped

The Ahit conversion team in the US (left to right): Squadron 109 Deputy A Haggai Ronen, Yossi Sarig, Nissim Ashkenazi, and Squadron 109 Commander Ohad Shadmi. Shadmi first flew an Ahit on 5 July 1967 in TA-4F 488 and the same day soloed in A-4E 458. (PC)

Possibly photos of Mystère 05's crash site, which was lost in a fatal accident on 15 July 1967. (PC)

the US suspension was temporary and would be lifted within a short time.

MYSTÈRE 05

The Six Day War ended in cease-fire, but the Middle East conflict continued and the USSR's rapid replacement of Arab losses—by the end of June 1967 EGAF ORBAT reportedly included more than 300 combat aircraft, roughly twice the number of the ILAF—fueled the resumption of hostilities.

The ILAF's participation in border clashes covered counterbattery bombardments and reprisal operations; the largest amount of the action was along the Egyptian-Israeli border, so Squadron 109—always oriented north towards the Israeli-Syrian border and at the time in scale down status—flew a relatively small number of operational missions from the end of the Six Day War until the introduction of the Ahit.

The number of Squadron 109 Mystères dropped from ten to nine on 15 July 1967, when Uri Even-Nir and Uri Keidar (flying Mystère 05) returned to Ramat David and Mystère 05 crashed nearby; Uri Keidar was killed.

In a mix of facts and fantasy and dates and places, AMV3 somehow managed to link an Egyptian claim on 14 July 1967 and an ILAF accident on 15 July 1967:

> On 14 July [1967]... As a pair of Israeli reconnaissance fighters approached the southern portion of the Suez Canal to find Egyptian artillery positions, the UARAF launched ten MiG-17s. These did not manage to intercept the original Israeli formation, but then clashed with another one and claimed two Mystère IVAs shot down (the IDF/AF denied any combat losses that day, even though admitting that one of its Mystères crashed, killing its pilot, due to engine failure).

The GKSR seems to have transformed AMV3's claim and context into a solid statement:

> On 14 July [1967] Egyptian MiG-17Fs intercepted a pair of Mystère IVAs intruding into Egyptian airspace near the Suez canal and shot down one of them...

Regardless of AMV3's assumptions and hints and regardless of the GKSR's supposed established fact, there is no known operational action of any kind of ILAF Mystères over the Egyptian-Israeli border on 14 July 1967, not a single ILAF Mystère was lost on 14 July 1967, and Squadron 109 Mystère 05 was lost in an accident on 15 July 1967.

The first thus far unearthed Squadron 109 post-Six Day War operational missions were also flown on 15 July 1967, when Squadron 109 launched almost its entire inventory of aircraft—eight Mystères in two four-ship formations—to attack Egyptian targets along the Suez Canal. One formation attacked and one formation was recalled; reserve pilot Asaf Ben-Nun attacked west of the Suez Canal in Mystère 44.

SUSPENSION LIFT

ILDF General Staff Branch Chief Ezer Weizman—ILAF Commander from 1958 until 1966—travelled to the US for two days of discussions (11 to 12 September 1967) to present Israel's case for lifting the suspension. Weizman requested Ahit deliveries starting in December 1967 as scheduled, approval for Israeli acquisition of twenty-seven

ILDF Chief of Staff Isaac Rabin (second from the left) visited Ramat David during December 1967, where he was photographed with ILAF Commander Moti Hod (third from the left) and Squadron 109 Commander Ohad Shadmi (fourth from the left). (PC)

Squadron 109's Mystère 82 was displayed during an open day for families of Ramat David service persons during winter of 1967 to 1968. Aviem Sella flew 4582 on 28 December 1967 on a 0:35 flight hour training sortie, during which quarter attacks at 3,000 feet were practiced. (PC)

additional Ahits and fifty F-4 Phantoms; the additional Ahits to replace Six Day War attack aircraft losses and the Phantoms as an alternative to the embargoed Mirages. From Squadron 109's perspective, the most important issue was that Ahit deliveries would not be delayed.

The suspension was lifted in October 1967, the same month that Ohad Shadmi and Haggai Ronen returned from the US.

The final Squadron 109 Mystère mission was flown on 21 November 1967, when four Mystères—Ohad Shadmi in Mystère 07, Haggai Ronen, Josef Aviv, and Dani Schleider—were scrambled to Jordan, where they napalmed and gunned armor and vehicles in the Karameh sector, east of Jericho.

Squadron 109 Commander Ohad Shadmi flew four sorties in Mystères during November 1967; Squadron 109 EP pilot Aviem Sella flew four sorties in Mystères during November 1967; and Squadron 109 reserve pilot Asaf Ben-Nun flew four sorties in Mystères during November 1967. During December 1967, Shadmi and Ben-Nun did not fly Mystères, while Sella flew seven sorties in Mystères. The wind

The Ahit's first flight in Israel on 1 January 1968 included Ohad Shadmi in Ahit 03 with Haggai Ronen and Zvika Hess in Mystères 34 and 44. (PC)

down of Squadron 109 Mystère operations continued as ILAF Year 1967 Term 2 ended.

AHIT ARRIVAL

ILAF Year 1967 Term 2 was Squadron 109's final term as a Mystère squadron; ILAF Year 1967 Term 3 was planned as the Mystère to Ahit transition term and, thanks to the lift of the US suspension, it was possible for the ILAF to adhere to planning. The plan was to retain Mystères at Ramat David for a short while after the arrival of the first Ahit shipment so it would be possible to activate Squadron 109 as a Mystère unit with a few regulars, plus EPs and reserves in case of emergency. For this reason, training with EP and reserve pilots continued, albeit on a smaller scale than usual: Squadron 109 EP pilot Aviem Sella flew four Mystère training sorties during January 1968.

The first four Ahits arrived at Haifa port the night of 29 to 30 December 1967; Prime Minister Levy Eshkol viewed the newcomers at Haifa on Saturday, 30 December 1967, and then the four Ahits were transported from Haifa to Ramat David during the night of 30 to 31 December 1967.

The first Squadron 109 Ahit flight was accomplished on 1 January 1968, when Ohad Shadmi departed Ramat David in Ahit 03 and regrouped with Haggai Ronen and Zvika Hess in Mystères 34 and 44, and the three-ship formation flew over ILAF air bases.

MYSTÈRE DEPARTURE

Eleven years and some two months after Squadron 199 transformed into Squadron 109, and some seven years after the initiation of efforts and plans to replace the Mystère in Squadron 109 service, the Mystère finally departed the Jezreel Valley on 8 February 1968, when nine pilots—regulars, EPs, and reserves, including Squadron 109 Commander Ohad Shadmi in Mystère 06 and Squadron 109 Deputy B Zvika Hess in Mystère 32—flew the last nine Squadron 109 Mystères from Ramat David to Tel Nof for reassignment to Squadron 116, thus ending the era (1956 to 1968) of Squadron 109 Mystère.

Squadron 109 Mystère's farewell parade at Ramat David on 8 February 1968. (PC)

Squadron 109 service persons bid farewell to the Mystère at Ramat David on 2 February 1968. (PC)

Squadron 109 pilots flying Mystères from Ramat David to Tel Nof on 8 February 1968: standing (left to right): Squadron 109 Commander Ohad Shadmi, Bina, Dagan, Squadron 109 Deputy B Zvika Hess, and Squadron 109 Deputy A Haggai Ronen; and crouching (left to right): Lavi, Yariv, Ben-Dov, and Even-Nir. (PC)

The last nine Squadron 109 Mystères at Ramat David on 8 February 1968 after the farewell parade and before the farewell flyover: 4506, 4507, 4515, 4525, 4532, 4534, 4544, 4571, and 4582. (PC)

Mystère 25 departs Ramat David on 8 February 1968. (PC)

Squadron 109 Mystère's final flyover of Ramat David, 8 February 1968. (PC)

Squadron 109 Commander Ohad Shadmi disembarks Mystère 06 at Tel Nof at the end of his ferry flight from Ramat David on 8 February 1968. (PC)

Squadron 109's final farewell photos from the Mystère at Tel Nof after the ferry flight from Ramat David on 8 February 1968: standing (left to right): Squadron 116 Deputy A Ehud Shelach, Squadron 109 Deputy B Zvika Hess, Lavi, Dagan, Squadron 109 Commander Ohad Shadmi, ILAF Commander Moti Hod, Tel Nof Base Commander Samuel Sheffer, Squadron 116 Commander Simi Saar, and Tel Nof Base Maintenance Squadron Commander Josef Kvodi; and crouching (left to right): Squadron 116 Deputy B Abraham Salmon, Ben-Dov, Bina, Even-Nir, Squadron 109 Deputy A Haggai Ronen, and Yariv. (PC)

APPENDIX:

ABBREVIATIONS, ACRONYMS, CODES, DEFINITIONS, AND TERMS

1LT Lieutenant
2LT Second Lieutenant
AAA Anti-Aircraft Artillery
AGL Above Ground Level
Ahit ILAF name for the A-4 Skyhawk, pronounced *ah-it*, translation Eagle
AIR1 ILAF Air Department Branch 1 (Organization)
AIR2 ILAF Air Department Branch 2 (Weapon Systems)
AIR3 ILAF Air Department Branch 3 (Operations)
AIR4 ILAF Air Department Branch 4 (Intelligence)
AIR5 ILAF Air Department Branch 5 (Training)
ALO Air Liaison Officer
AMU Air Maintenance Unit
AMUC *Arab MiG-19 and MiG-21 Units in Combat*, David Nicolle and Tom Cooper
AMV1 *Arab MiGs*, Volume 1, Tom Cooper and David Nicolle
AMV2 *Arab MiGs* Volume 2, Tom Cooper and David Nicolle
AMV3 *Arab MiGs*, Volume 3, Tom Cooper and David Nicolle
AOA Angle of Attack
ARM Anti-Radiation Missile
BDA Battle Damage Assessment
CAP Combat Air Patrol
CAT1 Category 1 accident: no damage
CAT2 Category 2 accident: damage repairable at unit level
CAT3 Category 3 accident: damage repairable at depot level

By June 1993, the ILAF Museum had painted Mystère 09 in a Squadron 109 scheme. (PC)

CAT4 Category 4 accident: damage not repairable
COL Colonel
CPT Captain
Deputy A Senior deputy in an ILAF squadron, term originated from Flight A Commander
Deputy B Junior deputy in an ILAF squadron, term originated from Flight B Commander
DOD Department of Defense
DZ Demilitarized Zone
EGAF Egyptian Air Force
EP Emergency Posting
ETAF Ethiopia Air Force
FAC Forward Air Controller
FOR Full Operational Capability
FRAF France Air Force
FY Fiscal Year (Israel's FY was from 1 April to 31 March)
G loaf factor
GCA Ground Control Approach
GCI Ground Control Interception
GKSR Gordon and Komissarov - Soviet and Russian Military Aircraft in the Middle East
GOI or GOIL Government of Israel
HAS Hardened Aircraft Shelter
IFF Identification Friend or Foe
ILAF Israel Air Force
ILAF Year April to March; divided into three Terms: Term 1 from April to July, Term 2 from August to November, Term 3 from December to March
IAI Israel Aircraft Industries, nowadays Israel Aerospace Industries
ILDF Israel Defense Force
ILMD Israel Ministry of Defense
ILNF Israel Naval Force (also known as Israel Navy)
IOC Initial Operational Capability
IR Infra Red

The ILAF Museum added Squadron 109's Mystère badge to 09 by February 1994. (PC)

JOAF Jordanian Air Force
LBAF Lebanese Air Force
LBR Light Bomb Rack
Level A Maintenance at squadron level
Level B Maintenance at base or wing level
Level D Maintenance at depot level
LOROP Long Range Oblique Photography
LTC Lieutenant Colonel
LTG Lieutenant General
MAN1 ILAF Manpower Department Branch 1 (Adjutancy)
MAN1 ILAF Manpower Department Branch 2 (Personnel)
MAJ Major
MAT1 ILAF Material Department Branch 1 (Logistics Organization)
MAT2 ILAF Material Department Branch 2 (Engineering Maintenance)
MAT3 ILAF Material Department Branch 3 (Maintenance)
MAT4 ILAF Material Department Branch 4 (Engineering Design)
MAT5 ILAF Material Department Branch 5 (Ordnance)
MAT5 ILAF Material Department Branch 6 (Logistics General)
MG Major General
MIOR Mission Order: MIOR included a prefix letter that denoted month and a counter that denoted number in month; for example, MIOR Lamed 115 was the 115th MIOR that AIR3 issued during December (1956)
MPH Miles Per Hour
OPOR Operation Order
ORBAT Order of Battle
OTU Operational Training Unit
PAI Pilot Attack Instructor
PDM Periodic Depot Maintenance
PLO Palestine Liberation Organization
PSP Pierced Steel Planking
QBR Quadruple Bomb Rack
QFI Qualified Flying Instructor
QRA Quick Reaction Alert
Raam ILAF name for Mirage 5, pronounced *ra-am*, translation Thunder
RATO Rocket Assisted Take-Off
RCU Regional Control Unit
RPB Runway Penetration Bomb; in Hebrew known as PPM - pronounced *pa-pam* - for *Petzatzat Pitzoach Maslolim*
RPG Rounds Per Gun
RPM Rounds Per Minute
RTB Return To Base
RWR Radar Warning Receiver
SAM Surface-to-Air Missile
SARH Semi Active Radar Homing
SEAB Suppression of Enemy Air Base
Shafrir ILAF name for RAFAEL air-to-air missile, pronounced *shaf-rir*, translation Royal Canopy from Jeremiah 43:10
Shahak ILAF name for Mirage IIIC, pronounced *sha-hak*, translation Skyblazer
SMB2 Super Mystère B.2, pronounced *sam-bad*; 2 in French is *deux*
SSM Surface-to-Surface Missile
T/W Thrust over Weight (thrust to weight ratio)
Tadmor Israeli developed proximity fuse for bombs set to explode at a certain altitude AGL; why the ILAF named a weapon system after the Syrian city Palmyra (Tadmor) is a riddle.
TFC Technical Flight Commander
TOT Time On Target
UAR United Arab Republic: a union between Egypt and Syria that was established in 1958 and disintegrated in 1961, but Egypt alone continued to be officially known as the UAR from 1961 until 1971.
UHF Ultra High frequency
UK United Kingdom
UN United Nations
UNEF United Nations Emergency Force (present in Sinai from 1956 until 1967)
UNTSO United Nations Truce Supervision Organization
USA United States of America
USG United States Government
USSR Union of Soviet Socialist Republics
VHF Very High frequency
Yahalom ILAF name for Matra R.530 missile, pronounced *ya-ha-lom*, translation Diamond

INDEX

The ILAF Museum's Mystère 09 received paint refreshment in 1999, but the harsh Negev Desert weather took its toll and, by September 2004, the Mystère was decidedly discolored. (PC)

The ILAF Museum's Mystère 09 (in March 2009) represents Squadron 109 Mystère's era, which lasted from 1956 until 1968. (PC)